Concept Work

Concept Work

Constructing Frameworks
for Folklore Studies

Jason Baird Jackson

INDIANA UNIVERSITY PRESS

This book is a publication of

Indiana University Press
Herman B Wells Library
1320 East 10th Street
Bloomington, Indiana 47405 USA

iupress.org

First printing 2025

Cataloging information is available from the Library of Congress.
ISBN 978-0-253-07430-0 (hdbk.)
ISBN 978-0-253-07431-7 (pbk.)
ISBN 978-0-253-07432-4 (web PDF)
ISBN 978-0-253-07433-1 (ebook)

CONTENTS

ACKNOWLEDGMENTS

For support, encouragement, and labor in the preparation of this book, I want to thank Director Gary Dunham and the whole staff of the Indiana University Press. I began my publishing career working closely with Gary, and it was a special pleasure to work on this book with him as he prepared to conclude an exemplary and transformative career in scholarly publishing. It has been rewarding to work in diverse roles with the Indiana University Press throughout Gary's tenure. I look forward to the good work that the press will accomplish in its next chapter.

Retrospectively, I now see that this book began to take shape during the fall of 2018 when I was on sabbatical leave and had the good fortune to serve as a Fulbright Specialist at the University of Tartu in Estonia. My three weeks in Estonia—working with the students, faculty, and staff affiliated with the Departments of Ethnology and of Estonian and Comparative Folklore (both part of the Institute of Cultural Research); the Viljandi Culture Academy, particularly its program in Estonian Native Craft; and the Estonian National Museum—were transformational for me and helped me start to think in new, more expansive ways about concept work in folklore studies. I am appreciative of all who organized and supported my visit, but I note in particular Elo-Hanna Seljamaa (then leading the graduate program in Folkloristics and Applied Heritage Studies), Ülo Valk (leading the Department of Estonian and Comparative Folklore), and Art Leete (leading the Department of Ethnology).

Amid other duties and dilemmas, the project moved slowly until the summer of 2024 when I shed, for a time, the last of my administrative duties and began a very fruitful period as a residential fellow at the Indiana University Institute for Advanced Study. For that opportunity, I am especially thankful for the staff and leadership of the institute: Patricia Ingham, Suzanne Godby Ingalsbe, Elizabeth Kang, and Wuerxiya.

The studies presented in this book owe much to conversations and joint projects pursued with not only many colleagues in China, Germany, Estonia, the United States, the Muscogee Nation, and elsewhere but also the many groups of graduate students that I have taught at Indiana University, the University of Oklahoma, and the University of Tartu. The list of colleagues and students-turned-colleagues whom I wish to thank is impossibly long, so here I limit myself to those who were most directly involved in the specific work of this book in its final phase. For their direct contributions to the introduction or to chapter 5, I thank Richard Bauman, Ray Cashman, Sandra Dolby, Henry Glassie, Jon Kay, Dina Kellams, and Moira Marsh. For including me in particularly relevant and inspirational convenings and discussions related to concept work in folklore studies and ethnology, I want to express my deep appreciation to Regina Bendix, An Deming, Surna, Jessica Anderson Turner, Ülo Valk, Yang Lihui, Tim Lloyd, Dan Swan, and, most especially, Dorothy Noyes. I thank here also my coauthors for chapter 2, Lijun Zhang and Johannes Müske. None of my teachers, colleagues, and friends should be held responsible for infelicities surely present in this work.

Not everyone who aspires to pursue research and teaching in the field of folklore studies is able to find their way to, and plant their feet securely in, a place in which such work is fully realizable. I count myself among the truly fortunate in having been granted the opportunity to do public and academic work in folklore studies and ethnology that is deeply meaningful. I hope that I can continue to find ways to welcome more, and more diverse, colleagues to the work and to help sustain the communities and institutions that might support them in it. In such contexts, I am especially thankful for each of my colleagues and students in the Department of Folklore and Ethnomusicology and the Department of Anthropology at Indiana University Bloomington. Like most of the chairs that have preceded them, Pravina Shukla (chair, Department of Folklore and Ethnomusicology) and Stacie King (chair, Department of Anthropology) have been valued advocates for me and my work. I thank them. This is a good place and a good time to also thank Executive Dean Rick Van Kooten of the College of Arts and Sciences for his support of me and my colleagues and students during a vexing era in academic life.

Perhaps because their vocation is focused on everyday life, folklorists and ethnologists usually find it impossible to separate homelife and work life. It thus takes special patience to live in a family with them. With appreciation for their constant support, I dedicate this book with love to my wife, Amy, and to our son, Eli, and our daughter, Joelle.

Chapters 1–4 were originally published in three key folklore studies journals, each with a generous author agreement permitting republication here. I thank the peer reviewers and journal staff who worked to strengthen the earlier versions of these studies, as well as editors Thomas A. DuBois and James P. Leary (*Journal of American Folklore*), Ray Cashman (*Journal of Folklore Research*), and Art Leete (*Journal of Ethnology and Folkloristics*). Acknowledgments and appreciation appropriate to each of the following studies can be found in the original articles.

Jackson, Jason Baird. 2013a. "The Story of Colonialism, or Rethinking the Ox-Hide Purchase in Native North America and Beyond." *Journal of American Folklore* 126 (499): 31–54. [Chapter 1]

Jackson, Jason Baird, Johannes Müske, and Lijun Zhang. 2020. "Innovation, Habitus, and Heritage: Modeling the Careers of Cultural Forms through Time." *Journal of Folklore Research* 57 (1): 111–36. [Chapter 2]

Jackson, Jason Baird. 2021. "On Cultural Appropriation." *Journal of Folklore Research* 58 (1): 77–122. [Chapter 3]

Jackson, Jason Baird. 2022. "Towards Wider Framings: World-Systems Analysis and Folklore Studies." *Journal of Ethnology and Folkloristics* 16 (1): 1–28. [Chapter 4]

Concept Work

Introduction

Concept Work in Folklore Studies

Humble theory recognizes that all our work is essay, in the etymological sense: a trying-out of interpretation, a provisional framing to see how it looks. In the absence of a better alternative, there is much to be said for the Enlightenment project. Science reduces reality in an effort to understand it but it also properly lays itself open to an ongoing process of collective correction and revision. While science as converted into institutional practice has often not lived up to its own ideals, its authority legitimating various kinds of oppression, we can nonetheless recognize that science's own ideology gives us the tools to make this critique and that there is still a qualitative difference in openness to revision between, let's say, evolutionary theory and intelligent design.

—Dorothy Noyes (2008, 40)

Précis

The phrase *concept work* as used in this book is a way of characterizing the grounded and iterative development of useful models and perspectives in the interpretative social sciences, among which I include folklore studies. It is an approach that does not adopt the totalizing ambitions associated with projects in grand theory (Löfgren and Wilk 2006; Noyes 2016, 11–16; 2019; Rabinow 2008; Rabinow et al. 2008; Stoler and Golub 2014; Zeitlyn 2022). The chapters gathered in this volume are instances of me pursuing such concept work for folklore studies. In chapter 3, for instance, I work to develop a useful-to-others general conceptualization or model of the social process known as cultural appropriation. Valuable illustrations of such concept work in folklore studies abound and include generative treatments of vernacular religion by Leonard Primiano (1995; Valk and Bowman 2022), critical nostalgia by Ray Cashman (2006), world heritage by Barbara Kirshenblatt-Gimblett (2006), inheritances by Regina Bendix (2009), resilience by Dorothy Noyes (2016, 410–37), and belief narrative by Ülo Valk (2021). This volume arises from my own slow, modest, extended effort to advance concept work in folklore studies, as this field is in dialogue with various local and regional traditions in the neighboring field of ethnology. The concepts at issue herein can be tagged as keywords: *colonialism, heritage, appropriation,* and *world-system.* After an exploration of these concepts, I close with a reflection on teaching concepts while introducing new folklorists to the discipline. The connection between my concept work and my work as a teacher is not unidirectional. Each of the chapters of this book began with ideas and discussions pursued with my students and students-turned-collaborators.

Introduction: Folklore Studies

While all readers are most welcome, this book is intended most centrally as a contribution to ongoing conversations among folklorists, including folklore students and community-based scholars of expressive and social life, regarding concepts suitable for present-day and future work on folklore. Even this paragraph's first sentence, the one that you just read, is already overflowing with what in this book are called concepts, and these concepts are central to the work that folklorists do when thinking about, writing about, teaching about, and sharing about folklore and the communities that carry and use it. Sentence one already suggests that *folklore* is a concept, as is *expressive life* and *social life.* These concepts are presumed meaningful to some kinds of people: *folklorists, folklore students,* and *community-based scholars,* and these kinds of people—and perhaps you did not know that such kinds of people even existed—are presented as if they share an interest in these topics. Perhaps you did not know that these topics were a thing either. You hopefully see my introductory point. This book can—and hopefully will—have diverse readers, but to the extent that I am addressing specific ones, they are folklorists, those who are seeking to become folklorists, and those who find value in, or who think they might find value in, hanging around and talking to people who engage with what folklorists call—sometimes with ambivalence and almost always with reflexivity—folklore.

To set the stage for the chapters that follow then, I begin with folklore as a topic and folklore studies as the field that takes that topic seriously. I then turn to the matter of concepts in folklore studies. I conclude the chapter with an overview of the five chapters that follow this introduction. As the book's title suggests, these chapters are examples of what I will call concept work in (and for) folklore studies. Of course, my hope is that other readers with other interests or backgrounds will find interest in what I will share here. Folklore studies is one way of apprehending the expressive lives and social circumstances of people and groups, and thus folklorists have long engaged with other fields with whom such broader interests are shared. Sometimes the work of folklorists has been found useful to scholars in neighboring fields and, thankfully, nonscholars have often been among the most devoted readers of works written by folklorists.

Definitions of folklore vary and debating them has been fundamental to the project of folklore studies (folkloristics) since the field's founding in the mid-nineteenth century (Bauman 1992b; Bendix and Hasan-Rokem 2012a; Klein 2001; Noyes 2004). Despite the disciplinary variation at the center of the work done by folklorists around the world and across time, those unfamiliar with the field may want to first know that folklorists everywhere attend—in disciplined and nuanced ways—to the vernacular knowledge, expressive genres, and everyday customs fundamental to social life across time and space. They also study the broader historical, political-economic, and social contexts in which vernacular culture does its work. The field thrives at the border between the humanities and the social sciences, maintaining durable ties to most humanities and social science disciplines. In some national contexts, folklore studies, as a field, is pursued independently of adjacent disciplines such as anthropology, ethnology, or literary studies. In others, it is pursued more fully intertwined with them. The varied and complex nature of the field—particularly its engagements with ethnology (i.e., the comparative study of cultural groups)—is at the heart of my own professional practice as both a folklorist and an ethnologist working jointly in a Department of Anthropology and a Department of Folklore and Ethnomusicology. Folklore studies in its engagements with ethnology is central to my career generally and to the work shared in this book particularly.

Like its peer disciplines in the humanities and interpretative social sciences, folklore studies is a complex global assemblage that preserves continuity with its own past and is constantly changing in response to a wide variety of internal dynamics and external stimuli. To a much greater extent than would be true for fields such as mathematics or optometry, folklore studies is practiced distinctively in local and regional linguistic, cultural, social, and historical contexts that have intimately shaped, and that continue to configure, its nature as a field. As scholars such as Alan Dundes (1999, 2005) have shown, folklore studies *is* a single international discipline—one characterized by an unusually multilingual body of scholars and scholarship, a shared body of theory, some common research questions, and a common history entangled with modernization (Bauman and Briggs 2006), nationalism (Abrahams 1993), provincialism (Noyes 2003), colonialism (Briggs and Naithani 2012), capitalism, and the present interstate system (chap. 4, this volume). Yet folklore and related disciplines are practiced in situated contexts—museums, archives, universities, public humanities programs, scholarly societies—that are localized, nationally and regionally networked, and highly varied. As Dorothy Noyes (2016, 6, 182) has stressed, folklore studies is a field that has specifically addressed, and thereby thrived in, particularly provincial contexts, and these varied local and regional situations mean that, despite its status as an international discipline, it is not a unified and harmonized field. It is a provincial one, with multiple centers, varied national and regional histories, and differing kinds of entanglements with the disciplines, government, civil society, heritage organizations, and ethnonational projects (e.g., Jääts 2019 for Estonia; An and Yang 2015 for China). Folklorists tack back and forth between harmonizing and centrifugal tendencies and, I argue, benefit from both dynamics. Folklore studies is plural and, probably permanently and profitably, preparadigmatic, despite the continued quest of some folklorists to achieve grand (i.e., broadly applicable and widely shared) and discipline-specific theory (Kuhn 1996; Oring 2019a, 2019b, contra Noyes 2019). Beyond being provincial—in what I see as a good way—Noyes observes in the epigraph shared above that folklore studies work can also profitably, or at least realistically, be seen as always provisional. These two characteristics of folklore studies—provinciality and provisionality—articulate closely to the kind of foci that I refer to in this collection as concept work.

Introduction 2: Concept Work

I face risks in calling the kind of thing that I am up to in this book concept work.[1] On one level, these paired words are not that hard to decode in a general scholarly context. The fuller implication would be something like *scholarly work on concepts of possible use to other scholars,* specifically the colleagues and students who are the most likely readers of any such work. In combination with folklore studies, the scope becomes more modest. I address my colleagues (including student colleagues) in folklore studies and in the closely aligned, and historically twined, field of ethnology, and my subject is some kind of work about concepts of disciplinary relevance. As these linked fields concern themselves with the everyday and expressive lives of people, then our concept work must have something to do with concepts relevant to the appreciation of human worlds and activities. My hope is that such a straightforward understanding holds true. On the one hand, concept work does not have to seem, and probably should not seem, overly esoteric. On the other, we know that it is a complicated matter for all or most disciplines and all or most human beings.

It may be best to keep things simple and get on with it, but I feel a scholar's obligation to acknowledge that concept work has also been subjected to concept work by other scholars. Every field has concepts and thus every field does conceptual work. Some fields—linguistics, psychology, cognitive science, and philosophy, for instance—devote a lot of attention to the *concept of* concepts. I do not propose wandering the halls of academe chasing after the meta-concept of concepts. But one effort deserves notice. Due to its presence in another part of the social sciences and humanities neighborhood in which I live, the varied linked efforts by a network of cultural anthropologists and allies doing concept work and thinking about the concept of concept work since the middle aughts is perhaps most relevant. The work that I and my own closest collaborators do differs in several tangible and significant ways from that of this network, but their efforts have been steadily on my radar, and I have followed them with interest, thus I touch on them here briefly.

As an illustration, two scholars in this network, Anthony Stavrianakis and Gaymon Bennett, discussed their and a colleague's ideas about concept work in a 2012 essay. Their views stress collaboration and two goals that new approaches to scholarly collaborations in and around (in their case) cultural anthropology might advance—"concept formation for orienting common work; and the formation of shared standards and modes of judgement." The authors continue, "Concept work is not an end in itself. It is always connected to the problems one wishes to think through, as well as the question of how one could make a judgment about the problems one is engaging. Thinking about the (collaborative) mode in which one makes judgments is necessary if one thinks that ethnography, understood as the description of how a group does something, is only one part of anthropology. Rather, concept work forms one part of a broader experiment in attempting to change both how anthropology can be practiced and the purpose for which it is practiced" (Stavrianakis and Bennett 2012). In a broad sense, I share such sentiments, and they are relevant to the work of this book. Provisionally working out understandings of concepts is part of a larger collective effort that includes multiple aspects.[2] Ethnography and the other methodological approaches important to folklorists and ethnologists—historical, literary, philological, comparative, object-based—are crucial, but our fields are not reduceable to our methods or to the grounded data that they produce. Elsewhere, Noyes (2008, 2016) discusses the nature of theory in our fields, arguing, as reflected in the epigraph and the works from which it is drawn, for a productive kind of theoretical modesty and an emphasis on iteration. Like methods, theories are not autonomous, and their development is not a goal in itself. Like methods and theories, concepts are also part of the ever-changing working repertoire with which folklorists and ethnologists pursue the goal of evoking and interpreting aspects of the human experience, past and present. For some workers in these fields, the work also includes addressing the possibilities of the future and, again for some, intervening in the world actively through public and applied endeavors or in movements for social change more broadly. One aspect of the issue of judgments, as evoked by Stavrianakis and Bennett, relates to such scholarship-grounded interventions. Work aiming to clarify and explore concepts is not the end but one essential part of the larger enterprise wherein these different aspects are integrated in a reflexive scholarly practice.

Some concepts in folklore studies have attracted a great deal of attention. They have been subjected to a multigenerational program of work. Even as they use and refine them, scholars in our linked fields also often point to these refined concepts as markers of professional identity. For American folklorists, at least, genre, performance, and tradition are among a small group of star concepts that we use, teach, and identify with (Feintuch 2003). Some newer concepts have joined them in the conceptual canon—heritage, surely; property, maybe; commons, perhaps. University-based folklorists teach seminars on these concepts, and they organize our work in diverse settings, both individually and collectively (chap. 5, this volume). Conceptual writings on them both shape our empirical work, and, in turn, such research work is the basis for the refining of these concepts. Theoretical change comes more slowly, but ultimately, such broader orientations shift in accord with the needs or lessons of the more day-to-day work of our fields. Concepts are intermediate between broad theories and empirical and, sometimes, applied and public-facing engagements.[3]

Work on concepts in folklore and ethnology has tended in recent decades to be dominated by two generic forms, one ancient as measured by the history of scholarship and the other comparatively young. This newer mode may perhaps be nearing a state of exhaustion due to overuse in the broader context of the humanities and social sciences. When folklorists write about concepts, they probably do so most often in encyclopedia entries. These are of great value to multiple readerships. I have written them, and I rely on them extensively in my teaching and research.[4] The challenge of the encyclopedia entry genre though is that such works are typically brief, and, as they are particularly aimed at students, they carry an obligation to synthesize shared wisdom. Encyclopedia entries are not the place, for instance, to contentiously reframe an issue for one's colleagues, and, by their nature, they are called into being because they are to treat already-established concepts deemed by the members of a field to be important. One does not often find such entries charting uncertain waters.[5]

Some of these qualities are shared by the keywords genre. Inspired by an essential and influential book by Raymond Williams (1976; Bennett, Grossberg, and Morris 2005), the number of published collections adopting the keywords approach in the humanities is now vast, even if folklorists have been more sparing in their deployment of it. For American folklorists, the most influential and durable keywords collection is *Eight Words for the Study of Expressive Culture* (Feintuch 2003), which I touch on more again below. In general, the keywords approach is more open to new insights and idiosyncratic presentations. A volume illustrating this potential with particular fullness is a collection of essays by a group of folklorists and ethnologists titled *Off the Edge: Experiments in Cultural Analysis* built around highly individualized and novel concepts and keywords used to present and promote fresh considerations of unexpected phenomena. The distinction between the conventional encyclopedia entry and the experimental effort in concept work is particularly visible and instructive in this case (Löfgren and Wilk 2006).

As with the authors writing in *Off the Edge*, but less playfully, I push somewhat in this volume against the tendencies inherent in the keywords and encyclopedic approaches. I do not claim that the topics that I take up are the conventional ones. In my choice of topics, I have tried to find a kind of frontier space in between accepted concerns and matters so distant from our disciplinary conversations as to be illegible or of little relevance. I do this in hopes of enriching, perhaps extending, those disciplinary conversations and frontiers. Part of this is not writing about established concepts or keywords (such as *text, genre,* or *tradition*); it is also about writing in an exploratory rather than synthetic way. In the chapters that follow, I am taking up matters that are mostly underdiscussed and about which I cannot offer a harmonized disciplinary view or even a provincial one. Of course, I would like to provoke healthy discussions among colleagues. The registers that I have chosen to write in reflect this hope.

The chapters gathered here, while of variable length, are longer than is typical for either keywords essays or encyclopedia articles. I did my best to cover the ground that I felt needed covering without exhausting potential readers with a long, forced march across rough scholarly countryside. Sometimes the length required arose from the fact that I could not rely on the intertextual nature of established and ongoing disciplinary discussions of established concepts such as tradition.

Even if I had the wits to pursue such a thing, I do not live a professional life that would allow for the careful writing of a long and comprehensive tome on established or seemingly needed folklore studies concepts. I have rather, instead, tried my hand at an activity that I hope many other colleagues will continue to join in. Here, as suggested in chapter 5, I include those students who do concept work themselves as they join the discipline. I, for instance, crave the chance to read fellow folklorists and ethnologists offering useful disciplinary conceptualizations of food deserts or microfinance or reflections on the nature of scenes or exurbs as a social base for folklore. There is little doubt for me that folklorists need to join discussions of, and to conceptualize for their own studies, such matters as anthropogenic climate change (Owen in Richardson et al. 2023), creative aging (Kay in Richardson et al. 2023), or decolonization (Frandy in Richardson et al. 2023). I note that European ethnologists can offer inspiration to their American folklore colleagues in this regard. Faced with a greater sense of urgency in rethinking their fields since the mid-twentieth century, European folklorists and ethnologists have attended to such conceptual issues quite vigorously, as with recent work on, for instance, posttruth societies (Bareither, Harder, and Eckhardt 2023) and silence in cultural practice (Seljamaa and Siim 2016). The journal *Ethnologia Europaea* has been a key hub for such work. The possibilities for fresh work on conceptual issues in folklore studies and in ethnology seem quite broad to me.

Introduction 3: This Book

Folklorists pursue understanding of a wide range of expressive forms and everyday conduct in a large variety of social contexts, but for many observers, the field is particularly associated with the study of oral narrative manifest in storytelling. While over its course, it will expand out to global scale, this book begins in earnest with a small narrative. In chapter 1, I revisit a very old story using quite old sources and old research tools and techniques, but with a new purpose. The broader topic is colonization, particularly as recounted in a widespread colonization narrative. In this chapter, I aspire to contribute to a growing literature in folklore studies that attends to the nature of and conceptualization of colonization. Important in its own painful terms, such work is also a necessary prerequisite for newer conversations about and engagements around the diversely conceptualized concept—and practice—of decolonization, both in the world and in academic fields such as folklore studies (Bacchilega and Naithani 2018; Briggs and Naithani 2012; Tuck and Yang 2012).

As evoked above, in 1995, the American Folklore Society published an issue of the *Journal of American Folklore* devoted to seven keywords of special importance to (North American) folklorists: *tradition, art, text, group, performance, genre,* and *context* (Feintuch 1995). This collection was later expanded to eight words (*identity* was added) to become the book *Eight Words for the Study of Expressive Culture* (Feintuch 2003). These eight concepts or keywords remain vitally important in folklore studies, but in the decades since 1995, others have gained prominence in the folklore studies lexicon. Perhaps the most often written about of these is heritage. Some of the reasons for this, and some of the key writings on this concept, are woven into chapter 2, where two colleagues (Lijun Zhang and Johannes Müske) and I endeavor to contribute to an already vital discussion on the meanings and significance of heritage. While not arguing against the emerging consensus view of heritage among European and North American folklorists, we take a different, we hope complementary, approach to heritage, situating it in relationship to two other categories of cultural existence—innovation and what scholars, drawing on a French term, call *habitus*, a word closely related to the English terms *habit* and *habitual*. Our purpose in chapter 2 is to help folklorists think about heritage in a temporal way in which cultural forms sometimes move into, and sometimes also move out of, a cultural categorization as heritage. The reasons why such an approach might be useful are explored in the conclusion of this brief chapter.

If heritage is a concept that has gathered in considerable attention from folklorists around the world over the past two decades—and this is an easy case to make on bibliographic grounds—there are other concepts that, while showing up in everyday conversations among folklorists, nonetheless do not appear much in their scholarly writings. Chapter 3 offers an example of this type of concept: cultural appropriation.

A constant presence in old and social media contexts, this phrase also figures prominently, but privately, in the oral discussions of folklorists and ethnologists, but it has resisted or evaded formal concept work, at least within our fields. While much of the cultural stuff that folklorists concern themselves with—treasured recipes and stories, beautiful festive costumes, arresting communal dances—bring joy or at least comfort into people's lives, evocations of cultural appropriation signal that the party is over and that pain has replaced pleasure within the social network. While it is a proposition that cannot be proven, folklorists and ethnologists have probably avoided conceptualizing cultural appropriation formally because it seems both intractable and painful. While the writings of folklorists are unlikely themselves to solve the underlying social problems that call cultural appropriation contests into existence, it is possible that we, as scholars or scholar-practitioners, can develop more nuanced understandings of what the phenomena entail and also use such improved conceptualizations in our work as allies and as educators at work among various publics. In chapter 3, I draw on older work in folklore studies and ethnology to develop tools for making sense of cultural appropriation contests in a general way.

Noyes (1995, 2012, 2016) has written several works framing more clearly "the social base of folklore." These works and the core sources on which they build are fundamental to the ways that my colleagues and I think about the *folk* in folklore. But the work is never complete, and there are many new avenues down which folklorists still need to wander as they consider all the social relations in which people put folklore to work and into motion. In relation to such questions, chapter 4 is a consideration of folklore and folklore studies in the context of what is perhaps the widest of social conceptualizations, the historically constituted global arrangement of people, ideas, processes, and resources that is the object of the approach to social research called world-systems analysis. As Noyes has previously noted in a general way, and as I observe in this chapter, folklorists and ethnologists have a lot invested in the study of the small-scale social "interaction order." I do not question this focus. It is one of our specialties in the scholarly division of labor, and it is central to my own efforts in the field. But folklorists once focused on nations, and it is not preordained that we must forever and only consider the intimacies and artistries of small-scale social engagements.

What commonalities of interest and purpose do folklorists and world-systems analysts share? What points of articulation might folklorists explore? How does folklore studies fit within the knowledge structures of the contemporary world? In chapter 4, I argue that even if folklorists return to their regular work after considering such questions, that regular work might be better for having at least contemplated the commonalities and differences characterizing what are probably the two polar ends of the social research continuum. Expressive communication in small groups (Ben-Amos 2020, 23–39, 203–24), of course, happens in the same world in which, for instance, national economies and transnational corporations rise and fall, profoundly impacting small groups—in numbers beyond counting—along the way. The impacts are not one way. For instance, global antisystemic movements, such as those that aggregated around the World Social Forum beginning in 2001, have often focused on the struggles of small, subaltern groups articulated in cultural rather than simply economic terms. Such movements, both historically and today, have relied heavily on expressive practices, such as parade and parody, that folklorists know well from generations of grounded study. Study of the current world-system needs folklorists and ethnologists, even if most are averse to large-scale analysis and fearful about the normative simplifications that they often associate with it. Without abandoning the study of expressive and everyday life in specific social settings, how might we augment a folkloristics of the interaction order with renewed attention to wider contexts and to the historical factors that shape them?

This volume concludes with a final chapter in which I turn from trying to do concept work in folklore studies to a reflection on my experience teaching concepts, and modeling concept work, for graduate students in my work as a professor of folklore studies at Indiana University. In particular, in chapter 5, I take as a starting point a book chapter written by folklorist Richard M. Dorson and published posthumously in 1983. In that chapter, Dorson describes his approach to teaching the introductory graduate seminar for new folklorists in what is today the Department of Folklore and Ethnomusicology at Indiana University. I am one of several faculty members who have taught the course about which Dorson wrote and which he initially established and presented. In my own chapter, I reflect on continuities and changes in this key course (as an example of similar cognate courses elsewhere), focusing on the place of concepts in the teaching of graduate students who are entering the field.

Across each of these substantive chapters, some reoccurring tendencies might be observed. In each instance, I am interested in usable disciplinary pasts that offer resources for the present without fetishizing ancestors or ignoring limitations in their works. While critique is important and while fresh starts are sometimes quite warranted, I am one who wants to know what came before and to fashion what I can from it. While I admire and value theory making—and theoretical debates—I share Noyes's (2008) orientation to what she calls "humble theory" and her appreciation of more focused, but still general, work that is more grounded in the rich social and cultural worlds that we can engage through our historical, ethnographic, philological, and comparative studies of actual cases and through our engagement with the cognate work of our colleagues and others. Although I aspire to pursue concept work that is more polycentric, that is, efforts that track concepts as they are perhaps differentially conceived of in multiple national or regional "traditions" of folklore studies, the work presented in this volume is specifically rooted in my own "Americanist tradition."[6]

Finally, my approach to concept work, as reflected in these chapters, is aimed at developing heuristics for effective teaching and for credible empirical work on folklore in its social and cultural contexts. Heuristic schemes or models are never understood as perfected. They are only a springboard for moving forward toward improved, or just more useful, approaches worked out in an iterative way. It is important to note, as a folklorist and ethnologist, that heuristics or models in this sense are actually quite familiar in that they are the same as or quite analogous to the rules of thumb, cultural schema, conventional wisdom, vernacular knowledge, metis, and so on that are cultivated and used around the world by the extraordinarily diverse individuals and groups with whom folklorists and ethnologists work.[7] The best way to build a barn or cook a stew or tell a tale is only the best way up to the point at which someone works out a satisfactory and generative new way to do such a thing. It would be an amazing thing if a student preparing to begin their own journey as a new folklorist or ethnologist next academic year were to craft much better accounts of any or all of the matters raised by me herein. In a world in which hope sometimes seems in short supply, this is a hope that I feel certain will be realized.

Notes

1. A recent collection of work by folklorist Dan Ben-Amos was also framed as being focused on concepts. In that case, the studies centering the book were among the most durable issues at the heart of the field, rather than emerging ones that might be seen as being on its periphery, as here (Ben-Amos 2020).

2. The idea of concept work also appears in the work of historian and anthropologist Ann Stoler, as reflected, for instance, in an interview that she did with Alex Golub. In contrast to the narrower ways that social theory is often taught to graduate students, she described "concept work, working with concept, as a much more provisional and creative project" (Stoler and Golub 2014). This perspective aligns with Noyes's (2008) view of work in folklore studies (Noyes and Staley 2024).

The larger story of the Anthropological Research on the Contemporary (ARC) collaboratory, which devoted much attention over a period of fourteen years to working out approaches to what it was overt about calling concept work, is far beyond my scope here. The arc of the history of ARC is particularly complex. A range of innovative scholarship was pursued and accomplished in a multifaceted set of social relations. The work of the group was reflexively documented throughout (although much of this has been lost or made ephemeral through the rapid decay of neglected digital platforms), making its lessons legible for outsiders interested either in the making of the scholarship or in the practice of scholarly collaboration. The effort also faced strains and concluded, at least for one of its principal leaders, in a mood that I read as profound disappointment (Rabinow 2018). This complex history gives me pause in my own work, as the self-conscious, reflexive prominence that ARC gave to concept work risks establishing the concept of "concept work" as a branded phenomenon bound (too) closely to this particular research group. I do not think that the group intended to make it such, and I do not think that such a framing would be helpful for the many fields wherein this essential activity, and this usefully simple phrase, are of continuing value. For the issue of "branded tropes" in concept work, see Chris Kelty's (2006, 8) reflection on "what Anna Tsing calls friction."

The work of ARC was about collaboration and not only concept work. In the same period, much of my own work has also involved collaboration (Jackson 2018, 2019, 2023a, but also Bendix, Bizer, and Noyes 2017). Relative to the ARC collaboratory, I valued how the group shared insights into its collaborative work, as these reports to the broader community are a resource for other efforts, including my own (Rabinow et al. 2008 is one particularly helpful source from this larger corpus). Concept work is the specific focus of a white paper by a number of ARC participants and interlocutors. It was circulated under a generous Creative Commons license, but the decay of the ARC website after the effort was disbanded leaves uncertainty of its continued availability. Readers seeking it online are advised to search on the full paper title given in my references (Rees 2007). Concept work also appears prominently in a forum published in the journal *HAU* (Faubion et al. 2016; Rabinow and Stavrianakis 2016). My citation of a collection of essays published in *HAU* should not be interpreted as an endorsement of the journal.

3. Related to keywords and concept work is the matter of what Noyes (2016, 6) calls "slogan concepts." There is slippage and overlap between what I am calling core or emerging concepts here and the kinds of catchy, short-half-life concepts that she is addressing *conceptually*. About this kind of concept, Noyes (2016, 413–16) writes, "The slogan-concept is an abstraction that seems to validate concrete realities, the name of a purportedly eternal idea used to launch a time-specific project, a tent providing shelter to actors coming from all directions." She goes on to identify examples (Nation, Diversity, Multiculturalism, Sustainability, among others) and to assess the usefulness and limitations of slogan concepts for policy and scholarship. It is beyond the scope of this introduction to represent her account, just note that I endorse it and note that it is fully relevant to the work that I am introducing and trying to do in this book. I urge consulting her full account.

4. Jackson (2006a) on the concept of diaspora is an example of my work in this genre. If one were seeking to compile the most comprehensive accounting of concepts in use in folklore studies and ethnology, one would have to resort to such encyclopedia entries, as it is in them that the wider range of concepts (from oikotype to colonialism) are named, claimed, and explicated.

5. Encyclopedia entries, significantly, are also not generally peer reviewed, and they most often arise out of the pursuit of financial gains by commercial publishers chasing after library sales. Importantly, and positively, they are typically overseen by highly talented scholarly editors. Folklore studies has benefited greatly by some excellent topical encyclopedia led by gifted scholarly editors.

6. For the "Americanist Tradition" in anthropology and folklore studies, see the work of Regna Darnell (Darnell 1973, 2001, 2021; Valentine and Darnell 1999). For polycentric concept work, I am beginning to scope out how this would work through comparisons of Estonian, Chinese, and North American perspectives. A hint of this approach is evident in chapter 2, where my colleagues, trained in

German and China, respectively, joined me in working out an approach to heritage cognizant of these three national contexts. More ambitious efforts include the Chinese-English Keywords Project (China Made 2019) and writings such as Yu Luo's (2018a, 2018b) studies of the Chinese concept of *yuanshengtai* vis-à-vis the "Western" concept of "indigenous" and Tim Thurston's (2020) work on "cultural carriers" (*wenhua zaiti*) in Chinese cultural policy. Broadly, the internationalization impulse evoked here aligns with calls to provincialize folklore studies alongside other disciplines rooted in Western Europe and North America (Noyes 2016, 2 after Chakrabarty 2000).

7. My list here is likely familiar to most folklorists and ethnologists, but *metis* may be unfamiliar. The term is conceptualized in James Scott's (1988, chap. 9; 2012) *Seeing Like a State*. I recommend it and the related *Two Cheers for Anarchism*, which I think of as an outstanding introduction to folklore, even as Scott does not use this term.

1

A Story of Colonialism and Its Lessons

Colonialism generated space for many kinds of new oral discourses: the colonisers talking about the colonized (which is largely known and studied) and the colonised talking about the colonizers. The later area of research remains almost untouched.

—Sadhana Naithani (2004, 10)

Introduction

Despite living in a world of rapid global communication, some apparent diffusions or, as we might say in the idiom of our era, some global cultural flows still surprise us.[1] A number of Native North American peoples tell a story that is best known among scholars as a motif from the legend of the founding of ancient Carthage by Dido. Identified by comparative folklorists as both a tale type and a motif, the story features colonists who trick the local inhabitants by asking for only as much land as can be measured with one oxhide.[2] Given the small size of a single hide, the locals agree, and then the colonizers proceed to cut it into a fine string with which they encircle much more land than was envisioned by the locals. Such stories are told as history, with different inflections, by groups whose ancestors were both the clever perpetrators and the honest victims of this fraud. While the presence of this story in the narrative repertoires of Native American peoples has been generally known since at least the nineteenth century, it has not been comparatively examined in the Americas, in contrast to the rest of the world, where it has been taken up by a long line of distinguished scholars (Köhler 1864, 187; 1900, 321). In this chapter, I offer a comparative assessment of the oxhide purchase in Native North America. Working outward from my own fieldwork experiences and the beginnings of a historic-geographic treatment, I seek to consider the story from the perspective of recent work relating to historical consciousness in Native North America and as a chance to establish an additional link between folkloristic studies of narrative and research in other fields more closely concerned with understanding the legacies of colonialism.[3]

"The Coming of the White Man"

In *Huron and Wyandot Mythology*, the rich collection of oral narratives that industrious Canadian folklorist Marius Barbeau (1915) gathered among these kindred but sundered peoples, we find a straightforward text that can open up the topic of this chapter. Titled by Barbeau, if not by his narrator, "The Coming of the White Man" was told to him in English in June 1911 by Mary McKey, a seventy-three-year-old Wyandot of the Bear clan then living in Amherstburg, Ontario (Barbeau 1915, xi, 271, 425).[4] As reported by Barbeau, this story, from among the Canadian Wyandot, goes as follows:

> When the white man was first seen here, in the old time, he began to barter with our ancestors. Nowhere could he step without coming across some red man, [all the land being occupied].
>
> The stranger came forth with a cow's hide, saying that he wanted a piece of land. The Indian, thinking that it was all about a piece of land the size of a cow's hide, agreed to the barter. The other fellow, however, cut the cow's hide into a string [wherewith to measure a large domain]. The Indian remarked, "This is the way the white man does. He cheats the Indian." And he had to give away the land which the string had measured. (Barbeau 1915, 271)

Ms. McKey's version, like those I have been told among the Woodland Indian peoples of Oklahoma, takes a motif and makes a compressed, stand-alone story out of it. It is this kernel of narrative, known to comparative folklorists by the new tale-type number ATU 927C*, that is the focus of this chapter (see Uther 2004, 566–67; previously it was type AT 2400, see Aarne and Thompson 1981, 539).[5] For purposes of this book, I follow the custom of the Woodland Indian peoples among whom it is told and label the narrative a *story*. This less-specific emic label enables me to evade several typological questions that might hinder the analysis that I aim to pursue. The folklorist's impulse might be to begin by treating that narrative as a legend, but among Woodland Indian people, the diffuse genre category *story* shifts responsibility for assigning truth value away from narrators and onto listeners, a process that now encompasses readers of this chapter (see Jackson 2003b, 206; Linn and Jackson 2004; Urban and Jackson 2004). For now, it is enough to note that Ms. McKey's version is a token of the story's simplest type. For ease of reference, I will call it the *oxhide purchase*.[6]

A year later, in June 1912, Barbeau was privileged to record another version, this time in Wyandotte, Oklahoma. The narrator from among the Oklahoma Wyandots was John Kayrahoo, a seventy-two-year-old member of the Porcupine clan who was a monolingual Wyandot speaker (Barbeau 1915, xi, 268–70). Mr. Kayrahoo's narrative is embedded within a larger story that elaborates further on the phenomena of "first contacts" in the Eastern Woodlands of North America.[7] His account begins by noting that the Wyandot, at the time when they first met Europeans, led an intertribal league in which the Delaware (also known by their ethnonym *Lenape*) "occupied the second rank." As the most coastal of its peoples, the Delaware were charged with guarding the shore and preventing any landings.[8] In this context, Europeans arrived in startling "cloud-like" ships, and the astonished Delaware failed to prevent them from anchoring. The Delaware were invited aboard and offered a rich array of heretofore-unknown manufactured goods. Echoing many of the known Delaware narratives on the same theme, the Wyandot version devotes rich attention to recounting the amusing experiments undertaken with these new goods. Particularly appealing to narrators up to our day is the image of iron axe heads that were mistakenly worn as necklace pendants rather than used as tools (cf. Bierhorst 1995, numbers 17, 22, 28, 40, 83, 203, 215; Rementer 2005).[9] In the Wyandot account, this episode ends in a moment of sincere friendship that is then broken with the oxhide purchase incident (Barbeau 1915, 268–69).

Mr. Kayrahoo's account of these early days continues as follows:
Then it happened that the white man wanted to purchase some land, that is, just the size of a cow's hide. The Delaware chiefs considered the matter, and agreed to grant the request, as a cow's hide was a small thing. The white man, moreover, could occupy but a small strip of land, since there were so many of them crowded on their ship, as if it had been a village.[10]

No sooner had the Indians signified their acceptance than the white men looked for the largest bull in their possession and killed it. Stretching the skin as much as they could, they cut it up into a tiny string. They went to see their Indian friends and informed them that they were ready. And then, with the string, they measured a large body of land by going around it. The Delaware at once objected that this was not the proposition which he had accepted, for he would not give more than the size of a cow's hide.

As it was done, however, the Delawares sent messengers to the Wyandots who were traveling in the western lands. As they came back, the Wyandots were astonished to find so many white people among the Delawares, and asked their friends what authority they had to let anybody thus intrude [on the Indian's] land, in their allies' absence. The Delaware replied to the Wyandot that it could not be helped. The white man had offered him everything he had and had been so good to him that he could not refuse him just the size of a cow's hide of land.[11] The Wyandot, having learnt how the stranger had cut the hide into a string, spoke in these terms, "So it is, and so shall it always be! The white fellow shall always undermine the Indian until he has taken away from him his last thing." (Barbeau 1915, 269–70)

In the final sentence of this section, Mr. Kayrahoo strives to make clear that this reported speech, the only direct discourse attributed to a Native speaker, is prophecy. He states, "This was a kind of prediction."[12]

In the remainder of the story, the Wyandot protest strongly against the Europeans, but to no benefit. According to Mr. Kayrahoo (Barbeau 1915, 270), "But it was of no avail, trouble and wars began. The white man was an invader, and the Indian was determined to defend his rights. The Wyandots found several tribes of Indians ready to unite and declare war upon the invader."[13] The urge to quote now completely overpowers my drive for economical presentation. Mr. Kayrahoo concludes his remarkable account as follows:

So a terrible war followed. The white man, as a last resort, used a disease germ against [his enemy]. When he saw the wind blowing towards the Indian, he uncorked the bottle in which the smallpox germs were kept and he let them run out. Overpowered by this calamity, the Indian had to come to terms, and he shook hands with him to show that they were to live together in peace.[14] After a compact had been reached, the white chief spoke to the Wyandot chief, saying, "Hereafter all the lands that I have purchased from the Delaware shall be mine and I will proceed to occupy them. We shall forever be friends and we must not refer to the past war between us. We shall, moreover, be your guardians and look after your business." (Barbeau 1915, 270)

With these words of the white chief, occurring in the story's only other moment of direct reported speech, Mr. Kayrahoo brings the story to a close, again offering an explanation of perfect clarity. He ends, noting, "The meaning of this was that the Indians had now fallen under the conqueror's government. The old-time saying has long been handed down among us, that we must adopt the white man's way, because we are now in his clutches" (Barbeau 1915, 270).[15]

Before examining the oxhide story comparatively, I wish to make one discourse-centered observation on it. In Mr. Kayrahoo's account, I noted the two moments of direct reported speech: the first, the words of the Wyandot chief, and the second, the words of the white chief. Both were offered as prophecy. If we permit them to be set, as the narrator intended, in the appropriate temporal frame, the Wyandot prophecy has certainly proven true, while that of the white chief is poignantly untrue. Mr. Kayrahoo's own commentary is so clear that one can almost hear his own voice in all of this. One can perhaps also picture a mental image of Barbeau, the young field-worker. The story ends categorically, with the phrase "we are now in his clutches." Having experienced many moments like this as a naive, young white ethnographer in the company of thoughtful, complex old Indian men, I can only imagine there were a few moments of respectful silence before someone made a joke and changed the topic—to the unpredictable Oklahoma weather, perhaps.[16]

Comparisons, Old and New

Having shared, in paraphrase and quotation, the texts that he collected, I owe Barbeau the first chance to comment on them. In a note to Mr. Kayrahoo's text, he wrote, "The above tradition is really a parable. It is difficult to see exactly to what historical facts it refers. In fact, it seems to characterize in a symbolic manner the whole problem of spoilation of the Indian's rights by the white invader" (Barbeau 1915, 268n3). I am not going to disagree with Barbeau in this view. Instead, I will try to take up and elaborate this reading, but first I would note that, for its day, this was a rather sophisticated, reflexive frame within which to place the text.

While Barbeau did not cite the comparative literature on the oxhide purchase as it then existed, he did acknowledge its presence in European tradition. He reported an English version told to him by one of his colleagues at Canada's Geological Survey.[17] This version, set somewhere in the north, accounted for British colonization of Ireland or Scotland. In his general discussion of Wyandot mythology, Barbeau (1915, 26–27) also offers one of the few historical interpretations by an Americanist of the oxhide purchase, suggesting, "Although the Europeans might have borrowed it from the Indians, it is more probable that the latter heard it from the neighboring European settlers here and embodied it in their own narratives."[18]

Despite being required to read the primary works of James Frazer as an anthropology student at Oxford University, Barbeau seems not to have fully made the connection between the Wyandot oxhide purchase (with its English analogue) and the European and Asian tradition that had already become a matter of scholarly discussion (Barbeau 2006). The story is best known among scholars as a motif from the legend of the founding of ancient Carthage by Dido, as narrated by Virgil in the *Aeneid* and explicated by other writers from antiquity to the present. It is this association that has generated a rich (and vast), if sometimes strange, bibliography for the story and, for our purposes, is a fact that possibly also opens up new lines of cross-disciplinary dialogue (Virgil 1995; see also Rose 1929, 309).[19]

While relevant works preceded it, a convenient point of entry for the older literature, at least for an English-speaking anthropological folklorist, is Frazer's 1888 contribution to the *Classical Review*, a short note titled "Hide Measured Lands." In it, he cites Virgil on Dido's founding of Carthage and then builds on work by Jacob Grimm (1881) and Reinhold Köhler (1864) by noting and summarizing five additional cognate texts culled from the literature: one each from the Tatar, Burma, Cambodia, Java, and Bali.[20] He concludes by claiming, "The wide diffusion of such tales confirms Grimm's conjecture (Grimm 1881, 538) that in them we have a recollection of a mode of land measurement once actually in use and of which the designation is still retained in the English *hide*" (Frazer 1888, 322; see also *Oxford English Dictionary* 1989, s.v. "hide," n²). This is classic Frazer: fascinating, sweeping generalization sprung almost instantly out of a rich ingathering of decontextualized but global particulars. Subsequent work has undermined the philological underpinnings of Frazer's (and Grimm's) survivalist argument concerning the measurement of land, but the texts noted did make clear that a phenomenon of worldwide interest was under discussion.

While the entire history of research on the oxhide purchase is beyond my scope here, a second dip into the bottomless well of Frazer's comparative thinking on such matters will prove fruitful. In his best-known work, the twelve-volume collection titled *The Golden Bough*, Frazer offers further discussion of the oxhide purchase. In this study, he found the story's deeper rationale in a Bantu charm used to protect a new town from witchcraft. This rite of the Bechuanas (a Bantu people) involved the sacrifice of a sacred cow whose eyes had been sewn shut for four days prior to being, on the fifth day, ceremonially killed and ritually feasted on. Afterward, the hide was cut into two-foot strips, which, having been prepared by specialists, were taken by messengers in all directions and pegged down in the roads leading to the new town. In Frazer's (1935, 249–50) understanding of Rev. W. C. Willoughby's (1905) ethnographic account, the Bechuanas town was then protected through its ritual encompassment by one of the people's sacred cattle.[21]

For Frazer, the Bantu rite and the oxhide purchase both deal with the founding of new settlements and involve ritual encompassment of the site by a hide. In his later work, Frazer (1935, 249–50) retains Grimm's belief that ancient systems of measurement are at issue here, but he goes further to argue that these techniques, at a deeper level, were born of the principles reflected in the South African ritual, namely, "that the mode of measuring by a hide may have originated in a practice of encompassing a piece of land with thongs cut from a hide of a sacrificial victim in order to place the ground under the guardianship of the sacred animal."[22]

Frazer's doubtful (for modern readers, at least) take is not the only one that a fuller history of research on the oxhide purchase would need to confront. The literature, for the Occident and the Orient, is substantial. Changing scholarly thinking on it is a mesmerizing topic, one that speaks to larger issues in the history of knowledge and knowledge production, among other things. In reflecting on Frazer's contribution to the larger literature, I would only note—beyond simply observing that later work has sharply criticized the philological basis of his measurement argument—that the small sample that Frazer offers contains an interesting pattern (Powell 1933, 311). The Burmese case is a local legend in which a slave tricks the king to whom she is enslaved. The Balinese instance is a matter of "indigenous" colonialism, celebrating provincials who trick their own king.[23] The Tartar case is situated within a context of Russian colonization of the East, while the Cambodian and Javanese examples speak to Western European colonialism, specifically, in these two cases, that of the Dutch. In trying to offer us a reconstructive history of universal human ritual and law, Frazer has actually sketched the basis for a quite different comparative framework.

In developing a new scheme for thinking about this story, we might acknowledge that such narratives are told as history, with different inflections, by groups whose ancestors were both the clever perpetrators *and* the honest victims of this fraud. I suggest that we also note that the historical contexts that give the story meaning vary on a continuum from purely local trickery through more "internal," if no less unwelcome, forms of colonization to the specific instance of global European colonialism that shaped the formation of the modern capitalist world-system (chap. 4, this volume). These patterns, in a small way, might help us begin conceptualizing a comparative folkloristics of colonial experience. Finally, while I, and the Native North American examples that I am most concerned with, place emphasis on the morality of the victims relative to the deviousness of the perpetrators, the story, as a type or a motif, exists within a wider, more complex framework where this aspect can cut both ways.

Frazer's Burmese and Balinese examples show this aspect, as they describe such tricks being used by clever but subordinated peoples against those who would rule them.[24] A famous and accessible instance of this type, one that can also introduce a related motif (K185.7), in which the trick hinges on the land being marked by foot travel is Leo Tolstoy's (1993) short story "How Much Land Does a Man Need?"[25] In this story, written in emulation of oral folktales, Tolstoy tells of a Russian peasant who, driven on by the devil through a series of ever-expanding land purchases, meets his end while seeking to trick a group of Bashkirs into selling him their rich and, to European eyes, underused lands. The Bashkir chief agrees to sell but explains that their going price is 1,000 rubles a day. Confused, the peasant asks how land can be measured in days. The chief explains that, as they lack a system of measurement, the sale will encompass as much land as he can encircle on foot before sunset. When the process begins, greed pushes him to go for broke, and he arrives back at the starting point at sunset, only to collapse in death at the feet of the chief. I hope that my poor summary has not spoiled the story, which James Joyce pointed to as the best short story ever written. The title question is answered by the peasant's servant, who buries him far from home in a six-foot hole on the steppe where he fell (Tolstoy 1993; beyond assertions found widely on the internet, one source on Joyce's praise for the story is noted in Ellmann 1983, 227).

However much we might doubt their answer, Grimm and Frazer were not wrongheaded in taking up systems of measurement as a proper ethnological topic. Like the better-studied matter of systems of marking time, variable conceptions of measurement get to the heart of how cultures articulate people with the worlds in which they live (for time, see Dinwoodie 2006; for measurement, see Hallowell 1942). I also think that, from the perspective of classic comparative folkloristics, Frazer was justified in grouping (as Stith Thompson also did in the *Motif Index* and in his 1946 study *The Folktale*) instances of deception in the measurement of land under the same heading, as he did in the case of the Balinese legend that he cites in the company of the oxhide purchase stories proper. In Frazer's (1888, 322, citing Van Eck 1880) summary, it goes as follows:

> The people of Tengagan, a district in Bali, formerly enjoyed the honour of keeping the herds of the King of Kaloengkoeng. It befell that the King's riding horse died at pasture. So the King commanded that the horse should be buried on the spot and that the land, as far as the smell of the carrion spread, should belong to the herdsman. Thereupon the people of Tengagan cut the carcass in pieces and each of them sticking a bit in his girdle set off to walk. They walked and walked till they had as much land as they knew what to do with; and that is why the district of Tengagan is one of the biggest in Bali.

This text from Bali seems ready-made for a tourist brochure, and, sure enough, one has no trouble finding Rutger van Eck's sketches of Bali, from which it derives, cited on the web in pages catering to those travelers or would-be travelers wishing to partake of what James Boon characterized as *The Anthropological Romance of Bali* (1977). I include it here not to pull our attention farther east but to connect, as Frazer did, the oxhide purchase with real estate deceptions undertaken on foot. This connection allows us to return to the Woodlands of North America and the people for whom we have the richest body of related texts and who, as Mr. Kayrahoo's story illustrates, can even take a starring role in versions told by other peoples.

Like the Wyandot, the Delaware peoples live today in diaspora—the product of an almost incomprehensibly complicated colonial history. The European American side of this story tells of the forced displacement of the Delaware peoples westward from their homeland in present-day Delaware, New Jersey, New York, and Pennsylvania and can account for their fragmentation into communities found today in eastern Oklahoma, western Oklahoma, Wisconsin, and Ontario. Generations of ethnographers, in league with some remarkable Delaware tradition-bearers, have, importantly, documented not only Delaware understandings of this experience in the stories that are my concern here but also the deeper conceptual issues at stake. Anthropologist Jay Miller in collaboration with Delaware elder Nora Thompson Dean has written of the Delaware concept of *kwulakan*, which, at the level of Delaware cosmology, characterizes how disagreement or conflict makes the land on which it unfolds dangerous.[26] In essence, such land becomes contaminated by ill will, a fate that can also befall other forms of property. As Miller (1975) notes, this unfortunate process was, from a Delaware perspective, a factor that motivated the Delaware to relocate westward to uncontaminated territories in the face of irresolvable conflict with those who colonized each of their successive homelands (for a sketch of Delaware migrations since contact, see Goddard 1978).

In this context, we find that Delaware historical consciousness has proven hyperattentive to the story of first contact and the many colonial transformations that it spawned (Rementer 2005). Before exploring this, I need to address the story's distribution in the Americas. I had begun consulting relevant text collections, and I queried the nine hundred members of the Society for the Study of the Indigenous Languages of the Americas (SSILA) in search of versions (Jackson 2006c). As scholars who generally know with great familiarity the text collections associated with the Native languages that they study, this seemed like, in the absence of a tale-type index for Native North America, an efficient beginning.[27] It is revealing that I only received negative responses from those studying languages other than Delaware, but three different scholars (Jim Rementer, Ives Goddard, and John Bierhorst) noted affirmatively the existence of Delaware texts. These are gathered in what is a model for Native North America, Bierhorst's (1995) *Mythology of the Lenape: Guide and Texts*. Delaware first-contact stories are the special focus of Rementer's (2005) important contribution to the collection *Algonquian Spirit: Contemporary Translations of the Algonquian Literatures of North America*. The topic was also taken up more recently in a broader collection edited by Camilla Townsend and Nicky Kay Michael (2023) that was published after this chapter was initially circulated as an article. That collection—*On the Turtle's Back*—provides rich context for the Delaware narratives evoked here.[28]

Abstracting and indexing all known Delaware texts, Bierhorst identifies seven versions, the oldest a late eighteenth-century text collected by John Heckewelder from an unknown narrator, the most recent told by Ms. Bessie Snake of Oklahoma's western Delaware community and collected by Jim Rementer and Bruce Pearson in 1978 (Bierhorst 1995, 17, 215; Rementer 2005).[29] These texts span both the full geographic range of the Delaware diaspora, from the Atlantic homeland to Canada and the Oklahoma groups, and the full history of ethnographic research relative to these communities. The texts are remarkably consistent across time, space, and narrators. All involve the oxhide purchase motif, and most include many of the other associated motifs, including the Native prophecy of European arrival, misunderstanding of European trade goods, initial experimentation with alcohol, and a clear condemnation of European trickery. Two of the stories repeat the deception, adding a second incident in which additional land is obtained when the colonists ask for only as much land as a chair will cover. Upon securing agreement, they proceed to unwind the long cord composing the chair's seat, which is used, as was the cowhide, to encircle a similarly large area (Bierhorst 1995, 22, 28).[30]

For Native North America, the distribution of the oxhide purchase seems limited relative to Native nations and local groups. While told in modern times in both eastern Canada and eastern Oklahoma, the oxhide purchase story's social history in the Woodlands seems clear-cut and its far-flung distribution is probably attributable to the dispersal of a small number of allied groups, although it may admittedly be ancestral to a larger number of Woodland peoples for whom we have no recorded texts. It goes back among the Delaware, Shawnee, and Wyandot to a time before these peoples were sundered.[31]

We also have published records of the story told among the Creek (Swanton 1928, 75–77) and the Yuchi (Euchee) (Wagner 1931, 156–64).[32] I have heard it told by personal friends among both the Yuchi and the Western Cherokee (see Jackson 2003b, 22, 294n10). These latter peoples, while conventionally viewed as being of the Southeastern Woodlands, rather than Northeastern Woodlands, culture area, all belonged to a region-wide social network before the so-called removal era, and this system was replicated in miniature in Oklahoma and, I am almost as certain, in eastern Canada. While the history of these social contacts over time is complex, it is enough to note here that it is understood in outline and that there is a chain of social interaction that can be demonstrated to connect all the known communities where the story is told (Jackson 1999; Jackson and Fogelson 2004; Waselkov with Jackson 2004).

The most stunning of the reasons for dwelling on the Delaware case, both within this book and for any broader investigation of contact and colonization narratives in eastern North America, is the fact that, in addition to possessing the richest body of narrative texts on these subjects, the Delaware also, uniquely, it seems, experienced a similar incident that has also been recorded in the annals of documentary history in the Western mode. Several generations of professional historians have devoted attention to the so-called Walking Purchase, a fraudulent treaty between the Delaware and the Pennsylvania colony, which was conducted in 1737.[33] The most eloquent and economical way of retelling this story is to quote the account of the event offered on the web page of the Delaware Tribe of Indians.[34] This is the Delaware community settled in eastern Oklahoma and the one that I am most acquainted with from my life and work in the region.

In Lenape history there is the story of the "Walking Purchase" which took place in 1737. William Penn had always dealt fairly with the Lenape, but after he returned to England his sons and other agents began to sell land to pay their creditors, and these were lands which were still owned by the Lenape.

In order to convince the Lenape to part with the land, the Penns falsely represented an old, incomplete, unsigned draft of a deed as a legal contract. They told the Lenape that their ancestors some fifty years before had signed this document which stated that the land to be deeded to the Penns was as much as could be covered in a day-and-a-half's walk.

Believing that their forefathers had made such an agreement the Lenape leaders agreed to let the Penns have this area walked off. They thought the whites would take a leisurely walk down an Indian path along the Delaware

River. Instead, the Penns hired three of the fastest runners, and had a straight path cleared. Only one of the "walkers" was able to complete the "walk," but he went fifty-five miles.

And so by means of a false deed, and use of runners, the Penns acquired 1200 square miles of Lenape land in Pennsylvania, an area about the size of Rhode Island! The Lenape people complained about the way the "walk" had been done. Lenape chief Lappawinsoe expressed the frustration and dissatisfaction of the Lenape when he said: "[the white runners] should have walkt along by the River Delaware or the next Indian path to it . . . should have walkt for a few Miles and then have sat down and smoakt a Pipe, and now and then have shot a Squirrel, and not have kept up the Run, Run all day."

Nonetheless, the Lenape felt honor-bound to fulfill what they thought their ancestors had agreed to, and thus began their movement westward. The Lenape were given place after place. Each time it was promised by the government that it would be their permanent home, only to have to move again. Their trek, which lasted 130 years, finally brought them to what was known as Indian Territory, now Oklahoma. (https://web.archive.org /web/20130602092147/http://culture.delawaretribe.org/walkingpurchase .htm, accessed June 6, 2024)

This bit of history is complex, and there is much that can be said about it (for additional treatments, see Fenton 1998, 398–99; Kraft 1986, 226–28; McConnell 1992, 122; Merrell 1999; Wallace [1949] 1990).

The topic of this chapter—like the symposium for which it was initially prepared—is the exchange of colonization narratives viewed in terms of what Dorothy Noyes (2006) has aptly described as a "context-sensitive philology." A "finding" of this project on the oxhide narrative, one proposed by Barbeau and foreshadowed by all the scholars who noted the story's "old world" provenance, is the very strong likelihood that Europeans were both the source of and motivation for the incorporation of the oxhide narrative into the living oral history traditions of the Woodland peoples whom I have discussed. That there is general consensus among academic historians about the facts of the Walking Purchase proves, for Woodland peoples at least, the more general validity of their tribal (or intertribal) historiography. Beyond this side of the story, we can also use the history/story of the Walking Purchase to speculate on the function that such narratives could play in the founding moments of colonial encounters.

The oxhide purchase story diffused to peoples of eastern Native North America from Europeans during the same time that Europeans were beginning to appropriate the lands of the region's Native peoples. In addition to offering Woodland Indian peoples a retrospective explanation of one of the ways that this was done, the story seemingly also provided Europeans with a practical strategy on which to improvise such takings in the moments that they occurred.[35] Even if a cowhide was never actually stretched and cut thinly as a means of deceiving Native landholders, the Walking Purchase makes clear that such thinking was not confined solely to the realms of popular legend among the colonial masses or the classical studies of colonial elites. For European narrators and audiences, such narratives seemingly were the aesthetic and ideological counterparts to the day-to-day realities of colonization, even as they provided, when rekeyed, the basis for Native claims, to both common human decency and the moral high ground in colonial and postcolonial North America.[36]

The Oxhide Purchase as Epitomizing Event

Whether it happened exactly the way that so many Woodland Indian narrators have reported it or not, the oxhide story rings true with the experience of their peoples and with a world in which events like the Walking Purchase, to say nothing of present-day deceptions, are known facts. Finding the scholarly language with which to deal with such instances has been a central part of folkloristics' disciplinary quest, as exemplified, for instance, by the multigenerational debate on the historical validity of "oral traditions" (Basso 1990; Lowie 1915, 1917; Dixon 1915; Eggan 1967; Goldenweiser 1915; Nabokov 2002; Sturtevant 1953; Swanton 1915). There are quite a few useful frameworks within which we might think and talk further about these issues. One that has proven helpful to me and to a number of my colleagues is anthropologist and ethnohistorian Raymond Fogelson's (1989, 143) notion of "epitomizing events," an idea that is just one in a series that composes a cross-cultural typology of "events and non-events."

For Fogelson (1989, 143), epitomizing events are "narratives that condense, encapsulate, and dramatize longer-term historical processes. Such events are inventions but have such compelling qualities and explanatory power that they spread rapidly through the group and soon take on an ethnohistorical reality of their own."[37] The best-documented example of an epitomizing event in Fogelson's work is the case of the Aní-Kutáni, a priestly class among the ancient Cherokee, who were overthrown by their own people when their rule became overly domineering. Fogelson (1984, 261) links the story of the Aní-

Kutánî to a series of other similar episodes in Cherokee historical consciousness. As narratives, these accounts all "appear to be efforts to encompass and
make intelligible seemingly impersonal, inevitable, and insidious processes
of change through the evocation of a real or fanciful, dramatic, epitomizing
event." Reframing the cases central to his analysis, he continues,

> It is also important to emphasize that these epitomizing events involve hu-
> man motivation and causation: Cherokees voluntarily accepted and then
> rejected the power of the Aní-Kutánî; they felt personally responsible for
> the smallpox plague by immorally fornicating in the fields; the extinguish-
> ing of the sacred fire was caused by the corruption of their political leaders
> in ceding their ancestral homelands to whites; and surely the sacred ark
> deserved greater protection from Delaware marauders. The Cherokees, in
> common with most peoples of the world, do not view history in terms of
> abstract, disembodied, invisible, immutable laws and forces. History is gen-
> erated by human action and, since the Cherokees believe that they are not
> only distinctive people, but the only "real people" in the world, their past
> and their destiny is self-determined. (Fogelson 1984, 261)

There are two moves here. One is understanding a different modality of history, as Barbeau began to do when he saw Mr. Kayrahoo's tale not just as a
stray bit of European folklore but as a parable documenting and commenting
on deeper truths about Wyandot colonial experience. The other, as Fogelson
notes, is recognizing that the narration of such history is an active means of
engaging and understanding a complicated and often unjust world. In the
analytic language of our day, these narratives represent a confrontation between the agency of creative narrators and structures that, no matter how
overwhelming or external in origin, are still always understood in local terms
and in ways that almost always place the local at the center of the global. As
Marshall Sahlins (2000, 417) has described the task, our work is to "examine
how indigenous peoples struggle to integrate the experience of the world
system in something that is logically and ontologically more inclusive: their
own system of the world."[38]

Thus, while I agree in essence with Barbeau's understanding of the tale as
something like a parable, my motivation in recasting this interpretation in Fogelson's terms is that doing so then places the narrative within a larger context
of Woodland Indian historical consciousness rather than simply explaining
it as something outside of the event- and document-centered historiography
of the Western tradition. As importantly, this approach sees in the story, in

its Native North American forms at least, not only the ugly domination at the center of the plot but also the creativity, resistance, cultural self-assurance, and moral indignation within which this plot is contextually enveloped in textual framing, in performance, and in local cultural meanings. Seen within a larger framework of Woodland Indian social, cultural, and historical thought, we can appreciate more fully what the story is saying, what social work it has been doing over the past several hundred years, and the ways that it has been localized to reflect enduring concerns in Woodland Indian life.[39]

Bad News, Revisited

In my view, among the most important contemporary contributions to the comparative study of North American Indian oral history as historical consciousness is Donald Bahr's 2001 essay "Bad News: The Predicament of Native American Mythology." This is a paper that is overflowing with provocative ideas and powerful insights born of a career-long engagement with the sacred narratives of Southwestern peoples. It is also a paper that offers a thesis (one among many) that crashes noisily and directly into the case of the oxhide purchase and its related narratives. The project I attempt in this chapter relates so closely to the concerns of Bahr's essay that I cannot avoid engaging with his arguments, but this brings about a difficulty that must be described briefly so as to avoid misunderstanding. Bahr's essay offers many general observations on the state and nature of American Indian mythologies, including the special predicaments that these face in the life of contemporary Native communities encompassed by the larger world and the competing discourses that we are all exposed to from many corners. While Bahr's essay is a complex, interwoven whole, I have here space to touch only on the point of greatest overlap with my concerns. This does an injustice to Bahr's complex, multifaceted argument and might mistakenly suggest that I disagree with every aspect of his position (Bahr 2001).

For Bahr (2001), the bad news is that, while they are immeasurably rich and complex, Native American mythologies are dying; slipping into the past, despite the prestige that communities might overtly accord to them. This is so because, while beautiful creations, mythologies face a new challenge in the modern world—to defend themselves against the charge of being untrue. To complicate their fate further, to serve in modern contexts, he argues, mythologies must address themselves to Native-White relations, which, in his experience, they largely do not do.

I need to note first that, by myth, Bahr means what folklorists generally mean—stories that are true to those who tell them and that serve as the basis for a coherent history of the world, one that usually begins with the events of creation.[40] The hallmarks of Bahr's conceptualization of Native American mythology are its emphasis, cross-culturally, on what he calls "Edenism," meaning events in the time before the normal order of the world was established and "parody," which is his quite effective way of characterizing the ways that American Indian mythologies relate to one another. On this aspect, he writes, "By parody I mean 'a work that is based on another work but is cleverly different from the other and is silent about the other's existence.' In other words, to parody is to take an idea from someone else and slyly change it so as to make it your own. Instead of contesting, parodies borrow and play" (Bahr 2001, 588). This view is, to my mind, a compelling recasting of the principles and findings of (Native North) Americanist folkloristics, including the foundational work of Franz Boas and his students, as well as that of Thompson and Claude Lévi-Strauss. The key here for Bahr is that parody is a different mode of cross-cultural engagement than contestation, which is the dominant means by which competing views of history engage one another in Western forms of historical consciousness.

In the context of the bad news, Bahr (2001, 3) holds that an emphasis on Edenic themes and on parody has served to suppress "historical dispute and the narrative of recent events." Like others, he sees the role of parody in mythology as central to identity formation in the context of small societies in interaction with neighbors. As for Eden, I despair of trying to say all that needs to be said. The best I can do is to cite a final relevant paragraph from Bahr's account, using it as a final frame for a new comparative approach to the oxhide purchase and its congeners. Bahr (2001, 589) continues,

> Edenism is more difficult to explain. Although I can see that all peoples may need an Eden, at least an account of ancient origins and creations, I cannot see why this should preclude literary attention to recent events. Where is the culture of resistance, which is so important to scholars of the fate of today's tribal peoples? I do not find it in native American texts from the twentieth century, at least not in those of the "old school," which were told as history and which, as explained below, I call "myths." Tentatively I say that a liking for Eden distracted the tribes away from producing an oral literature of resistance, but I cannot say why this occurred.

You can probably see where I am going with this. Bahr argues that American Indian mythologies, while including prophecies of the coming of white people, generally come to a conclusion the day before the Europeans arrive on the scene. This may be, as a statistical matter, a general tendency, but then the kind of comparative but contextual folklore study that is foreshadowed in the work of Fogelson and Bahr has new work to do. In light of Bahr's arguments, what do we make of the oxhide purchase and the significantly larger corpus of first-contact and postcontact stories of which it is a part in the old narrative repertoires of Woodland Indian peoples? The generalization does not seem to hold up in this region, where contact and postcontact themes extend almost seamlessly the fabric of the mythology. I do not yet know why, but I think that a combination of comparative and contextual methods, old and new, when combined with the existing texts and new collaborative fieldwork, might help us find out. One set of factors that might be at play are the very different histories of contact that differentiate the experiences of Native peoples on the Eastern Seaboard and in the Southwest where Bahr has worked most intensively.

Folklore Studies, Comparative Colonialisms, and a Context-Sensitive Philology

When I was initially taking up this project, the School of Advanced Research Press published a book titled *Archaeology of Colonial Encounters: Comparative Perspectives* in its Advanced Seminar Series. In it, a group of archaeologists struggled to reconceptualize the way that their field approaches questions of colonization in light of the central importance accorded to studies of European colonization in many fields over the last several decades (Stein 2005). The contributors adopt a comparative frame and consider more than just the origins of the current global order; thus they are trying to develop conceptual tools for understanding colonization in such times and places as the ancient Mediterranean and Mesopotamia and pre-European California and Mesoamerica. The challenge for them, as I think it is for folklorists, is to find ways to simultaneously pluralize the historical colonial encounters about which we speak, while preserving a middle path between, on the one hand, homogenizing such studies into a unified theory of all things colonial and, on the other hand, treating each particular case as distinct, unrelated, and incomparable.

Although the oxhide purchase is a small bit of narrative, it has a wide reach in time and space and, as we have seen, it engages with some big and important issues in the history of human affairs. This characterization has, of course, long stood as part of folkloristics' self-understood definition of its object. In sharing some stories about this story, I have tried to continue to come to grips with what new work folklore studies might engage in now and in the future. This is a larger question of concern to many in the field. How might we preserve the accomplishments of our predecessors—the neglected comparative tools of the historic-geographic method, being just one example—while undertaking work that both incorporates all that we have struggled to learn to this point and engages with the deep human concerns, anxieties, and conflicts of our own age? What kind of stance—disciplinary, interdisciplinary, antidisciplinary, postdisciplinary—might best enable folklore studies to pursue such work with such a relationship to the field's pasts? What kind of partnerships, new or revitalized, might such work necessitate? These are among the questions that I have been asking, and I have been grateful for the chance to think and talk about them with the various interlocutors who have helped me in this project.

I wish to close by reminding myself, and you, of the human contexts that ground this work. I heard the oxhide purchase story told most recently at sunrise on the morning of September 29, 2005. I had, at that point, been awake for twenty-seven hours. The context was the wake and funeral for a Yuchi woman whose meaning and importance to me was, and remains, indescribably large and profound. She was, among other things, one of the Yuchi women who raised me, as an exercise in charity or perhaps as a social experiment, a second time— watching out for me, feeding me, and teaching me as an adult what proper Yuchi children learn while kids. While the Sun, one manifestation of the Yuchi Creator, came over the horizon, I was assisting the eldest Yuchi chief in the preparation of the herbal medicine to be used as a purifying wash by the mourners after the funeral party returned from the grave site. The woman's husband joined us, and we sat telling stories of all sorts, as is the custom at an all-night wake among the Yuchi and their Woodland Indian neighbors. In the course of our conversation, the widower—who is also a friend and teacher—recounted for the chief and me the story of the oxhide purchase. A Cherokee, he had learned it in his own community circle. For me, the moment brought back multiple memories and associations, as the woman whose passing we were marking was the daughter of the elderly Yuchi man who, in my first week as a fumbling ethnographer, had told me this story for the first time. Neither of these tellers, whose first languages are not English, had read the published texts that I have since consulted; neither had school-age lessons on Dido's founding of Carthage. The oxhide purchase thus continues to circulate and give meaning not only to the past that it describes but also to the present in which it remains important enough to be told by smart, serious people who are concerned with the way the world is and determining how one might best live within it. I have been fortunate to have had teachers patient enough to try to teach me such things.

Coda

In the time since this study was first authored and circulated, the specific literature on folklore, folklore studies, and colonialism has grown. In my opinion, the central work in English is Charles L. Briggs and Sadhana Naithani's (2012) article "The Coloniality of Folklore." Debates about and efforts to advance decolonial practices in some of the societies within which folklore studies is practiced (with the United States and Canada among them) have given urgency to the work of situating folklore studies as a field in relationship to colonial and postcolonial situations and decolonial practices. My thinking on these questions has been particularly shaped by my engagements with Native American individuals, communities, and nations in present-day Oklahoma since 1993. The published work that speaks most directly to the issues that I am evoking and that provides an intellectual and political context for it is Eve Tuck and K. Wayne Yang's (2012) widely cited article "Decolonization Is Not a Metaphor." The two articles just mentioned were in press at the same time as the original version of this chapter. All were offered at what I take to be the start of a new period of discussion and activism that I see as ongoing.[41]

Notes

1. In the spirit of Anna Tsing's (2000) work, I would stress that, despite popular and social science rhetorics emphasizing the newness of contemporary global flows—and of what is presently called globalization more generally—global interconnections are both long standing and, in significant part, matters of cultural circulation—a topic that has a long history as a focus for research in folkloristic and anthropological research. The historic-geographic approach in folklore, in both its Americanist (Boasian) and Finnish forms, is a key part of this genealogy.

2. Specifically, specialists in folk narrative research identify the narrative that is my focus in this chapter as tale type AT 2400 (in Thompson 1961) or ATU 927c* (in Uther 2004). It is also a constituent motif within tales, where it has been cataloged as K185.1 (in Thompson 1966).

3. In considering the contribution that folkloristics can make to interdisciplinary inquiries into colonial situations, I absolutely do not wish to suggest that important work in this domain has not already been undertaken. Numerous scholars have already contributed vitally to this project. Illustrative of the trend are works by Kirin Narayan (1993), Susan Rodgers (2003), Dorothy Noyes (2007), Donald

Haase (2010), and especially Sadhana Naithani (2001a, 2006, 2008, 2010), whose investigations have been particularly fruitful and influential beyond the field. While progress has been made, I feel that Naithani's (2006, 51) characterization of the field holds true: "Surprisingly few folklorists have taken up research on the relationship between colonial hegemony and oral discourse." Of course, a great body of folklore research—from Franz Boas on the Northwest Coast of North America to Henry Glassie in Northern Ireland—has been pursued in, and meaningfully addressed, colonial contexts.

4. Standard anthropological sources on the Huron and Wyandot include Tooker ([1964] 1991), Trigger (1987), and Barbeau (1915, 1960). An extended bibliography of Wyandot ethnography and history can be found at http://www .kshs.org/p/american-indians-in-kansas-a-bibliography/13534#wyandotte, accessed June 6, 2024. For background on Barbeau, see his autobiography (Barbeau 2006), the biography by Nowry (1998), the edited collection *Around and about Marius Barbeau* (Jessup, Nurse, and Smith 2008), and the more focused examination of his Wyandot studies by Nurse (2001).

5. An introduction to classic, comparative folklore studies, out of which the motif and tale-type indexes emerged as research tools, can be gained in Dundes (1999). The narrative at issue in this chapter was interpreted comparatively in a very brief fashion by Thompson (1946, 198–99). Richard M. Dorson (1946, 121) noticed it too and treated it briefly in his study of "Comic Indian Anecdotes." For Dorson, the narrative illustrated Native people's appreciation for humorous anecdotes that portrayed the endless battle of wits staged between Native and colonist. For Dorson (1946, 122–23), stories like the oxhide purchase and the famous sale of Manhattan account provide the ground for their inverse, humorous stories of Native deceptions of gullible settlers.

6. In contrast to other widespread Native North American narratives, no single title of either folk or scholarly origin has been attached to the story examined here (in the Americanist literature). Aarne and Thompson called it "The Ground Is Measured with a Horse's Skin (Ox-Hide)" (1981, 539; this label is retained in Uther 2004, 566–67). Other names include "cowhide purchase myth" (Swanton 1928, 76), "The White People as Still Fooling Us" (Bessie Snake in Rementer 2005), and "Dido's Purchase of Carthage" (Bierhorst 1995). As noted below, no standard tale-type index has yet been developed for Native North America.

7. For a classic work on the subject of first contacts, see Schieffelin and Crittenden (1991). Grumet (1995) explores Native American-European contacts in the context in northeastern North America.

8. The reality of such intertribal leagues and their special place in Woodland history and historical consciousness is an established and important topic in the region's scholarship. Kinship terms were used for Native nations whose ties to one another were expressed in the idiom of family relationships. Different groups

framed each other using different kin terms at different moments, but in this system, the Delaware were often characterized as the grandfathers to other Woodland
peoples (see Trowbridge 1939, 9, 55).

9. Key motifs of these contact stories include, in addition to the "axe heads
as ornaments" element, the existence of prophecies that foretold the arrival of
Europeans and their novel material culture, the strangeness of European ships,
and varying strategies for testing the safety and effects of alcohol on first exposure.

10. Note the sense conveyed here that the Delaware felt sympathy for and wished
to extend hospitality to the newcomers. This sensibility is easily recognizable in
present-day attitudes related to hospitality among Woodland Indian communities,
at least those that I know in Oklahoma. Even the most casual non-Indian visitors to
Native family or community events are struck by the extent to which hospitality to
strangers is prioritized as of paramount concern (see Jackson 1998).

11. Woodland norms of corporate (collective) reciprocity are shown to be at work
here. Norms and forms of intergroup reciprocity are a focus of Jackson (2003b).

12. For the literature on Woodland Indian prophecy, see Tom Mould's (2003)
contextual study of Mississippi Choctaw practices and beliefs.

13. Anticolonial wars of resistance engaged in by intertribal alliances, such as
that evoked here, are now well documented in the Eastern Woodlands during the
colonial and early American periods. See, for instance, Dowd (1993, 2004), Sugden
(1999), and Edmunds (1983).

14. Notice that if a conventional war had been fought, without recourse to an
immoral weapon of mass destruction, the allied tribes would have prevailed. For
an analysis of smallpox legends and history in the Americas, see the work of Mayor
(1995). As noted by Mayor (1995, n. 3), Dundes (1993) lamented in print that no one
had yet studied legends of the intentional introduction of smallpox via blankets
(Mayor's topic) or the uncorked bottle (at issue here and in many other extant
texts). The vast literature in folklore studies focused on legend is beyond the scope
of both this chapter and my competencies, but I would note that the historicity of
legend is a subject taken up by Tangherlini in his (1990) survey of legend theory.

15. A third Wyandot, Mr. Allen Johnson, served as interpreter for Barbeau's
work with Mr. Kayrahoo; thus, we have three Wyandots to thank, along with Barbeau, for their efforts to make this story available to us. As we pause to reflect on
the people behind these narratives, I might note that the Oklahoma Wyandot
community of which Mr. Johnson and Mr. Kayrahoo were a part is descended from
those Wyandot people who moved west from Huronia, the tribal homeland at the
east end of Lake Huron, over the course of the conflicts that this story encapsulates,
and that they resided successively in present-day Ohio, then Kansas, and finally
northeast Oklahoma (contra Nurse 2001, 439) where they are located today. For
a discussion of the movements of various Wyandot and Huron communities, see
Tooker (1978), Heidenreich (1978), and Morissonneau (1978).

16. A different kind of analysis of a very worthwhile sort could pick up here and consider this and related texts from a discourse-centered point of view, attentive, in particular, to the questions of reported speech and "voice" (in the sense derived from the work of Mikhail Bakhtin) to which I only allude here. I have sought to contribute elsewhere to such work (performance- and discourse-oriented folkloristics and linguistic anthropology), but here I am seeking to return, in a small way, to older comparative and historic-geographic approaches in folkloristics that were, to a degree, displaced with the rise of performance-oriented research. Nonetheless, a consideration of this and related texts in discourse terms would prove most enlightening and would, I believe, further enhance our understanding of them and the colonial contexts that shape their meanings.

17. The teller was F. H. S. Knowles, who "heard the tradition in England" (Barbeau 1915, 26). A modern Canadian telling, used to explain the history of a cathedral built in colonial St. Johns, Newfoundland, is given in Clark (1970). To clarify the context for Barbeau's report, the Geological Survey was the organizational home for the National Museum of Man and the Canadian national research programs in anthropology and folklore studies.

18. In connection with this issue of the direction of the story's diffusion, I would note that the comparative evidence from the Woodlands region suggests that Swanton's guess that it was a recent (late nineteenth or early twentieth century) borrowing by his Muscogee (Creek) consultants from their own schoolbooks is surely incorrect (Swanton 1928, 76).

19. A full folkloristic study of the literature on the Dido legend would demand great linguistic and bibliographic skill as well as considerable resources for translation assistance. A sense of the scale of the literature involved can be gained by doing a full-text search on *Dido, Carthage,* and *hide* in the HathiTrust Digital Library or the Google Books collection. Such a search mainly just reveals the English sources. Sarah Iles Johnson and William Hansen both generously helped orient me to the sources and provided valuable leads. Not all of their assistance is reflected in this chapter, but their suggestions were very valuable as background for this work.

20. It may (or may not) eventually prove relevant that the Cambodian and Javanese summaries given by Frazer (1888, 322) make special reference to a Dutch colonial contact situation, as do most of the Delaware examples gathered in Bierhorst's guide (1995, numbers 17, 22, 28, 40, 83, 203, 215) and studied by Rementer (2005). For accessible biographical sketches for Jacob Grimm, Reinhold Köhler, and James Frazer, see the introductory notes provided by Dundes (1999).

21. Having consulted Willoughby's text, I can note that Frazer does not distort what is reported there, although interesting details are omitted, the most relevant of which is the fact that the thong is first cut in a long, single strip, like those in the oxhide purchase stories. I do not know if Willoughby is judged to be reliable

as an ethnographer of southern Africa. A generous obituary published in *Nature* discusses his work (Anonymous 1938).

22. Note that in the *Golden Bough*, Frazer (1935) also cites one more example, not found in his previous article. This is a "Hottentot" instance that explains European settlement in South Africa. Frazer (1935, 250n1) is citing Arbousset and Daumas (1842, 49). An English translation of this volume is available in Arbousset and Daumas (1846) wherein the relevant version of the oxhide tale appears on page 25.

23. The Newfoundland instance given by Clark (1970) might be classified similarly, as it represents a victory of marginalized British colonials over the Crown.

24. The story, in this mode, recounts one expression of subaltern resistance (tricking the powerful) in the context of another (narrating a tale of resistance). In a full global study of the documented texts, it would be interesting to see what patterns are revealed. The "weak instigator" stories may be common in certain parts of the world relative to the "morally upright victims" stance taken in Native America. Such a pattern could correlate not only with local narrative systems and local cultures of history but also with different colonial contexts. Below, I suggest that such comparative folkloristic work offers an opportunity for the field to engage in the larger scholarly conversation on such topics as power, resistance, hegemony, imperialism and colonialism, and what James C. Scott (1987) referred to as "everyday forms of peasant resistance."

25. The relevant motifs for "Deceptive Land Purchase" in Thompson (1955–58) begin with K185.1 (the "ox-hide measure") and continue through many variations on the theme K185.2 through K185.14. I hope that an enterprising scholar will take up the whole corpus.

26. Jim Rementer has noted for me that the notion of *kwulakan* centered on "food over which there has been an argument or dispute, but that [Mrs. Dean] thought the concept might be extended to anything that became taboo" (Rementer, personal communication, May 25, 2011).

27. The as-yet-unrealized dream of a tale-type index for Native America is too large a topic to explore here. Americanists have discussed the problem for generations and continue to rely, for the time being, on a "catchword" system, although it is possible to use the numbering and naming scheme developed in Claude Lévi-Strauss's work on mythology, particularly the *Mythologiques* (1969, 1973, 1978, 1981), as a common frame of reference for the narratives discussed therein. For the catchword system and the hope for a proper "Concordance of American Myth," key sources include Swanton (1907, 1910), Thompson (1929, 271–72), and the valuable documentary history authored by Darnell (1973). Very useful in this connection is also Dundes (1963). Jacobs (1966) is a brutally harsh assessment of "oral literature" studies that touches on this specific matter from a different point of view. While a tale-type index has not been completed, Thompson (1929) provides a rich start to such an effort and has

often been used as a provisional index. While also a provisional effort (and not containing a discussion of AT 2400/ATU 927C*), Remedios S. Wycoco's (1951) neglected dissertation on American Indian tale types should be mentioned in this connection as well. For England and North America in general, see the tale-type and motif index developed by Baughman (1966). For type 2400 and Motif K185.1, Baughman noted two English examples and the Woodland Indian ones cited by Dorson (1946).

28. *On the Turtle's Back* also includes a version of the story of the oxhide purchase by Julius Fouts, a storyteller of the Delaware Tribe of Indians (Townsend and Michael 2023, 111–13).

29. Rementer (personal communication, May 25, 2011) reports that elder Nora Thompson Dean, drawing on Delaware oral tradition, recounted the story in a presentation for an academic audience in 1980. Present for the event, he recalls an unknown professor smugly commenting that the story was the Dido tale and asking, "What do you think of that?" Rementer reports that she replied, simply, "Nothing." Rementer recalls, "Soon Herb [Herbert C.] Kraft got up and said the Delaware probably learned the story because some whites had tried it on them." Kraft was a specialist in the study of Delaware history and archaeology.

30. Bierhorst treats the oxhide purchase, which he names "Dido's Purchase of Carthage," and the "Land Sale with Chair Deception" as separate but related motifs. I suspect that had the "Land Sale with Chair Deception" been widely known to the Europeanist folklorists, they would have grouped it with the oxhide purchase (as part of K185, for instance). Another text attributed to the Wyandot (Woodman 1924, 7–11) also situates the coastal encounter among the Delaware and focuses on the unwound chair incident. I do not understand the documentary context of this text (which was one of two used by Dorson 1946, 121), but it enriches the corpus under consideration.

31. As partial and suggestive evidence of this proposition, see *Shawnese Traditions: C. C. Trowbridge's Account*, an early nineteenth-century manuscript edited for publication by Vernon Kinietz and Erminie W. Voegelin (Trowbridge 1939). Trowbridge, who possessed considerable knowledge of the Native peoples of the region, recorded a Shawnee account that contained all the major elements found in the Wyandot and Delaware narratives. Trowbridge (1939, 10), who knew all three peoples (and others to whom they were allied), wrote, "They [the Shawnee] say that no other nation was with them upon the arrival of the whites, notwithstanding the Wyandots & Delawares both tell the same story in substance." In an editorial note at this point in Trowbridge's account, Kinietz and Voegelin acknowledge, "This tale is of Old World origin" (n. 6).

32. Based on discussion given in Dorson (1946, 121), it at first appeared that the story had also been documented among the Micmac. As the Micmac of eastern Canada are a coastal Algonquian-speaking people (like the Delaware),

this would have fitted neatly with the regional patterning discussed here. Dorson's source is Mabel Burkholder (1923, 20–23). Her work is a popular literary anthology that shows (without discussion) the signs of heavy intervention by the editor/author. (She writes [1923, 7] of "gathering" legends from "all parts of Canada," but the work does otherwise signal its status as an edited volume.) In the case of the oxhide purchase tale, close comparison indicates that Mr. Kayrahoo's story as recorded and published by Barbeau is Burkholder's unnamed source. I believe that she substituted the Micmac in place of the Delaware so as to achieve her evident literary goal of producing a Canadian anthology. The story may be told among the Micmac, but I do not have access to a reliable source on this point.

33. The link that I am making here between the "legend" of the oxhide purchase and the "history" of the Walking Purchase was made before me by Eugene S. McCartney (1927). I learned this after making the connection on my own.

34. The author of this account is Jim Rementer, who composed it on behalf of the tribe. I appreciate his allowing me to reprint the material here.

35. Shakespeare scholar David Scott Wilson-Okamura has pointed to the ways that Dido's colonization at Carthage served the real poetic, rhetorical, and political purposes of early modern colonial leaders, including on the Eastern Seaboard in North America. He also tracks the movement of such Virgilian themes in Shakespeare's *The Tempest* (2003, 716).

36. Historian Joshua Piker has noted that, in addition to enabling Native peoples to claim the moral high ground in the colonial encounter, stories like the oxhide purchase also serve to illustrate the validity and accuracy of Indigenous traditions of prophecy. This theme is particularly present in Mr. Kayrahoo's text. Both effects are a part of a more complex notion of resistance, one that goes beyond the kind of military resistance that Mr. Kayrahoo describes in his narrative (personal communication, June 11, 2011).

37. Folklorist George E. Lankford—a scholar who has given extensive consideration to themes such as those raised in this chapter—has fruitfully suggested that the category of "cliché-legend" might also capture the nature of stories such as the oxhide purchase that I am considering here via Fogelson's model of epitomizing event. Lankford suggests that under some circumstances a "historical account is not as desirable in continuing narrative traditions as a generalized legendary account that can represent the actual event." Using the example of Ozark narratives of Civil War–era violence (drawing on Johnston 1976), Lankford (personal communication, July 10, 2011) has developed a compelling account for the motivations that would explain a preference for a diffuse legend over a tight, historically specific narrative. Lankford also recognized that the oxhide purchase narrative, as an example of a first-contact narrative with something of an absurd character, partakes in the spirit of Trickster narratives that are highly

developed throughout Native North America. Like the white men in the oxhide purchase, the Trickster is powerful but also both absurd and immoral. Lankford argues, quite rightfully I think, that only a Trickster-like being would get away with such an amoral and outlandish scheme as that described in the oxhide purchase. In Lankford's account, the Trickster provides a model for the difficult task of making sense of the "white man." The literatures on Tricksters and white people behaving in contrasocial ways are too vast to cite, but consider Radin (1956) and Basso (1979).

38. For applications of Fogelson's model of "events and non-events," see a number of the chapters gathered in Kan and Strong (2006). Without much elaboration, I framed the Yuchi version of the oxhide purchase in this way in Jackson (2003b, 22–23). Noyes (personal communication, June 19, 2011) has usefully noted that while the kind of acceptance of responsibility for tragedy that Fogelson is chronicling here does represent a kind of assertion of agency in the face of overwhelming structural realities, it also constitutes a means of denying the power of such impersonal forces. Moving from a culturalist analysis to a personalist one, she recognizes something similar in Anglo-American personal narratives in which it is easier to claim responsibility for failures than to face a sense of powerlessness that comes from accepting that there are things in every life that are beyond our individual control. Much more could be done with the theoretical issues raised by these materials.

39. It should be clear that I feel that this story deserves further study. This would require, of course, going back and looking at the particular texts with an eye on the specific details in light of the local cultural contexts. Additional work would also be enhanced by performance analyses of actual enactments of the story in community contexts. Another valuable tack to take in considering such stories will be to follow the lead provided by Hasan El-Shamy (1995, xiii; 1997) in his work on narrative and Noyes (2003) in her studies of festival and recognize that narratives such as the oxhide story can be viewed as important expressions of vernacular social theorizing. In this case, we might glimpse in the oxhide story a fragment of an Indigenous theory of colonialism as social process.

40. Bahr (2001, 589–90) is actually much more interesting than this in his conception of myth, which also acknowledges that whoever uses the word *myth* is positioning themself as a disbeliever relative to someone else who is believed to believe the story in question, who, in other words, sees it as history. In using the word *myth* in this book, I am trying to connect my arguments to existing scholarship. I am painfully aware that Native people—and probably all believing peoples—dislike the term *myth* in English when used in relationship to narratives held to express the sacred phenomenon or deeply valued stories because it connotes falsehood in everyday English. This conundrum is why I so often use the

phrase *sacred narrative* where others might stick with *myth*. The larger problem of in-group terminologies and comparative typologies is at issue here (Ben-Amos 1976a; see also Dundes 1984).

41. Separately from the larger context of decolonial thought and folklore studies, the earlier version of this chapter (Jackson 2013a) figured in a debate on theory in folklore studies (Oring 2019a, 2019b; Noyes 2019).

2

Innovation, Habitus, and Heritage

(WITH JOHANNES MÜSKE AND LIJUN ZHANG)

Language was considered by Boas not only as a part of ethnological phenomena in general, but even as "one of the most instructive fields of inquiry," and his motivation is thoroughly remarkable: "The great advantage that linguistics offers in this respect," Boas tells in his magnificent introduction to the *Handbook of American Indian Languages* (1911 [70–71]), "is the fact that, on the whole, the categories which are formed always remain unconscious and that for this reason the processes which lead to their formation can be followed without the misleading and disturbing factors of secondary explanations, which are so common in ethnology."

—Roman Jakobson (1944, 189)

Introduction

Since the 1990s, folklorists have become self-conscious and more deliberate in their use of the English language term *heritage*. In earlier periods, the word was regularly used rather casually with a taken-for-granted patrimonial meaning.[1] Today, the term—often qualified with the prefix *cultural* and differentiated into "tangible" and "intangible" modes—is a matter of theoretical debate and policy significance. Even as it may be coming to share the spotlight with newer "slogan concepts" such as resilience, heritage is a phenomenon that is now ubiquitous in the larger social worlds that folklorists study, and it is prominent among the concepts with which we work.[2] Said differently, heritage is something that folklorists think about and a concept that we think with. In this chapter, we first evoke some current thinking on heritage in English-language folklore studies. From there, we present a complementary model of heritage that locates it within the flow of cultural history and in relationship to other aspects of culture. Cultural heritage—that which is shared—is often paired with cultural property—that which is not shared—with the two notions composing something like the opposite sides of the same coin. Here, we describe a model in which heritage is instead situated in relation to two other modalities of culture: innovation and *habitus*. We use the term *habitus* somewhat loosely here, and it is not necessary to adopt this concept as articulated, for instance, by Marcel Mauss (1979) or differently by Pierre Bourdieu (1994) to engage our model. We touch first on concepts of heritage, returning to these other modes of culture below.

American folklorist, performance studies scholar, and museum curator Barbara Kirshenblatt-Gimblett (1995, 369) characterizes heritage as "the transvaluation of the obsolete, the mistaken, the outmoded, the dead, and the defunct." She goes on to emphasize the role of exhibition and other performative modes in giving heritage forms a second life. Such exhibitions can happen in museums but also take many other forms, including festivals, ethnographic descriptions, and archiving. Discussing heritage further, Kirshenblatt-Gimblett's (1995, 369) now-canonical treatment notes, "My argument is built around five propositions: (1) Heritage is a mode of cultural production in the present that has recourse to the past; (2) Heritage is a 'value added' industry; (3) Heritage produces the local for export; (4) A hallmark of heritage is the problematic relationship of its objects to its instruments; and (5) A key to heritage is its virtuality, whether in the presence or the absence of actualities." Kirshenblatt-Gimblett's model of heritage is particularly suited to contexts such as cultural tourism, museum displays, and salvage ethnography where past/present disjunctures are often prominent. In her more recent work on heritage, she has tracked the ways that global heritage initiatives have the effect of converting local cultural diversities into a paradoxical global commons in which the local is made available for extralocal consumption and economic appropriation out of a global public sphere that heritage policy helps construct (Kirshenblatt-Gimblett 2004, 2006).

American folklorist Dorothy Noyes has built on Kirshenblatt-Gimblett's model, stressing the role that heritage plays in negotiating modernity, including in identity politics and political economy. Whereas the folklorist's concept of folklore provided a medium for political recognition within modernizing nation-states, Noyes notes how heritage represents a preferred form of economic development under globalization. Noyes (2014a) stresses the negative consequences of heritage policies when pursued as identity or economic development strategies.

> When a collective tradition is reduced to an emblem of identity and/or a
> tourist attraction, it becomes less available for all the other uses of tradition:

to socialize children, to learn and practice skills, to compete for status, to maintain memory, to provide entertainment, to worship divinity, to negotiate conflict, to contemplate the meaning of life. Complex performance traditions evolve in societies with scarce resources to serve a range of purposes. They are especially important in helping people to negotiate rapid social change. When they are removed from everyday use by heritage protection, the foundations of the community can be destroyed instead of strengthened.

For further exploration of heritage's negative externalities, we particularly recommend Noyes's volume *Humble Theory* (2016).[3]

Work in critical heritage studies by Kirshenblatt-Gimblett, Noyes, Valdimar Tr. Hafstein (2012, 2018b), Regina Bendix (2018; Bendix, Eggert, and Peselmann 2013), Kristin Kuutma (2016), and others on whom we draw emphasizes the praxeological dimension and places a special focus on the social construction of heritage. The theoretical work we aim to contribute to here builds on this agent-centered approach to situate heritage (as one mode of cultural life) in relationship to two other manifestations of culture—innovation and the normative culture that is fundamental to everyday life across societies. Existing critical heritage theory discusses in detail the complex implications of heritage processes but less directly addresses the place of heritage as a cultural mode in the everyday lifeworld as experienced by individuals and groups through time. Inspired by both existing theories of heritage and rich ethnographic work on life in heritage-filled communities, our model is an effort to work toward a treatment of heritage as a kind of culture that people live with every day. We write in a provisional-but-theoretical idiom, but we are mindful of our ethnographic experiences and those of diverse colleagues in our field.[4]

Culture and Metaculture

The scholars mentioned here are just a few among numerous English-speaking folklorists and ethnologists theorizing the social status and ramifications of heritage.[5] Engaging and extending this work requires understanding the German American culture concept that is a key inheritance of American folklore studies via Franz Boas and his students. As suggested by the work of Kirshenblatt-Gimblett and others theorizing heritage, an associated concept of metaculture—that is, cultural expressions or representations that are about cultural expressions or representations—is also necessary.

For those new to such discussions, we note that the word *Boasian* is generally used to refer to scholarly work attuned to research questions, findings, methods, principles, and theories associated with a research line in American anthropology (inclusive of American ethnology) and folkloristics pursued by Franz Boas and his students (Jackson 2000, 2010; Stocking 1998; Darnell 1973, 2001). Many articulations of the Boasian culture concept are available to us. Because of its succinct relevance to a concept of metacultural awareness, we turn here to a formulation offered by Boas's student Alfred L. Kroeber in his 1948 text *Anthropology: Race, Language, Culture, Psychology, Prehistory*. Regarding culture, he writes, "Now the mass of learned and transmitted motor reactions, habits, techniques, ideas, and values—and the behavior they induce—is what constitutes culture" (1948, 8).

In the same work, Kroeber (1948, 245) addresses the dynamics of unconsciousness and consciousness of culture. On the first, he argues, "The quality of unconsciousness seems to be a trait not specifically limited to linguistic causes and processes, but to hold in principle of culture generally." While linguistic phenomena, such as grammatical gender, had provided a generative domain for Boasian cultural theorizing (cf. Boas 1911, 63–70; Silverstein 1979), Kroeber importantly is flagging the general capacity of cultural phenomena to manifest relatively low levels of individual and shared awareness. While in Boasian ethnology this quality of culture had a number of ramifications beyond our scope here, we note that it is this same phenomenon that also underpins our vast literatures on social norms and the interaction order (Goffman 1963, 1971). They are at issue, for instance, in the breaching experiments that we most often associate with the work of Harold Garfinkel (1991). Performance-oriented folkloristics inherited interests in the relative degree of consciousness of cultural phenomena down several lineages, including the fundamentally Boasian ethnography of speaking (Boas 1911 as reflected in Hymes 1974), interactional sociology and social psychology (Goffman 1974 as reflected in Bauman 1975), and Roman Jakobson's (1960 as reflected in Shuman and Hasan-Rokem 2012, see also Jakobson 1980) poetics.[6]

As in psychoanalysis and ethnomethodology, Boasian ethnology attended to the movement from relatively unconscious to relatively conscious. Kroeber (1948, 245) continues, "A custom, a belief, an art, however deep down its springs, sooner or later rises into social consciousness." In the Boasian framework, this could happen in a variety of ways emerging from both extraordinary and everyday life experiences, for instance, in the lived experience of rapid cultural change or through diverse, normal experiences of intercultural contact (e.g., travel, intermarriage, pilgrimage, ethnography, or migration). In the American approach rooted in Boasian concerns, we also see the ways that individual variance in reflective disposition shapes intrasocietal variation in metacultural awareness. We recognize this in the key interlocutors who often star in American folkloristic ethnography. Like Packy Jim McGrath, the subject of Ray Cashman's (2016b) study of Irish worldview, such consultants reel us in with their higher-than-usual awareness of, and capacity to critically reflect on, their cultural surround.[7]

If metaculture is cultural expressions or representations that are about cultural expressions or representations, the fullest available treatment of metaculture, to our knowledge, can be found in Greg Urban's (2001) *Metaculture: How Culture Moves through the World*. Our arguments here are particularly indebted to Urban's theoretical work. We do not fully unpack the concept here, instead introducing it just enough to frame our perspective on heritage as a kind of metacultural process or state recognizable through its cooccurrence with elaborated metacultural discourses. Heritage discourses and practices are canonical instances of metaculture. As Urban (2001, 3) writes, "Judgments made by natives about similarities and differences—continuity with the past and change—are part of what I will call metaculture, that is, culture that is about culture."[8]

In building on the contemporary concept of metaculture carried forward from this classic theory of culture, the model we introduce here emphasizes the theme of relative metacultural awareness present in individuals and that can be hypothesized for typical individuals within collectives. This awareness has a snapshot character in time and focuses in any given instant on a particular cultural form, expression, value, or complex. Theoretical work on metacultural awareness owes much to scholarship on metalinguistic awareness, work that has in turn shaped understandings of linguistic ideologies, including work on language loss that is relevant to the kinds of heritage phenomena of concern here (Silverstein 1981; Irvine 2012).

Innovation/Habitus/Heritage: A Heuristic

The kinds of theories of heritage that we have evoked are complementary to each other, touching on different aspects of a multifaceted whole. Our model is offered in this spirit of complementarity with the hope of supplementing constructively critical perspectives that are particularly focused on formal heritage policy. Our model situates heritage as one of three "ideal type" manifestations of culture, placing it alongside innovation (i.e., those aspects of culture overtly marked as new) and habitus (i.e., culturally derived and individually embodied dispositions, norms, and taken-for-granted practices)

FIGURE 2.1. (FACING) To evoke the three modalities of culture under discussion, my coauthors and I point to three examples from the material culture of North America. *Top* is an Apple Watch from 2015, a (then) innovative technology that was for a time the focus of considerable metacultural discourse (face-to-face conversation, press articles, reviews, etc.). *Middle* is a plain man's pocket comb, an object that is generally taken for granted. Neither new nor markedly old, it exists in the realm of everyday practices without being the focus of much attention or discussion outside of specialist contexts such as barbershops. *Bottom* is an Eastern Cherokee white oak splint basket (from the collections of the National Museum of Natural History, Smithsonian Institution). While baskets of this type among the Cherokee were initially innovations adopted from Europeans after contact, such baskets today have passed through a period of everyday normality to become emblems of Cherokee cultural heritage. Community heritage initiatives help celebrate, promote, and preserve such basketry. *Apple Watch image (2015) by Yasunobu Ikeda via Flickr (licensed CC BY-SA 2.0). Black Plastic Pocket Comb image (2015) by Crisco 1492 via Wikimedia Commons (licensed CC BY-SA 4.0). White Oak "Market Basket" by Eastern Band Cherokee Basket Maker Agnes L. Welch, circa 1961, from the William C. Sturtevant Collection, Department of Anthropology, National Museum of Natural History, Smithsonian Institution. E437563-0.*
Image by Jason Baird Jackson.

(fig. 2.1).[9] All three are here situated in relation to the passage of time in the flow of cultural history. We do not frame the model in this way here in this chapter, but it is also possible to treat these three modes of culture ethnologically or geographically, in relation to movement in space rather than to time. This prospect suggests the ways that our model is intended as a contribution to the broader renewal of historic-geographic, historical, and comparative approaches in a plural tradition of folklore studies that remains attentive to the tasks of performance ethnography (for related arguments, see chap. 1).[10]

The scheme that we present here was developed initially by Jackson and Müske. L. Zhang's (2018, 2024) ethnographic work on heritage practices in China has further enriched our thinking relative to the proposed model. Horizontal movement to the right in fig. 2.2 represents time's passage. Relative degrees of cultural self-consciousness are represented by height or depth relative to the centerline.

Cultural forms positioned above the centerline are ones manifesting some relative degree of collective self-consciousness. This is manifest in their being the focus, for instance, of significant metacultural discourse. An example from Zhang's work is a type of fortresslike, monumentally scaled, rammed-earth

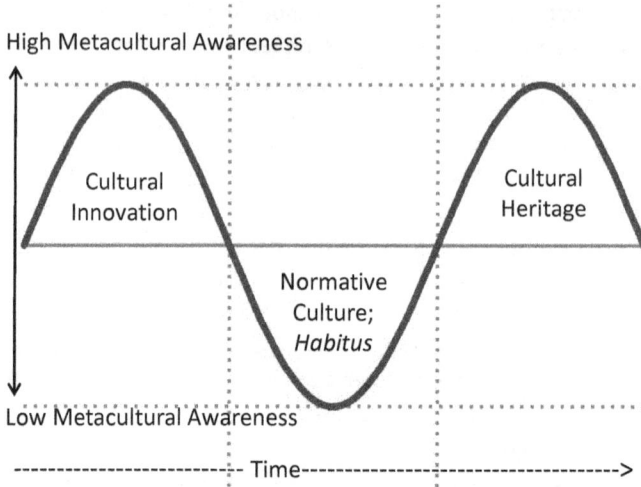

FIGURE 2.2. A heuristic diagram characterizing innovation, normative culture, and cultural heritage over time and in relationship to metacultural awareness. Figures 2.3–2.5 offer examples situated at different points along the continuum of this model.

domestic building found in a rural part of China's Fujian province. Formerly just a local home type, these buildings, known now as the Fujian *tulou*, are marked as cultural heritage properties from the global to the local levels and are the subject of much self-conscious discourse as well as vigorous economic, political, and legal activity (fig. 2.3) (L. Zhang 2018, 2024; UNESCO 2018). The Patum of Berga, as documented by Noyes (2003, 2016, 337–79), has similarly become a matter of ever-greater self-consciousness as it has become entwined in what Bendix and her colleagues have characterized as "heritage regimes" of an extralocal sort (Bendix, Eggert, and Peselmann 2013).

Cultural forms positioned below the timeline are ones that have faded into the social and cultural background. They are unremarkable in the literal sense that they generate little metacultural commentary on their status. Whether in the form of the cultural traits studied by Boasian ethnologists or as Geertzian "local knowledge," culture of this sort has long been the primary concern of American cultural anthropology. It is also a focus for much contemporary European ethnology, with its current theorized passion for quotidian practices (SIEF 2014, 2017). Taken-for-granted assumptions, everyday routines, commonplace commodities, norms of conventional conduct, Maussian "body techniques," and so much else in our lives and in the lives of all people have

FIGURE 2.3. An example of cultural heritage that would be situated on the right above the centerline in figure 2.2, "[Fujian Tulou] are inscribed as exceptional examples of a building tradition and function exemplifying a particular type of communal living and defensive organization, and, in terms of their harmonious relationship with their environment, an outstanding example of human settlement" (UNESCO 2018). Fujian Tulou were inscribed on the UNESCO World Heritage List in 2008. *Image by Gisling (2007) via Wikimedia Commons (licensed CC BY-SA 4.0).*

this character (fig. 2.4). As American ethnology/cultural anthropology and European ethnologies have regularly demonstrated, this core of culture has a low degree of self-consciousness, but this does not mean that it is unconscious in the psychoanalytic sense. Ethnographic inquiry, the necessities of child-rearing, and cross-cultural travel, among other techniques, have long helped individuals and groups gain a reflexive sense about their everyday lives. Still, the modes of culture positioned below the horizontal line are distinct in that they are separate from two other modes of culture that do especially attract heightened metacultural awareness and discourse.

In this treatment, the two aspects of culture seemingly most divergent in other ways are shown to share a key quality—metacultural prominence. New technologies, new social innovations, and the latest fads and fashions, along with much else marked as "new," are commonly matters for public discussion

FIGURE 2.4. An example of normative culture or habitus that would be situated below the centerline in the middle of figure 2.2, an everyday bowl of rice—neither innovation nor heritage.
Image by International Rice Research Institute (IRRI Photos 2009) via Flickr (licensed CC BY-NC-SA 2.0).

and debate (fig. 2.5). Similarly, obsolete technologies, moribund customs, long-standing-but-disappearing ways of life, and eroding values are also often matters for public discussion and debate.[11] In both modes, metacultural prominence correlates with cultural self-consciousness and is made manifest in varied discourses and social interventions.

While heritage is a special concern of folkloristics— an outgrowth of its status as a kind of recasting of our nominal object (i.e., folklore)—folklorists also have a tradition of studying innovation. We see this at the core of the Boasian version of the historic-geographic method, with its concern for the adoption-or-not of diffused cultural traits as well as with the historical invention of new cultural forms (Boas 1940, 281–89, 290–94; Lowie 1940, chap. 20; Kroeber 1948, chaps. 8–14). While American folklorists have not tended this tradition particularly well, it is fundamental today in the social-science-turned-business literature on innovation diffusion, a literature in which social difference—for

FIGURE 2.5. Situated to the left above the centerline in figure 2.2, cultural innovations take many forms, including fads in fashion, technology, and design. Decorated with reflective tape, so-called Tron cars (resembling vehicles in the 1982 movie *Tron*) captured the imagination of young adults in urban China as well as Western journalists around 2014 (Diaz 2014).
Image by Sebastien Cosse (2015) via Flickr (licensed CC BY-NC-ND 2.0).

example, early adopters versus laggards—has taken the place of spatialized cultural groups (Rogers 2003; Gladwell 2002).

In a different way, Noyes's (2016) work on "hardscabble academies" points to the social contexts in which vernacular innovations arise and are adopted. In general, however, concern for innovation has grown less pronounced in autonomous American folkloristics as it has drifted from its ethnological roots. There are always exceptions to any generalization, though. We acknowledge that we can see one kind of renewed interest in new cultural forms in, for instance, contemporary American folklore work on new media genres (Blank 2008). Think, for instance, of the folkloristics of cleverly captioned photographs (a.k.a. image macros, memes) circulating in social media.

In the ethnological culture history framework informing this chapter, innovation is, for instance, at the center of revitalization movements as well as being fundamental to the local adoption of diffused cultural forms (Harkin

2007). It is also a key motif in the Americanist biographical tradition, as reflected in the life histories of innovators in "traditional" societies as well as the stories of individuals who so often experienced missionization, colonization, migration, and other modes of radical cultural change (cf. Brandes 1979).[12] Culture brokers, innovators, and those whose personal stories center on significant levels of dramatic social change—three prominent types of ethnographic consultants—all generally share higher-than-average levels of metacultural awareness relative to both that which is new and arriving and that which is old and departing (Casagrande 1960).

The vast space below the abstract self-consciousness borderline has been referred to and discussed in a number of ways. In Boasian approaches, it is the main share and normal mode of culture. It is also recognizable as the embodied cultural practice that Mauss, and Bourdieu after him, characterized as *habitus* (Mauss 1979; Bourdieu 1994). This semiconscious and generally unquestioned (in everyday life) mode of culture is built up out of cultural content that originates ultimately in innovation. Innovation from this perspective includes not only the modern sense of invention but also other quite varied forms of cultural change, both the intentionally directed and the seemingly random. While every cultural form begins at some point in space and time, innovations usually appear in individual lives and collective experiences having circulated from elsewhere. To adopt a diffused cultural expression is thus also to innovate, as the contemporary literatures on innovation adoption stress (Rogers 2003).

As those of us who were children prior to the availability of mobile telephones or the public internet have witnessed, these are model innovations in the sense described here. For younger adults and children in most parts of the United States—individuals who have never lived without them—both are rapidly moving into the realm of unremarkable everyday culture. Every day, all around the world, people are experiencing the normalization of previously innovative cultural forms, whether those innovations began as inventions (e.g., in vitro fertilization in the United Kingdom) or importations (e.g., sushi in the urban United States).

Innovations such as robotics, artificial intelligence, self-driving cars, nanomaterials, vat-grown hamburgers, or weaponized "insect" drones are marked for conscious discussion (these are examples recently under discussion in the United States or Europe) because they are new and are entering the cultural system, often causing some anxiety in the process. Heritage is marked for conscious discussion because it is old, is valued favorably by someone, and is perceived or feared to be leaving the cultural system (Jackson 2007). Innovations are at the beginning of their cultural careers, while heritage is seen as, or feared to be, at the end of its time as lived cultural practice.

Here we intersect with the core of Kirshenblatt-Gimblett's model (1995). She speaks of heritage giving cultural forms a second life after they would otherwise become obsolescent. This could conceivably be a long-term fate. Alternatively, the heritage phase could be relatively brief—something like a period of mourning prior to the complete loss of its object.

To think through the distinction that we raise here, consider the basket-making practices found today in some Native American communities and in Japan. With baskets no longer widely used as tools of physical labor, basketry was, in some but not all possible contexts, reframed as an important expression of cultural heritage, with linkages to art markets, tourism, personal and museum collecting practices, and the expression of local (in Native American contexts) or national (in Japan) identities. This has been a multigenerational and ongoing project in these societies, with changes developing within the heritage period, as with the decline of heritage baskets sold to tourists in Native American societies and the rise of heritage baskets that are understood as works of fine art. Contrastively, folklorists around the world have found themselves documenting and heralding the work of the "last" practitioner of a once-vital expressive form or culturally rooted custom. While such "lasts" are not always actually the last, sometimes they are. Folkloristic documentation, celebration, and lamentation of obsolete-to-moribund heritage can happen in a very brief period of time. Many folklorists have been told by earnest, elderly interlocutors, "No one wants to learn it." Such folklorists have sometimes been surprised when someone does want to learn it, but some folklorists have also seen prophecies of disappearance proven true.

Importantly, not all culture forms experiencing obsolescence are recast as heritage. The elders among the Yuchi people with whom Jackson has worked as an ethnographer were deeply committed to the revitalization of their unique "heritage language" but had no desire to return to the practice of hauling home muddy drinking water in barrels in wagons from distant sources. In every society open to heritage-making, doing so is a selective process unfolding within particular regimes of value.

Most interesting to contemplate and follow are instances in which heritage comes to be transformed back into habitus. Heritage endeavors,

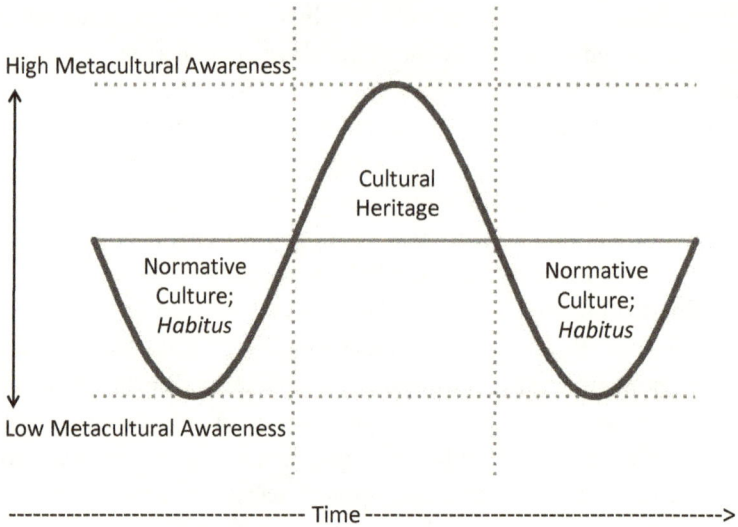

High Metacultural Awareness

Cultural
Heritage

Normative
Culture;
Habitus

Normative
Culture;
Habitus

Low Metacultural Awareness

------------------------------- Time ---------------------------------->

FIGURE 2.6. A version of the heuristic diagram evoking the renormalization of heritage. Note that the abstract model is drawn like a wave, but there is no necessity that cultural changes be either rhythmic or gradual. In this case, a revitalized and renormalized heritage item might persist with stability in an ongoing way.

particularly locally initiated and controlled preservation efforts in small-scale, community contexts, *have* moved in this way, often intentionally. A child raised amid a successful cultural revival can perceive a renewed state of vitality not as a persistent heritage intervention but as a local norm (fig. 2.6).[13]

When everyday culture is born again out of heritage work, the wave line of heritage goes back below the self-consciousness line. While we may think that such a transformation is relatively rare from the perspective of a narrow definition of heritage, this is a fundamental effect of many successful "revitalization movements" as well as of diverse cultural "revivals." When Jackson once expressed anxiety about the seeming unidirectional quality of her model of heritage, Kirshenblatt-Gimblett (1998b) was quick to point to her own work on klezmer—the musical genre rooted in the cultural history of Eastern European Jews. She has tracked a recent postheritage (postconservatory) stage characterized by increased innovation and what we might call renormalization. This more recent period of renewed vitality followed a period of strict preservationist activity. This conserva-

tionist period logically followed the genocide, destruction, and displacement of the Holocaust (1933–45) and World War II (1939–45)—historical
events that had effectively ended the kind of communal life in which the
music previously flourished.[14]

Conclusion

The model we offer here has been visualized in the form of a wave, but it
is important to recognize that this is a heuristic for interpretive work, not
data from an experiment in social physics. The aim of the visualization is to
capture aspects of cultural historical processes that we think are, at some
level of generality, reoccurring in the social worlds that folklorists and ethnologists both study and live within. In any particular "real world" case,
the line charting the career of a cultural form and people's metacultural
relationship to it would be irregular and distinctive. For a great many parts
of the cultural worlds in which we all live, the forward-moving line long
ago sank below the consciousness line. Only a small number will ever rise
above it again. Especially for those exhausted by the expressions of heritage
that we are already managing, safeguarding, preserving, reviving, monetiz-
ing, fighting over, and so forth, this fact is perhaps a source of relief. Surely
no one would want to give a second life to the entire global repertoire of
interconnected human practices and values from both past and present.
Heritage is salient because it is selective and, as Kirshenblatt-Gimblett (1995,
369) stresses, a "mode of cultural production in the present" and is thus an
outgrowth of present-day preoccupations.

    In closing, we note again that our heuristic is offered as a complement
to existing theorizations of heritage. Work by Jackson and others in Native
American communities has suggested the value of such a complementary
approach (fig. 2.7). In such communities, there is a tremendous amount of
heritage activity (the English word *heritage* is often explicitly used for it),
but this activity—in contrast to circumstances in various other parts of
the world—is not driven by nonlocal tourists, political agendas, scholarly
programs, or economic development schemes, even as such phenomena
are certainly also present in Native North American communities. An approach that is compatible with such grassroots kinds of heritage endeavors
and that can easily attend to situations in which these activities achieve
the goals set for them by community heritage workers seems valuable to
us. A model that includes innovation and everyday normative culture

FIGURE 2.7. Reestablished in their community in 1994, many of the younger women and girls of the Duck Creek Ceremonial Ground shown here dancing the Yuchi ribbon dance in June 2016 have never known the absence of this important ceremonial dance. A self-conscious effort made by their elders laid the groundwork for a (re-)new(-ed) normal.
Photo by Jason Baird Jackson.

helps in several ways. Among these is fostering the recognition that innovations are often leveraged in the service of heritage and that heritage programs and initiatives themselves are often innovations and not just interventions.[15]

The use of the latest digital technologies such as smartphone apps for Indigenous language revitalization efforts provides an increasingly widespread illustration of our own moment. Soon such things will probably seem normal. Our work here is offered in the hope of better accounting for the nature of such shifting heritage situations outside of the UNESCO heritage sphere. We also have aimed to suggest the value of reanimating older ethnological findings and frameworks in the service of current scholarly tasks. Folklore studies, European ethnology, and cognate fields would benefit, we hold, from a reengagement with their own heritage as well as renewed attention to such social, cultural, and historical phenomena as invention, innovation, diffusion, the nature of everyday and quotidian cultural forms, revitalization, revival, endangerment, obsolescence, traditionalization, and grassroots heritage-making projects.

Notes

1. For the ways that folklorists have iteratively debated, formulated, described, and critiqued the concept of heritage and how heritage debates relate to earlier ones around "folklore" and newer ones related to, for instance, "resilience," see Noyes (2016). The literature on heritage is now vast in folklore studies, ethnology, and neighboring fields. The field of inquiry is also international in scope, with particular strengths in the three scholarly languages represented by the coauthors of this chapter (English, German, and Mandarin Chinese). We regret that we can only draw on a small portion of this literature in this project. Hafstein (2012) provides a survey for folklore studies; a German introduction to the concept and field is provided by Tauschek (2013). Those seeking an introduction to heritage studies in China can begin with An and Yang's (2015) English-language contextualization of folklore studies in China since the late 1970s. For the closely related concept of cultural property, see Skrydstrup (2012). See also n. 3, below.

2. "The slogan-concept is an abstraction that seems to validate concrete realities, the name of a purportedly eternal idea used to launch a time-specific project, a tent providing shelter to actors coming from all directions" (Noyes 2016, 412). For "slogan concepts" and for "resilience" as an example, see Noyes (2016, 410–37).

3. In addition to Noyes's writings, we point in particular to the work of Kristin Kuutma (2013, 2016) and Regina F. Bendix (2018), including the rich body of work produced by the cultural property research group that Bendix co-led (Deutsche Forschungsgemeinschaft [DFG] Interdisciplinary Research Group on Cultural Property 2018). We also recommend the overview of heritage scholarship offered by Icelandic folklorist Valdimar Tr. Hafstein in *A Companion to Folklore* (2012). Drawing on our international field and his own important scholarship, Hafstein (2012, see also Hafstein 2018b) does an excellent job of synthesizing the critical folklore studies literature on heritage theory and policy. For illustrative ethnographic case studies exploring the local impact of formalized heritage policies, see Foster and Gilman (2015) and L. Zhang (2018, 2024). For case studies of state-level heritage policies and practices, see Bendix, Eggert, and Peselmann (2013) and Maags and Svensson (2018).

4. Even the seemingly simple expression *our field* is complex, as each coauthor operates within and feels an attachment to multiple and differing disciplinary positionalities in multiple local, national, regional, international, and interpersonal

social network contexts. We sometimes write here as if folklore studies is a coherent, unified discipline neighboring to but distinct from cultural anthropology,
ethnology, and adjacent fields, but we are very much aware that this is a tactical
simplification and also a misrepresentation of a much more complex landscape,
past and present. Situated in multiple provincial contexts but aspiring to enact an
aspirational international scholarship, we are uncomfortably aware, for instance,
of how much relevant scholarship (in English and many other languages) we are
failing to engage in this effort. For one of several useful evocations of the plural
state of the fields in which we are engaging, see Bendix (2003).

5. In a contribution to the *Journal of Ethnology and Folkloristics*, Markus Tauschek (2011, 57) offered an earlier reflection on heritage theory in relationship to
metaculture and a biographical approach to cultural forms. Among his concerns,
though, is the belief that tracking the transformation of habitus into heritage implies a "teleological 'historical trajectory.'" As discussed later in this chapter, we
have endeavored to show that heritage can be converted into habitus and not solely
the reverse.

As work on our article unfolded slowly over a period of many years, Michael
Dylan Foster was pursuing an important ethnographic project on the impact of
national and international heritage interventions on local ritual masking practices
in rural Japan, particularly on the visiting deity customs found on the island called
Shimo-Koshikijima. Foster (2017) draws on many of the same sources that inspire
our work here to both interpret his case and offer a conception of metaculture compatible with but distinct from the one that we use in this article. Foster is working
with a conception of metaculture in which this term refers to transcultural phenomena (such as UNESCO heritage designations), whereas here we use *metaculture* to refer to those aspects of culture (local or translocal) that are themselves about culture.
(Related is what Immanuel Wallerstein calls geoculture, as discussed in chap. 4.)

6. Richard Bauman's work on storytelling offers a now canonical example. In
accounting for the work of Texas storyteller Ed Bell, Bauman noted the way in
which, over time, his storytelling performances were staged in increasingly formal
settings for audiences with decreasing familiarity with the local cultural contexts
from which his stories derived. Telling stories for formally constituted audiences
in cross-cultural contexts increased Bell's self-awareness of his storytelling practice
and of the passive cultural knowledge that his stories demanded in their source
context. A range of techniques were used by the narrator to recalibrate his stories
for new audiences, prominent among them being the introduction of rich metadiscursive commentary. The shifts chronicled by Bauman (1986, 78–111) are closely
linked to the kind of increased metacultural awareness that performance provokes
and that we are evoking in relation to heritage.

7. Given American folklore studies' emphasis on excellence in expressive performance, we often see the individuals with whom we work—as their communities of-

ten also do—as "stars" relative to the exercise of their talents vis-à-vis the aesthetic or expressive practices for which they are deemed masters (i.e., "star performers"). But folklore studies, cultural anthropology, and field linguistics also have a history of recognizing "star informants"—ethnographic consultants who are particularly adept at the work of cultural or linguistic translation and explication across cultural differences (see Cashman, Mould, and Shukla 2011, 12; Silverstein 1981 addresses related issues). From the perspective developed in this chapter, star informants—but also artists who cultivate the skills needed to perform in cross-cultural settings— are often those with higher-than-typical metacultural awareness or consciousness. As Ray Cashman, Tom Mould, and Pravina Shukla note, star performers can sometimes, but need not also, be (capable of being) star informants (2011, 12–14).

8. For traditionalization as a closely related metacultural practice, see folklore studies and linguistic anthropology work cited in Jackson (2013b, 74–85, 216–18). Similarly, for treatments of linguistic and cultural "endangerment" (a related metacultural discourse about the potential "death" of linguistic varieties or cultural forms) in this perspective, see Jackson (2007) and Moore (1999).

9. Readers seeking orientation to the methodological concept of ideal type as used here are directed to the classic formulation developed by German sociologist Max Weber (1949, 89–99). A classic Chinese development of the concept inspired by Weber can be found in the work of Fei Xiaotong (Fei, Hamilton, and Wang 1992, 8). For a current assessment of ideal-type methods, see Swedberg (2017). Our use of habitus owes more to the earlier formulation of Mauss (1979) than to that of Bourdieu (1994). As noted above, one need not embrace the concept of habitus to engage our model. Routines, for instance, as described by Jespersen and Damsholt (2014, 26, drawing on Ehn and Löfgren 2010) fall into this zone. Any word or words describing generally-taken-for-granted and uncontroversial cultural norms or forms or practices or techniques will work. In this chapter, we also characterize our formulation as a "model." For clarity, we note that the sense of model that we have in mind is heuristic, that is, "a description or analogy used to help visualize something (such as an atom) that cannot be directly observed" (*Merriam-Webster* 2018).

10. The claim, just made, that there is a distinction between what we outline here and a space-centered ethnological analysis may require additional explanation. Both kinds of analysis—temporal change within a society and spatial patterning of difference across societies—figured prominently in the American ethnological approaches on which we draw here. While we are not here presenting ethnographic evidence from particular societies, such ethnographic (and historical) experience in particular lifeworlds most clearly informs our argument. A geographic analysis would instead focus not directly on the immediate experience of life with an innovation-turned-norm-turned-heritage phenomena in time but instead on comparative evidence from across different societies in some form of contact with each other and thereby constituting a spatial network across which cultural forms can (but do

not always) circulate (through diffusion, forced acculturation, missionization, etc.) as innovations, becoming normalized (and sometimes made in turn into heritage) within particular societies. Such a project could, for instance, consider the diffusion of a practice such as the ritual use of the peyote cactus or the spread of online dating applications on mobile phones as they pass from society to society in space (a process that does have a temporality). Such a project would rely on a great deal of comparative data whereas our arguments are mainly informed by ethnographic sensibilities. For instance, what is it like for people to talk about innovations or heritage in particular societies and how does such talk change over time as people normalize innovations or heritage-ify (disappearing) norms? A comparative account of the sort evoked but not pursued would instead ask questions such as what kinds of metacultural discourse accompany diffusion events across space in situations of intercultural encounter and how does the metaculture of cultural change across spatialized social contexts impact lived experience of the sort of concern to us here?

11. As an example of this dynamic we offer a case from Müske's work in Switzerland, where it has long been common for church bells to be rung on every quarter hour. This is a time signal and not done for liturgic reasons, although the practice is not completely unconnected from its religious background. In recent times, this custom has become more and more contested by some individuals living in many areas, as it is perceived as "noise." This view means that such bell ringing is vanishing as a taken-for-granted custom and is at the same time a more and more reflected-on event in everyday culture. In 2010, the Swiss federal court judged that such ringing church bells belong to Switzerland and that there "is a public interest in maintaining this tradition" (Müske 2015, 77–78). In defense of bell ringing, the court acts as a heritage-making actor in a context in which such bells were already becoming metaculturally salient under conditions of changing cultural values and social practices.

12. Making sense of experiences of radical versus gradual social change (i.e., colonized Native American societies vis-à-vis modernized peasant ones) may partially account for differences distinguishing older American and Northern European ethnologies of innovation. Notably, the framing of innovation as a topic for scholarship in folklore studies given in this chapter is particularly US centered. Innovation is addressed in other disciplinary settings very differently. Astrid Pernille Jespersen and Tine Damsholt's (2014) careful characterization of the ways, past and present, that innovation and everyday life intersect as concerns in Danish ethnology is an instructive illustration of this distinction.

13. Instances abound in Jackson's observations of Native North American societies. Müske offers the example of southern German *Fastnacht* (carnival), which has undergone a strong revival since the 1980s. Like so many "traditions," young people, but also middle-aged adults, cannot remember a period characterized by less intensity, and most people think that current festival customs are hundreds of years old. Today the Fastnacht has been promoted as intangible cultural heritage by

the German UNESCO Commission (folklorists have contributed to the application process and are participating on the board), and there have been arguments against such recognition since many protagonists think that the Fastnacht is not "ripe for the museum" (as the German expression goes).

14. She discussed this matter with Jackson (personal communication) during the annual meetings of the American Folklore Society in Salt Lake City, Utah, held October 13–17, 2004.

15. As one thoughtful reviewer of this chapter observed, it might be reasonable to treat innovation and heritage not just as sharing the characteristic of metacultural prominence but as being conterminous. Put more simply, all heritage *is* innovation in its own moment in time. Adopted fully, a constructivist view of heritage situates it as a human-made construction in the present. While such a construction has, as most folkloristic definitions stress, recourse to the past, it can certainly be seen, from one analytic point of view, as simply one kind of innovation.

We propose, and invite others, to continue working on formulating a model that can more fully incorporate this insight. Our emphasis here retains an interest in the biography of cultural forms moving unidirectionally (but not teleologically) through time. In this context, it seems useful to differentiate between a cultural form that is being argued about because it is new, and one that is being argued about because it is old. It might be better, given our goals here, to say that it seems useful to retain differentiation for when a single cultural form that was once argued about in the context of its newness is today being discussed in the context of its oldness and concerns about its disappearance. Beyond our concern for difference over time, there is the hope that our conception is compatible with grassroots heritage endeavors. Those activities are human creations in the present, of course, just as UNESCO listing activities are, but an ethnography of local heritage work would be difficult to pursue with an analytic metalanguage that completely disregarded local cultural emphases on pastness. Scholars who have attempted to negotiate discussions of traditionalization—or, still harder, the so-called invention of tradition—with members of communities invested in questions of cultural continuity have regularly faced this dilemma (Briggs 1996; Jackson 2013b, 74–85, 216–18).

3

On Cultural Appropriation

There's a strange paradigm of people wanting to pursue cultures that aren't theirs, but they step over the line when they start claiming to be those ethnicities and speaking for people of those ethnicities.

—**Chief Ben Barnes, Shawnee Tribe (in Hilleary 2017)**

Introduction

Folklorists and ethnologists speak regularly about issues of cultural appropriation. I have been party to numerous serious, thoughtful discussions of the theme with fellow scholars in my fields, and because most of my adult life has been twined with the lives of Indigenous friends and colleagues, I have had rich access to the ways that the issue is a catalyst for pain, reflection, and activism. Even without direct contact with aggrieved or impacted communities or individuals, cultural appropriation debates frequently appear in media reports and across social media feeds. In the English-speaking world at least, cultural appropriation stories pass in front of us in a steady flow, even if we choose not to attend to them. There are sophisticated writings on the subject too, but even when written by journalists, activists, or scholars with direct experience or knowledge germane to the topic, these tend to be authored from near the front lines of specific cultural contests. This is logical and good, of course, and I have followed both news and analysis of cultural appropriation throughout my career, but folklorists and ethnologists still lack general models and heuristics with which to assess this steady flow. Here, I attempt to work on this general, conceptual level. My goal in this chapter is to provide a framework within which folklorists can consider instances of appropriation and refine their thinking about the phenomena. I am not suggesting that appropriation must be inscribed as a keyword among the most central and durable concepts of folkloristics, but because it has been a reoccurring theme in the lives of the communities that we engage with and the cultural forms that we study, I hold that it deserves conceptual attention.[1]

My aim is to complement important specific discussions of cultural appropriation with a general heuristic or model. This could be thought of as both a model of and a model for work in folklore studies and ethnology. My proposition is that scholars in folklore studies and ethnology have developed resources that can help us think in cross-contextual ways about cultural appropriation. If brought together as a framework, such an account could be useful as we approach new particular cases as scholars or as we take up further work as allies or self-advocates in the projects of scholarly activism. As with heritage and other matters of interest to these fields, cultural appropriation is both a scholarly framework and a phenomenon in the wider social world. Such instances require intentional efforts of conceptualization.[2]

Appropriation in the Roster of Kinds of Cultural Change

American ethnology and folklore studies were always concerned about change, even before the phrase *cultural change* came to prominence. Prior to taking up work on acculturation, which foregrounded concern for change after contact with colonial influences, historic-geographic work centered on questions of cultural innovation, diffusion, adoption, and adaptation. This work sought to reconstruct local and regional patterns of historical change with or without the benefit of written sources. Only the most extreme forms of functionalist ethnography in the mold of British social anthropology purposefully bracketed out questions of change (Lesser 1985, 53–68, contra Radcliffe-Brown 1952; see also Mintz 1985a; Lesser [1933] 1977; Strong 1936).

In my training in folklore studies and cultural anthropology (American ethnology), significant emphasis was placed on issues of "culture change" as this has generally been framed in the Americanist tradition. I took a whole graduate seminar titled Theories of Cultural Change (after Steward 1955), and various kinds of cultural change were always under discussion. These ranged from stark instances such as revitalization movements (Wallace 2003; Harkin 2007), enslavement (Mintz 1985b), and the rise of capitalism (Weber 1958; Thompson 1967) to relatively less painful ones such as folk revivals (Cantwell 1996; Sacks 1997), small-scale practices of traditionalization (Bauman 1992a), and the invention of dessert (also Mintz 1985b). An interest in modalities of cultural change has continued throughout my career, even as scholars have grown less typological about cataloging them and as they have come to see change as a constant in all social life, a view that perhaps reduces the need to be overt about marking one's studies as studies of "cultural change."[3]

In the long run of scholarly work, however, our fields have cataloged and described quite a roster of modes of cultural change. Naming and characterizing all of them is a bigger task than this chapter can contain, but it may be useful to evoke something of the range and then to situate cultural appropriation among them. One key thing about the wider list is that the terms have active names. These aspects of human existence are experienced as processes. *Missionization* or *modernization* or *enculturation* or *assimilation* or *creolization*, for instance, all end in *-tion* or *-ion*, which in modern English is used in nouns that are the result of a verb. Missionaries missionize and thereby attempt to produce conditions of missionization. In folklore studies and ethnology, we have systematically worked our way through our inventory of key concepts, making them active, processual, and agentive in this way. In doing so, we have added them to the set of cultural change concepts. Static tradition became traditionalization, a metacultural, discursive means by which individuals and groups create continuity-mindedness in the flow of history and change through the mobilization of people for certain kinds of action and through the inculcation of particular values (Jackson 2013b, 74–85, 216–17). Folklore studies' nominal object has undergone this change also, with attention focusing on folklorization (McDowell 2010; Mendoza 2000; Hafstein 2018a; Briggs 2012; Paredes [1973] 1993). Heritage has likewise spawned heritagization (Hafstein 2018b).

Not all processual modalities of culture change take the *-tion* ending. Genocide is an important example of a culture-change noun overflowing with horrifying action but without the *-tion* ending. The English *-cide* suffix, referring to death, shows up in other especially grim modes of cultural change, as in *linguicide* (a more active version of language death). While most of the *-cide* words are subsocietal (e.g., *suicide, regicide, infanticide*), they carry powerful social and cultural implications and effects, even if they are probably not thought of as varieties of culture change in the same way that innovation, migration, or genocide are.

Before addressing some of the most relevant forms of cultural change, I would like to observe that global histories of folklore studies and ethnology are entwined with processes of social change of the sort that I am discussing here, with modernization and colonization producing, for instance, such phenomena as traditionalization and revitalization but also fostering, if not producing, the rise of these fields of study (Briggs and Naithani 2012; Bauman and Briggs 2006). The matters at issue can be read in various ways, but as a scholar whose work attempts to grapple with issues of continuity, and not just change, reaching back to precolonial, and thereby premodern, contexts in the Americas, it is my sense that some parts of the roster of culture-change concepts are applicable in diverse times and places, whereas others are specific to the formation of the current capitalist world-system. To suggest this is not to deny the particularly strong salience of nationalism, modernization, and colonialism to the concerns of and rise of folkloristics. I discuss these matters in a different way and in greater depth in chapter 4 (this volume) on folklore studies and world-systems analysis. Here, it might be easiest for me to just suggest that I think that cultural appropriation is a particularly salient matter in the early twenty-first century, but that I also believe that processes deserving of this label can occur in other settings, including precolonial Indigenous ones. At the same time, there are reasons, some of which are explored below, for cultural appropriation being more prominent in some times, places, and social positionalities than in others. Different culture-change concepts have to be assessed and reassessed in changing scholarly practice and in different cases in which they might be applied. At the very least, folklorists subscribing to the "modernity changes everything" paradigm are likely to agree that such modes of culture change as diffusion, urbanization, domestication, and invention have been with humanity for a very long time.

To situate cultural appropriation in this larger matrix of modalities of cultural change, I have to pluck from the bundle those that I will argue are most immediately proximate to it. While heritage and property will reenter the discussion below, here I focus first on diffusion, acculturation, and assimilation. These three processes have a very deep scholarly history of relevance. This is especially true with diffusion, which was a founding problem for these disciplines in their modern forms. Acculturation and assimilation were taken up intensively in the mid-twentieth century.[4]

Diffusion

Discussions of diffusion in American folklore studies and cultural anthropology (American ethnology) are one part of a much wider history of international scholarly investigation into diffusion in which European ethnological and folk narrative research also played a significant role. While preceded by research concerns that are largely consigned to the dustbins of disciplinary history, diffusion stands at the head of our modern genealogies of respectable topics that respectable ancestors studied. Even if diffusion per se does not animate the work of most contemporary folklorists and ethnologists, we are trained to understand some of its basic characteristics, we read some classic works related to its study, and we walk around witnessing its continued presence in our lives. Trying to shake students out of seeing diffusion and the associated historic-geographic methods as matters of the past, I have long drawn their attention to contemporary interest in diffusion in business schools, where the study of innovation diffusion is at the heart of how multinational corporations strive to spread their new products widely (Rogers 2003).

There are many definitions and conceptualizations of diffusion available. Due to its richness and sophistication, and its standing as a synthesis of early American ethnology (inclusive of much folklore studies), I often return to Alfred Kroeber's (1948) textbook *Anthropology*. In the context of a longer and very rich discussion that I highly recommend for its interest and artistry, Kroeber (257) follows a discussion of cultural tradition with a conceptualization of diffusion.

> Now allied to this receptivity of its own past is a receptivity that every culture shows toward cultural material worked out by other cultures. Such acceptance of foreign elements and systems of course constitutes a geographical spread; and the designation most in use for it is "diffusion." Such spreads occasionally are rapid, but often they require a considerable time interval. Accordingly, much of what is acquired by diffusion from outside also has its origin in the past, much as what a culture receives by internal handing-on of traditions; but the characteristic of diffusion, the emphasis of the process, is on transmission in space.

Along with further theoretical reflection, Kroeber (257) goes on to offer a fantastic account of the cultural provenance of a wide range of elements in "American" culture, thereby making clear for his audience the centrality of diffusion as a historical process of cultural change for all known societies. In doing so, he also notes how, typically, "once acceptance is made, the source is played down and forgotten as soon as possible." We should keep this later dynamic—the denying or downplaying of origins—in mind as we approach cultural appropriation.[5]

If we look at the list of "American" cultural traits that Kroeber (1948, 258) identifies, from a Germanic language full of French words written on Chinese paper with Phoenician alphabet and German printing to the global food basket from which Americans eat, most (the Native American "contributions" being a possible exception) are not seen as vexing instances of taking. The temporal distances separating us from these acquisitions may account for some of this, but much cultural transmission through social or geographic space is accepted as relatively "normal" or desirable by the parties involved. Consider so-called Scandinavian design in general and the products offered around the world by the multinational firm IKEA in particular. Such furnishing may not be equally appreciated by all residents of the global ecumene (Hannerz 1989) or capitalist world-system (Wallerstein 2004), but on average, the residents of Sweden (IKEA's home country) do not oppose the spread of assemble-at-home modernist furniture or their national meatballs, nor do those who line up to purchase them in places like Cincinnati or Beijing.[6] In keeping with American-ist theories of diffusion, IKEA products do often require localization, as was discussed for India in the *New York Times* (Goel 2018, "Ikea Opens First India Store, Tweaking Products but Not the Vibe") and other media outlets. Here is a good place to evoke one of folklore studies' more esoteric but beloved modes of cultural change, *oikotypification,* the term used in folk literature research (after von Sydow 1948) for more complex instances of the localization of dif-fused folk narratives (Clements 1997; Laudun 2006).

More could be said, but a hallmark of diffusion as I am describing it—based on established literatures in folklore studies and ethnology—is that diffusion is a widely occurring process of cultural change involving the movement of cultural forms, values, practices, and technologies from one social setting to another. The "arrival" of such a diffused cultural element changes the recipient society or group, sometimes to a small degree, sometimes extensively. Not all cultural forms are put on offer by potential source societies, and not all poten-tially recipient societies are open to every possibility offered. Diffusion can be subtle and interesting along a range of variables; for instance, as Claude Lévi-Strauss observed across his oeuvre, societies often create new cultural forms in which they invert the forms or practices that they recognize among their neighbors (e.g., Lévi-Strauss 1982). This is a special version of what is called stimulus diffusion, but it also relates to complex practices of social boundary maintenance (Kroeber 1948, 368–70; Barth 1969). The issues central here also relate to the discussion of parody (after Bahr 2001, 588) presented in chapter 1.

There are many nuances, and the study of diffusion is closely related to the study of innovation. As I have already suggested, a diffusion from one perspec-tive is actually an innovation from the perspective of the society in which it "arrives." As colleagues and I have suggested in modeling innovation in relation to habitus and heritage, an innovation often co-occurs with a metacultural discourse of newness (chap. 2, this volume; Urban 2001; Urban, Baskin, and Ko 2007). In the present context, it is useful to return to Kroeber's point about forgotten origins. In terms of the arguments offered in chapter 2, the process of forgetting that Kroeber describes would mark the transition of an innovation into the realm of normative, unremarkable, taken-for-granted culture. Appropriations can be similarly normalized, although the aggrieved memory of wrongs done can also be actively preserved, thereby preventing this transition.

Some part of the pain in contemporary appropriation debates arises when one side channels our scholarship and cites diffusion as a healthy, "normal" cultural process, refusing to see that appropriation is different from diffusion for this very reason—that not all parties are accepting of the process of cultural movement or flow involved. I return to metadiscourses of anguish below, but as is probably evident, I argue for a rich, granular corpus of terms and characterizations of culture-change processes, and I reserve diffusion for those instances in which both the source and the recipient societies are for the most part not particularly troubled by the transmission. Diffusion is most easily applied to cases in which all parties (to the extent that we can speak approximately and theoretically about "all" parties) are pleased with or indifferent about the transmission.[7]

Acculturation

Acculturation's scholarly history is long, but not as long as diffusion's. Acculturation, as a theorized kind of cultural change, was a project embraced by American ethnologists (including many who also identified as folklorists), but it lacks a strong presence in folkloristics separate from ethnology. In American anthropology, as elsewhere, the study of diffusion (and innovation) was closely linked to the reconstruction of cultural histories manifest in historical or memory ethnographies and regional ethnologies. Acculturation studies in the US represented a reorientation in which the object was not to conduct ethnographic work that would allow for the reconstruction of past ways of life but instead to focus on the present social dynamics that were confronting social groups experiencing change. This applied particularly but not solely to instances of forced cultural contact, as among Indigenous groups experiencing ongoing European colonization.

The addition of acculturation studies in American anthropology is closely associated with a key document known as the "Memorandum for the Study of Acculturation" authored by Robert Redfield, Ralph Linton, and Melville J. Herskovits (1936, 149). While it was preceded by work relevant to the study of acculturation—in general and in particular societies—the memorandum legitimated this research question. In it, the authors define acculturation as a mode of cultural change as follows. Note how they seek to position it in relationship to related-but-not-the-same processes.

> Acculturation comprehends those phenomena which result when groups of individuals having different cultures come into continuous first-hand contact, with subsequent changes in the original cultural patterns of either or both groups. (NOTE: Under this definition, acculturation is to be distinguished from culture-change, of which it is but one aspect, and assimilation, which is at times a phase of acculturation. It is also to be differentiated from diffusion, which, while occurring in all instances of acculturation, is not only a phenomenon which frequently takes place without the occurrence of the type of contact between peoples specified in the definition given above, but also constitutes only one aspect of the process of acculturation.)

In the parenthetical note just cited, the authors treat several of these processes as overlapping and, in some ways, coconstitutive. For ease of exposition and for heuristic purposes, I treat the modes of cultural change as distinct, but I am not arguing against what the memorandum's authors are saying. In their terms (as in mine), cultural change is a broad category encompassing a number of types. I am treating diffusion, for instance, as distinct from acculturation, but in their terms, it is reasonable to see acculturation as the result of an aggregation of diffusion events taking place in particular contexts.

Later work on acculturation brings out some of the distinctions that I am making and sets me up to introduce assimilation and then return to appropriation. Present-day authors have retreated from categorical pronouncements of the sort that I am about to evoke. This is both because they come off as judgmental and because later work has often shown matters to be more complex and nuanced than such pronouncements would suggest.[8] With that caveat in mind, I note that classic work on acculturation generally used this term to describe broad cultural configurations arising from situations of cultural contact. This fostered comparative judgments about, for instance, an ethnic group or a particular village being more (or less) acculturated. While I am framing this as a kind of scholarly assessment, ethnographic work in Indigenous societies has shown that these judgments are also common in local life, as when the residents of one Indigenous village characterize themselves as more "traditional" or "conservative" and see a rival community as less so. (Such judgments can be reversed, with one community expressing pride in being more "progressive" and claiming that conservative neighbors are "backward.") Such intracultural discussions typically are based on an intergroup dynamic in which a group, Indigenous people for example, are under pressure from a large and more powerful (often non-Indigenous, often historically more recent, and colonial) population.

Among scholars today, this sort of discussion is often awkward and embarrassing, whether encountered in a remote community or in an older work of scholarship, but it remains necessary to understand what the study of acculturation is about. Typically, such assessments, as with work on acculturation generally, arose from circumstances in which a relatively more powerful group was in sustained contact with a less powerful one. This power dynamic is central to the larger discussion that I am pursuing here. Most often, in the Americanist context at least, acculturation studies were pursued in acknowledgment of colonial contexts. Ethnographic studies of acculturation generally focused on the ways that put-upon, colonized peoples adjusted to a constrained and difficult existence alongside dominant and dominating colonizing groups. It is worth noting, however, that power and demographic differentials existed among precontact Indigenous groups, and these situations could also be analyzed within the framework of acculturation.[9]

Power differentials in colonial and settler society contexts are a relevant factor, but as assessments of relative acculturation suggest, this is also largely a gestalt characteristic. In contrast to diffusion, where individual cultural traits (practices, texts, foods, etc.) are the focus, acculturation is a broader, more pervasive characterization of change. A village resists or does not resist acculturation as a wholesale matter, whereas a story or a song or a style of hat might or might not diffuse. As I noted above, acculturation as a broader kind of phenomenon could be seen in a large aggregation of diffusion events. In colonized communities generally resisting acculturation, we see marked differences between, for instance, acceptance of European metal tools (often welcomed) and European religions and values (sometimes resisted vigorously). For considering assimilation and appropriation, the power differential aspect is the one to keep foregrounded, even as trait versus gestalt (or configuration) helps us further distinguish diffusion and acculturation.

Assimilation

While acculturation is a way of conceptualizing a powerful and pervasive kind of cultural change under (most often) conditions of unequal, intergroup contact, assimilation, as generally used, carries a strong aura of intentionality on the part of the dominant group and is a more unidirectional process. The term is also regularly used beyond colonial situations, as when nation-states devise policies that aim to "assimilate" immigrant and refugee groups. This way of thinking about assimilation frames it as programmatic (i.e., as a matter of intentional policy). In popular understandings of assimilation, cultural forms do not just diffuse; they are actively pushed from the more powerful source group to the weaker target group. While proponents in positions of power will often speak of individuals and groups choosing to assimilate, assimilation efforts are done *to* people. The degree of coercion involved can be highly variable. As evoked in the memorandum, acculturation studies anticipated (and discovered) ways that both parties in cultural contact situations would reshape each other. In contrast, dictionary and scholarly definitions of assimilation emphasize its unidirectional nature. Assimilation is about how majorities attempt to reshape minorities in their image, sometimes with considerable coercion, often under structural conditions of inequality and relative disadvantage.[10]

The literatures on assimilation are especially vast due to the huge range of global situations, past and present, in which something like assimilation has taken or is taking place. The key thing here is to see again the power dynamic (stronger-weaker, larger-smaller, group-to-group) and to acknowledge that, while some individuals and groups may feel open to "being assimilated," this should not be assumed to be a universal reaction. Even when not overtly coerced, as when Native American parents insisted that their children learn English and abandon their Indigenous languages so as to avoid deeper forms of suffering and to take "advantage" of "opportunities" in the dominant society, "choice" under pressure is not exactly choice. Many individuals and groups may feel open to, even eager to, pursue cultural change on their own terms, but it is different when they are forced to do it on the terms spelled out by a dominant group. In assimilation, a dominant group actively transfers its lifeways to a subordinate group. This can be empowering, or it could deepen the receiving group's subordination. The real-world contexts can be highly variable, but the power differentials and the direction of the cultural movement are constant.[11]

Appropriation

In ideal-type terms, diffusion or "cultural exchange" takes place in piecemeal transactions between relative equals without coercion being the dominant motivation.[12] By contrast, acculturation takes place in situations of contact characterized by relative power imbalances and refers to broader contours of change. Because it is not about the movement of a single trait from one group or society to another, it becomes possible to speak of acculturation going in both directions (mutual influence) despite the demographic, economic, and other inequalities characterizing the contact situations. Like missionization, revitalization, and other modes of cultural change, assimilation often has an active character, with someone actively pursuing a program of change. Like missionization and unlike revitalization, assimilation is outward-focused. There is a sense, at least from a certain point of view, that it is done *to* an external party. Assimilation shares this quality with appropriation.

As I am modeling it here, appropriation is a structural inversion of assimilation. In assimilation, a powerful group imposes aspects of its culture on an economically, politically, and demographically weaker target group. This is most clear in situations that scholars have overtly characterized as "forced assimilation" (see Lesser [1933] 1977; Strong 1936). In a framework of appropriation, in contrast, the powerful group takes aspects of the culture of the subordinated group, making them its own. If the subordinated group was happy or indifferent about a particular instance of such adoption, neither we nor an on-the-ground observer would resort to the label *appropriation*. *Diffusion* or *acculturation* (depending on the nature of the situation and our analysis) would serve us as labels, but in cases of aggrievement, appropriation fits. Appropriations are typically a source of pain, and feelings of loss or violation, for source communities—often resulting in concrete negative consequences—even as appropriating groups either do not perceive or refuse to attend to these wider consequences. As noted above, those who take up cultural practices from aggrieved, subordinated groups often cite diffusion as a healthy part of (inter)cultural life, fundamental to the practical business of everyday living and valuable for the construction of multicultural societies, to which all participants "contribute." To this macrodefense is often added a microdefense of appreciation, in which those accused of appropriation stress that they take up forms or practices out of respectful admiration. These macro- and microdynamics are easy to see in nearly any appropriation controversy, including in the brief examples given below. The four neighboring modes of cultural change are illustrated schematically in figure 3.1.

**Schematic Representations of Diffusion, Acculturation,
Assimilation, and Appropriation**

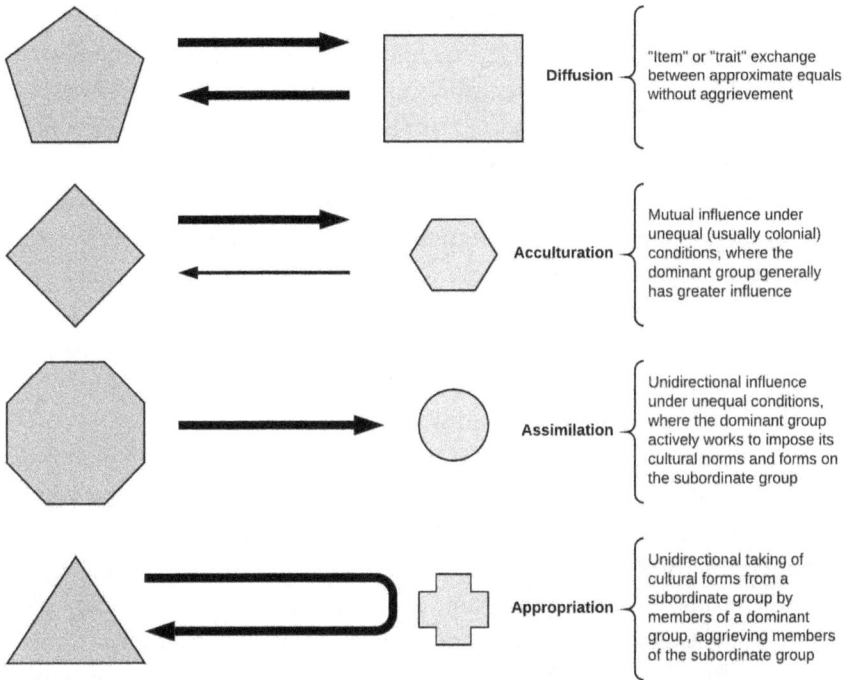

FIGURE 3.1. In this representation of the four modes of cultural circulation under discussion, the differences in shapes only serve to evoke eight different hypothetical societies. The relative size of the shapes suggests the relative power of a society in relation to the other in its pair. The arrows characterize the direction or directions taken by the cultural circulations being modeled by each of the four concepts. The arrow of lighter weight pictured in connection with acculturation is intended to suggest that, while bidirectional, acculturation situations are marked by asymmetrical or unequal exchange between the linked societies.

Illustrating the Framework

Some instances of appropriation reported in the popular media can help illuminate the framework proposed here. These instances have been chosen because they are easily recounted. There are much more complicated and painful cases available for consideration. While I think that the framework should be useful for addressing such cases, I pass over them here for economy of presentation. Examples of such cases would include many that are observable in relationships between Indigenous peoples and dominant European populations in the four main Anglophone settler societies—Canada, the United States, New Zealand, and Australia. US examples would include the phenomena of fraudulent claims and enactments of Native identity by both individuals and groups, "American Indian" sports team mascots, the unwelcome use of Native American religious practices and ideas in non-Native "new" religions and spiritualities, the production and sale of fraudulent Native American arts and crafts, and the commercial exploitation of Native American designs by large, non-Native corporations (e.g., see Aldred 2000; Brown 2003; Bruyneel 2016; Parsley 1993; Sturm 2011). The literatures relating to specific appropriations are large, and I encourage those unfamiliar with them to read the work of Indigenous authors who have explained the damage caused by appropriation and the ways it creates broader harms to Native communities.[13]

As a student of material culture in general and dress in particular, I use three cases of cultural appropriation in the domain of clothing and adornment. These progressively more complex instances can help illuminate the general framework. While simpler in relation to the kinds of cultural appropriation instances evoked above, they are still complicated and tap into larger networks of history, culture, and conflict. In presenting them briefly, I want to stress that they, too, could be unpacked and discussed in much greater depth.

Before taking up the examples, I want to underline that not all instances of cultural appropriation are equally troubling. To stick with typical Native American responses—there are reoccurring experiences that provoke, for instance, eye rolling and the shaking of heads, and there are reoccurring experiences that provoke deep anger, tears, profound feelings of grief, and impassioned activism. When, for example, a European American evokes vague family lore to claim to have "some" Native American ancestry, eyes typically roll. When a European American incorporates a fake Native tribe and makes money selling "tribal" ID cards that enable those who buy them to fraudulently get set-aside (US) state government contracts intended for Native-owned firms, Native American observers will usually feel justifiable anger.[14]

Different intensities of response to acts that are framed as cultural appropriation prompt recognition of other differences worth noting before examining some examples. Appropriations attributed, for instance, to profitable corporations are often read differently from those playing out at the individual level. Those involving financial gain or the telling of lies or the breaking of laws are often seen differently from those arising from simpler differences of under-standing between the parties. As my examples suggest, some kinds of appro-priation contests are easier to understand and to narrate in the public sphere. As media reports suggest, clothing-centered examples are common, and I think that this is in part because they are easy to recognize and easy to mediatize. Given the way that clothing functions in European American societies, cloth-ing examples have the effect of gendering cultural appropriation discourse, suggesting that women are the primary agents of appropriation or consumers of appropriative products. I worry about this perception and would observe that the more egregious kinds of cultural appropriation practices—sports team mascots, for instance, or complex and often criminal forms of ethnic fraud—are usually perpetuated by organizations or groups led by men. Within fashion as an industry, men often hold decision-making and economic power. Men are involved in a range of cultural appropriation phenomena, but these are often vexingly hard to explain and do not lend themselves to easy social media uptake/outrage or rapid journalistic exposé.[15] Saying that a Halloween outfit is offensive because the wearer is being insensitive and undermining the dignity of the people (mis)represented is a much simpler matter than explaining how the federal recognition of Native nations works in tandem with the Native American Graves Protection and Repatriation Act of 1990 and why a group of county commissioners in some midwestern US county cannot simply hand over human remains to any claimant group that shows up and asks for them.

"appropriate culturation"

In March 2014, Christina Fallin, daughter of then-Oklahoma governor Mary Fallin, posted to Facebook a photograph in which she wore an eagle-feather headdress. While there are some special circumstances in which women in Native American groups of the Great Plains might wear such a headdress, they are, in this region, closely associated with Native American men and in all cases are seen as important emblems of respect and prestige—one gen-erally reserved for important Native leaders and elders. Christina Fallin is non-Native and had already, in a controversial photoshoot at the Oklahoma governor's mansion, established a polarizing reputation for circulating im-ages of herself deemed by some in the state as inappropriate to the governor's mansion as a state symbol. When the image of Fallin wearing the headdress was posted, there was a significant backlash among Native American observ-ers who were joined by non-Native allies and critics of Christina's mother, Governor Fallin. While Governor Fallin is a Republican in a state dominated by the Republican Party, she was at the time of the headdress episode on the path to becoming the least-popular governor in the US and in the history of Oklahoma (Buettner 2018).

For Native American people, this was hardly the first instance of inappropriate use of such a headdress by a non-Native person. It was hardly even the first case covered widely in the media. Thus for Native critics, the fact that non-Native people keep doing this and ignoring their pleas for cultural respect is deeply frustrating (coverage of the broader phenomena is summarized in Lynskey 2014). That an important cultural object associated with solemn occasions and older, respected male leaders keeps being worn in casual and sometimes erotic ways by younger, non-Native women is particularly upsetting. When outrage followed Christina Fallin's photo posting, she offered a now-classic form of nonapology in which she refused to address the substance of criticisms, noting instead, "Growing up in Oklahoma, we [non-Native Oklahomans] have come into contact with Native American culture institutionally our whole lives—something we are eternally grateful for." As reported in the *Tulsa World*, Fallin (then age twenty-six) continued, "With age, we feel a deeper and deeper connection to the Native American culture that has surrounded us. Though it may not have been our own, this aesthetic has affected us emotionally in a very real and very meaningful way" (Eaton 2014; see also Bain 2018; Keene 2014; Murg 2014; Zezima 2014).

In defending herself against criticisms, Christina Fallin describes a kind of entitlement that she feels and that she seems to suggest all Oklahomans should feel. Appreciation for visual aspects of Indigenous culture that are ubiquitous in the state, in her account, opens the door to making these one's own. Note the curious word *institutionally*. I am hard-pressed to interpret this, but my best guess is that this refers to institutions (such as museums) that make objects like feather bonnets visually accessible to non-Natives outside of the norms and cultural contexts of Native community life. I close this evocation by pointing out that when Christina Fallin (or her bandmate) posted her image to her band's social media, she/they captioned it "appropriate culturation." Despite claims to the contrary (Murg 2014), this inversion of the phrase *cultural appropriation* signals that they knew exactly what they were doing in her posing for the photograph and then circulating it publicly. The caption suggests that her actions were intentional and were courting (further) controversy or making a political statement.

Native people are a minority in Oklahoma despite their large numbers relative to other US states, and the state being home to thirty-nine federally recognized Native nations. While their own tribal governments are increasingly important economic and political actors in the state, Native people in Oklahoma continue to face a great range of difficulties and lack the power to decisively impact state politics. Although I do not want to frame the matter categorically for all situations and contexts, they are generally in a subordinate position relative to Oklahomans of European ancestry, particularly leaders such as Governor Fallin. As reflected in Christina Fallin's words and actions, we have a classic case of a non-Native person claiming rights to and taking a cultural practice that is not hers by right of local Native practice and values. She should have known better, and her caption suggests that she did know better. When confronted with the hurt that she caused, she chose to formally assert her claims to Native culture (on the common basis of appreciation) rather than to apologize or engage Native people on the underlying issue. I offer this as a classic instance of cultural appropriation.

"To be honest, I'm finding it hard to work up much in the way of outrage about this"

Due to costume controversies, the American holiday of Halloween at the end of October is now the season for cultural appropriation discussion and debate in the US, but in 2018, a UK newspaper got a head start. German Oktoberfest celebrations offered a less-expected instance of costumed appropriation. The *Guardian* offered an unattributed September 10 piece titled "Oktoberfest Dirndl: Is It Ever OK to Wear 'Sexy' Versions of Traditional Dress?" The subtitle offered further detail, explaining that "visitors wearing 'pornographic' Alpine outfits at the Munich beer festival have been accused of tasteless cultural appropriation" (*Guardian* 2018). While the piece touches on the wearing of dubiously modified versions of traditional Alpine folk dress (dirndl) by American and Australian tourists of both genders, the associated image (of a cisgender woman wearing the sexy version of the Oktoberfest dirndl) makes clear that the women's outfits are the ones most clearly under discussion.

The piece is an instance of the paper's "Pass Notes" genre, which are presented as "A quick chat designed to tell you everything you need to know about a story you don't need to know about." The title and subtitle play it straight and evoke (unattributed) concerns about cultural appropriation and debasement. In what follows, both a position against such misuse and one that finds such objections ridiculous are presented quasiconversationally. We do not get quotes from either side of the implied debate, just anonymous journalistic representations of the two positions. Both sides evoke "cultural appropriation" directly, but the case against this being an actual instance of cultural appropriation is made in a lighthearted tone to suggest that any objections are, in this instance at least, ridiculous.

The piece is too short and elliptical to be certain, but it seems that the author or authors, or at least the representation of the doubtful commentator, cannot believe that millions of tourists traveling to Munich to wear sexy peasant wear and drink a lot of beer is worthy of being understood as cultural appropriation. Anyone who knows the seriousness of devotees to traditional forms of folk dress in northern European nations would be more willing to entertain the possibility that the objections are real and justified, in at least some German circles. One would love to know more about the matter on the ground, even if the *Guardian* treats it as something we "don't need to know about." Be that as it may, I raise this case not because of the quality of the reporting but because it points to certain perceptions held by those with liberal politics in English-speaking countries like the United States and the United Kingdom. Cultural appropriation can be seen to be a real thing, but not a real thing that Germans could reasonably experience, at least not with respect to folk costumes worn during what is now a major tourist spectacle. Note that I cited a full-throated critique of the cultural appropriation of Native American dress from the *Guardian* in the headdress case above (Lynskey 2014).[16]

Subordinated minority groups—particularly Indigenous groups—experience cultural appropriation. If Germans are on any side of this equation, it would be, the logic seems to go, as appropriators.[17] A left-leaning UK paper in the end makes light of the claim that German vernacular culture could be debased and misused by non-German tourists in league with German purveyors of Oktoberfest experiences. The dubiousness of the cultural appropriation claim, in the eyes of the naysaying voice in the *Guardian* piece, seems to rest on its nonaccord with the model described here, in which appropriators are in a more powerful position than those whose culture forms are being appropriated. This view, of course, aggregates all Germans into a common body. A committed devotee to German ancestral dress may receive no direct benefit from Oktoberfest tourism, but because some Germans do and because Germany is a powerful state with global influence, the idea that its citizens could be victimized and thus aggrieved is dubious. The German case as presented by the *Guardian* not only underlines the issue of relative collective power but also highlights again the unavoidable facts that appropriation is constructed in metacultural discourse about cultural practices and that this discourse, by its nature, is constructed around two opposing sides in which one is aggrieved and one questions the aggrievement.

"My culture is *not* your prom dress"

The variables in play can be seen more complexly in a final dress and adornment case. In the United States, the senior-most grades in high schools regularly hold an elaborate celebratory dance known as "prom."[18] Attendees often wear formal dress, including tuxedos and formal gowns. During the spring of 2018, a young woman in Utah chose to wear a style of Chinese dress (*cheongsam* or *qipao*) that has come to be seen as culturally significant, especially in the context of the country's Han majority, in which this dress style has come to fill the same slot as the "nationalities dress" worn by the nation's minority peoples. My first firsthand experience with this type of dress was when Chinese museum colleagues brought them to the United States to wear at the openings for the Quilts of Southwest China exhibition in its US venues (MacDowell and Zhang 2016). In that context, the qipao dress was worn as a sign of affiliation with Chinese national culture, one especially appropriate for majority women without appropriate minority-style dresses.[19]

In Utah, as is now normal, the non–Asian American woman who chose to wear the Chinese dress to her high school prom posted images of herself and her date on social media. This generated a passionate backlash from Chinese American and Asian American observers who took offense at her decision to appropriate a sign of Chinese culture for her own use. Journalistic sources on this controversy are abundant and easy to locate, so I do not dwell on all of the details, such as her motivations, American reactions and counterreactions, or the young woman's response to the controversy. The key factor that causes me to bring it forward in this context concerns a later turn taken in the reporting. Journalists and their readers found a special interest in the divergence in reactions separating Chinese (and Asian) American critics and various persons-on-the-street in China (Qin 2018; see also Moon 2018; Rossman 2018a, 2018b; Schmidt 2018; Seely and Rossman 2018; Yang 2018; R. Zhang 2018).

The crux of the Chinese response was appreciation for the woman's choice. The commentators from China relayed by journalists appreciated her appreciation and saw no problem with her wearing it for this special occasion. On a microlevel, the Chinese and Chinese American voices said different things, embracing or being offended by the use of the dress. On a group level, the aggregated, synthesized "Chinese" response is in accord with a national policy of soft power, in which appreciative signs of non-Chinese engagement with Chinese civilization are not only welcome but also actively cultivated through a range of overseas investments and government initiatives. The Chinese voice as represented by journalists is confident, not embattled. By contrast, and in accord with the perspective that I am taking here, the Chinese American view (also a journalistic synthesis) is an upset one. The statements of Chinese or Asian American critics are born out of experiences of racism and subordination in the US that the Chinese commentators have not experienced and, if unexplained, would have difficulty understanding. My reading of the journalism here is reinforced by a discussion of the case with Chinese colleagues and acquaintances in China during the summer of 2018.

As in other cases, the student who wore the dress also had many defenders among European American observers. Many of my own friends found it hard to muster disapproval for the wearing of the dress, as many of them share with the student an appreciation for world cultures in general and textile arts in particular. I will not attempt to adjudicate the case myself, but the special difference separating fabrics hanging as art on a wall and fabrics fashioned into clothing and worn on the body is significant. Both are performances, but one is closer to the center of personal identity. Given all that we know about the important nexus of clothing and identity, it should not surprise us that dress practices are a particularly hot node in cultural appropriation debates. The student did not bring a dress to school on a hanger for a show-and-tell activity; she wore it on her body during an important rite-of-passage ceremony.

Power dynamics are important for understanding cultural appropriation contests. The prom dress case provides an opportunity to think imaginatively about conditions of authorization. Beyond the vexing problem of "playing" embodied identities that are not our own, there is always the situational context. The story of the prom dress would have been very different, I feel certain, if such dresses had been worn to prom by all of the women participating in a high school Chinese language or culture course. In this scenario, we could imagine the students having been instructed and encouraged in their wearing of such dresses by a respected Chinese or Chinese American teacher. While the initial social media outrage might have looked the same at first, the follow-up debates would have looked very different. My thinking on this point has been profoundly shaped by Native North American values relating to relationality and responsibility.

Relationality and Responsibility

Non-Native observers often misconstrue the reactions that they get when they enter into complex encounters with specific Native communities, perceiving such communities to be more bounded and exclusionary than they actually, in practice, are. If confronted by a question such as "Who are you?" non-Natives often think about this in an egocentric way (i.e., in individualistic rather than collective terms). In many Native communities, the simple question "Who are you?" is not as hostile as it sounds to non-Native American ears. "Who are you?" is a short way of saying, "Who are you related to? Where do you fit in the web of social relations that I perhaps also fit into?" Relationships relate closely to mutual responsibilities. People who are connected in relationships can expect (supportive) things from one another. Responsibility involves being held accountable to others and being able to hold others accountable as well. Sound work on the topic of Native American kinship speaks to these themes as do programmatic statements relative to Native American and Indigenous studies and ethical research in and with Indigenous communities (Deloria 1988, 1998, 24–37; DeMallie 1998; Fixico 2003, 75; Justice 2016, 30; Moreton-Robinson 2017). With respect to issues of cultural appropriation, they can help us see issues of context, particularly the question of human relationships and mutual responsibility.

In a public context, I was given a kind of jacket known in English as a Yuchi (or Euchee) jacket. The garment has a complex cultural history, as its origin can be found in the diffusion of European men's jacket styles into the Native American communities of eastern North America during the British colonial period (Jackson 2013b, 125–38). Today, though, coats of this type are, for the most part, no longer worn by non-Native people in the eastern United States. They were localized in Native American communities and have become a worn symbol of specific Native identities among the Yuchi and, with material variations, a few Native groups who are or were their Native neighbors. There are contexts in which it makes local sense for me to wear the Yuchi jacket that I was given, and there are other contexts in which it would not make sense or be appropriate. The key issue I am raising, though, concerns relationality and responsibility on my part and the part of others. If someone were to take offense at my wearing the Yuchi jacket that I was given, is there some respected Yuchi person who would speak up on my behalf, explaining not only the jacket and its contexts but also me and my relationships in the process? On my side of the equation, I am being judged in an ongoing way by my Yuchi friends, who monitor the question "Am I conducting myself in a responsible way and in a way worthy of my relationships with them and with others?"

I could elaborate on this point further, but I have evoked the theme enough to circle back briefly to the case of Christina Fallin and also the prom dress incident. If Christina Fallin was connected in a meaningful relationship with actual Native American Oklahomans knowledgeable about the headdress that she chose to wear, there is little likelihood she would have worn it. If she had worn it, she would have faced informal sanction and not just mediated criticism. She did not wear it as an outgrowth of her face-to-face relationships with Native peoples of the Great Plains but as an outgrowth of her lack of such relationships and her participation in a dominant culture in which Native signs are ubiquitous but Native people are not. In the case of the dress, our assessment of the situation would be wildly different if there were Chinese American individuals standing beside her, endorsing her participation in and accepting responsibility for her engagement with their cultural practices. This would have also entailed holding her responsible for their trust in her. Instead, she was read as engaging in a consumer practice (purchasing a dress as an individual) in a colonial global marketplace that cares little about the feelings of those whose signs, objects, and practices are pulled into its orbit. Of course, intercultural relationships and responsibility in the sense I am evoking them here play out in small-scale ways. In a contemporary idiom, they are hard to "scale up" to a societal or global level.

Other Models of Cultural Appropriation

Among the most regularly consulted general treatments of cultural appropriation is *Borrowed Power: Essays on Cultural Appropriation* edited by law scholars Bruce Ziff and Pratima V. Rao and published in 1997. In their introduction, Ziff and Rao evoke a broad range of contexts characterizable as cultural appropriation, noting not only this breadth of application but also the conceptual ambiguity of both culture and appropriation. Writing as legal scholars with an appreciation for cultural processes and cultural identities, they are attuned to the ways that cultural appropriation intersects with wider heritage and property discourses and practices. They include valuable discussion of the ways that cultural appropriation debates are predicated on conceptions of social insider and outsider and how cultural appropriation is flagged in relation to both rivalrous and nonrivalrous objects. For my purposes, the strength of

Ziff and Rao's account lies in the way that it foregrounds power differentials among the parties to appropriation events. Their essay also usefully disentangles varieties of appropriation events and the different kinds of critiques that underpin different kinds of appropriation.

In my view, Ziff and Rao (1997, 4) are least effective when it comes to sorting out the kinds of cultural movement or circulation that, I would hold, are analytically adjacent to but not the same as appropriation. Thus, in their account, diffusion is explored as a kind of appropriation, a position that leads to seeing appropriation as "pervasive phenomena" that "happen all around us in a vast number of creative domains." This line of thinking leads to a very expansive conception of appropriation in which it takes on qualities that I associate here with diffusion, acculturation, and assimilation. The authors express real concern about cultural appropriation and aim to cultivate nuanced responses to it, thus this treatment of diffusion is not in full accord with other things that the authors say in their essay. The stance that all diffusions are appropriations poses problems that I have aimed to evoke here. I have emphasized revisiting these neighboring domains in part on account of this aspect of Ziff and Rao's influential treatment.

As I do in figure 3.1, Ziff and Rao (1997, 6) also attempt to portray cultural appropriation in a heuristic diagram. Unlike the one that I offer, their diagram attempts to capture an extremely wide range of variables. Anyone concerned with the topic would do well to consult it, and it is my hope that my simpler heuristic will have value as a complement to the model that they offer. Theirs might be read as a relatively comprehensive inventory of factors that enter into and are generated out of appropriation episodes and debates.

In suggesting at the start of this chapter that folklore studies and ethnology had small literatures on cultural appropriation relative to the frequency with which we discuss and observe cultural appropriation phenomena and discourses, I have to underline that this is a relative, not absolute, lack. It is a lack most prominent in the absence of canonical overviews akin to those we regularly consult and teach on topics such as group (Noyes 2012), tradition (Noyes 2009), heritage (Hafstein 2012), and performance (Bauman 2012). In addition to works already cited elsewhere in this chapter, there are other key works in this realm that have shaped wider scholarly discussions. As I noted in a 2006 review, Michael F. Brown's *Who Owns Native Culture?* is a key survey of cultural property and cultural heritage issues organized around vexed contests, often discursive, sometimes also legal, of the sort that are often framed as cultural appropriation (Brown 2003; Jackson 2006b).[20]

Heritage and Property

While not the central point here, my concern with cultural appropriation is also linked to considerations of cultural heritage and cultural property. The literatures on these two phenomena, particularly the literature on property, overlap extensively with the case study literature on cultural appropriation. Cultural property is regularly evoked and sometimes actually leveraged for the defense of cultural forms against unwanted appropriation. We see this, for instance, in India's prior art database projects, which aim to prevent the appropriation of vernacular medicine practices and their enclosure by corporate actors (World Intellectual Property Organization 2011; Hansen and VanFleet 2003), or in the development of intellectual property-like laws that aim to, for instance, protect the market for Indigenous arts and crafts from inauthentic works made by non-Indigenous actors (Brown 2003, 215–16; Evans-Pritchard 1987; Wood 2008) or to protect the market for regionally marked artisanal goods and foodstuffs (May et al. 2017). We see it also in the development by Kimberly Christen, Jane Anderson, and their colleagues of a sophisticated system of licenses and labels that aim to discourage cultural appropriation and encourage respect for the local property concepts and values that should, but rarely do, travel alongside cultural forms and practices originating in Indigenous and other localized communities (Anderson and Christen 2013).

On the heritage side, appropriation claims and grievances threaten to arise whenever and wherever local vernacular culture is deployed for profit in markets. Examples are many, for instance, when outside tour operators seem to profit most from heritage tourism initiatives that focus on the richness of a local cultural community (Zhang 2024). Of special interest to me are the local-global heritage dynamics of an appropriative character that were flagged most compellingly by Barbara Kirshenblatt-Gimblett (1995, 2004, 2006) in her series of essays theorizing heritage. As discussed in chapter 2, in Kirshenblatt-Gimblett's approach, heritage is made in a process in which selected aspects of culture are given a new context, one that valorizes them and places them into a dramatically new metacultural framework, shifting them from the realm of everyday life into the world of the exhibition, the museum, the safeguarding strategy, the list, and the regulatory regime. Some cultural forms move further; they are not just made into heritage, they are lifted up onto national and international stages through heritage policies and practices operating at and above the level of states.

When a cultural form is made into heritage, not only is it celebrated as important and worthy of preservation, but its social base is also expanded to include nonlocal actors who are encouraged to care about its status. Along the way, heritage objects are carried out of intimate domains and pushed, often by nonlocal actors, into national or international commons. These commons are themselves constituted through legal, political, and policy actions of this sort. When cultural forms are placed into these extralocal domains, however, they become accessible to, and on a rhetorical level to "belong to," a wider range of actors (i.e., as "national heritage" or as part of the "universal heritage of humanity"). At the same time, they are thereby marked for possible further appropriation. They can inspire new kinds of copying, of course. The extensive documentation and publicity accompanying heritage initiatives can facilitate this. They are also, paradoxically, positioned to be enclosed and made into property by those who might appropriate them and then introduce value-added changes to them, modifications that can sometimes make them eligible for privatization via patent, copyright, and other intellectual property regimes. I try to illustrate such transformations, from local culture through heritage and on to enclosure in figure 3.2, a scheme that was initially developed by participants in my 2004 Contesting Culture as Property course based on the work of Kirshenblatt-Gimblett and others whom we were then reading.

The full relationship among appropriation, heritagification, and properitization warrants extended and further discussion by others. My aim in raising these linkages here is to note that they are explored in recent work and that they remain important for further research and conceptualization. I also aim to urge readers interested in appropriation to see how it is now bound up closely with heritage and property, two of the most important concerns for twenty-first-century work in folklore studies and ethnology.[21]

Lateral Appropriation

I recognize that articulating a heuristic for understanding cultural appropriations will prompt objections and require caveats. This is true of simplifications in general, and it will surely be true for a simplification of a complex matter that is fundamentally about painful contests waged on the ground in cultural life and in metacultural discourses about those grounded experiences. I cannot fully anticipate all possible reservations, but I want to frame one at the close of this chapter, as it arises from ethnographic work and ethnological reflection well known to me. I offer it in its own terms and as an illustration of how the model I articulate here will need to be further refined.

Global Transformations of Culture and Property Today

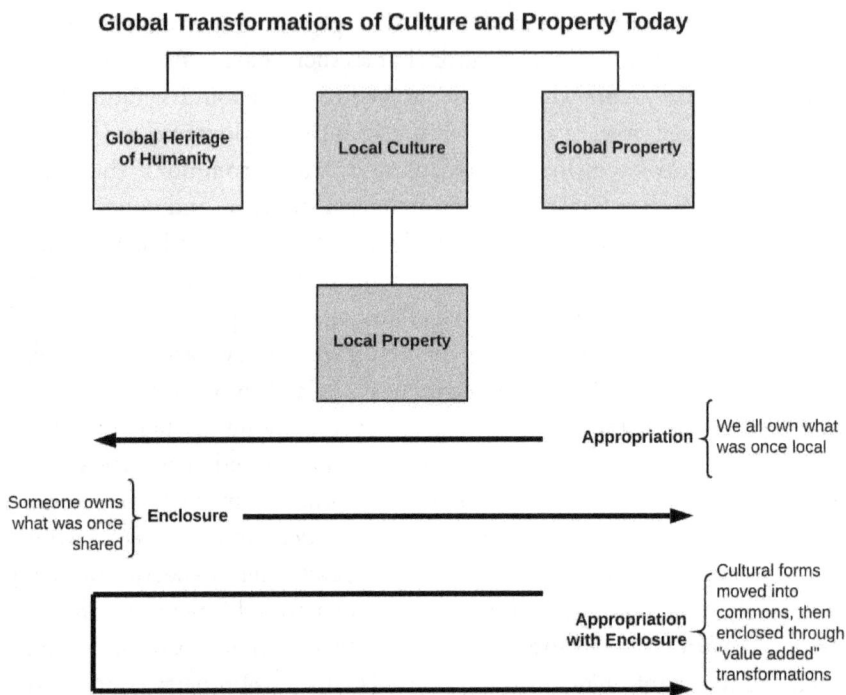

FIGURE 3.2. In this scheme for representing the connected relationship between the social construction of heritage and property, the arrows represent transformational movement between categorizations presented at the top of the diagram. Within a heritage and property framework, appropriation, often at the national or international level, turns local culture, including local culture understood as property, into national or global heritage. Enclosure is an inversion of appropriation in that once-local cultural forms are turned not into widely shared global heritage but globally recognized (usually corporately owned) property. A more complicated transformation is presented at the bottom of the diagram. It first involves turning local culture, including local culture understood as local property forms, into global heritage, thereby positioning such forms within a global commons. Once placed there and "shared," Western intellectual property regimes allow for "value-added" modifications that enable corporations and other actors to enclose them as property.

In a contribution to the *Journal of Folklore Research*, two close collaborators of mine—Daniel C. Swan and Michael Paul Jordan—reflected on their research collaborations over the course of many years with the Kiowa, a federally recognized Native nation living in present-day Oklahoma in the United States. In discussing the ways that leaders of the Kiowa Black Leggings Warrior Society (KBLWS) sought to use defensive documentation as part of a

strategy aimed at preventing appropriation of their dances, songs, and ceremonies, Swan and Jordan (2015, 74n23) note,

> Power undoubtedly plays an important role in shaping the form cultural
> transmission takes, particularly where interactions between indigenous
> communities and members of settler colonial societies are concerned.
> However, the model presented by Ziff and Rao (1997) fails to fully account
> for the concerns the leadership of the Kiowa Black Leggings Warrior
> Society expressed regarding the potential appropriation of the organiza-
> tion's intangible property. The model Ziff and Rao offer is based on a binary
> opposition between dominant and subordinate groups and does not ac-
> count for cultural borrowing between groups that occupy similar structural
> positions. It should be noted that the KBLWS is as concerned with prevent-
> ing other indigenous groups from utilizing its songs, dances, and regalia as
> it is with stopping members of the dominant Anglo society from exploiting
> these cultural forms. From the perspective of the KBLWS, any unauthor-
> ized performance of its songs and dances represents an act of appropriation.

Swan and Jordan's objections to Ziff and Rao's perspective would extend to
aspects of the account that I am offering.

Knowing something of the ethnographic case that they are reflecting on—
and many like it from other parts of Native North America—I share the view
that a general approach to cultural appropriation has to take such instances
into account. Until we have a better nomenclature and framework for such
instances, I propose that they might be qualified as *lateral* cultural appropriations, meaning instances in which groups worry about (and experience)
"horizontal" appropriations from groups occupying comparable circumstances, existing at similar scales, and in equivalent positions of power. Such
instances share with more power-imbalanced cases the quality of aggrievement and nonconsent. The Kiowa instance is not a hypothetical one, as many
Kiowa feel deep anger over the ways that other Kiowa songs, dances, and
ceremonies (particularly the gourd dance) have been taken up and practiced
by non-Kiowa, both Native and non-Native. Historical instances of stealing
songs and dances are documented widely in Native North America (Jackson
2014 explores an instance and Jackson 2010 addresses some of the legal and
theoretical issues at stake).[22]

Essentialist? Just Like Authenticity?

The KBLWS possesses a distinctive set of songs, dances, material objects, and
ceremonial practices, and, as its work with Swan and Jordan has documented,

the group is eager to prevent these from circulating in unauthorized ways outside of its ceremonial organization (Swan and Jordan 2015; Jordan and Swan 2014). The kind of cultural knowledge that they are eager to safeguard is an instance of what famed ethnologist and folklorist of the Native Great Plains Robert Lowie (1928) characterized as incorporeal property—what we would today call intellectual property. Across this region, the ceremonial dance forms held and practiced by men's societies were and often still are closely guarded and highly valued by those to whom they have been bestowed. The foundational literature in American folklore studies and ethnology related to issues of cultural property was established through the study of such dance practices among the Native American societies of the American West (Jackson 2010).

If sympathetic ethnography of Native American dances as collective property can serve as a canonical case for the recognition of a real-world worry about and experiences of cultural appropriation, a different body of dance ethnography can ground a critique of cultural appropriation as an interpretive framework. Salsa and belly dance can center this counterargument. Sheila Bock and Katherine Borland (2011) have made a strong case against seeing the borrowing of dance practices from distant or "other" source communities as cultural appropriation. In doing so, they marshal a formidable body of sophisticated folklore studies work to suggest that cultural appropriation is a problematic frame because it does not recognize the complex, networked nature of social life and because it suffers from the same problems of essentialism that marred classic conceptions of authenticity, tradition, and culture itself (see also Kenny 2007 for a parallel study of belly dance). Bock and Borland adopt a constructivist (contra essentialist) perspective that is also generally my own. I have argued elsewhere in ways similar to those they adopt (Jackson 2003a, 136–38; Jackson 2013b, 176–79; Jackson and Levine 2002; Waselkov with Jackson 2004, 694–96; see also n. 8 here).

What can we make of this conundrum? Partially, the difference between the case of the Kiowa men and that of the women who belly dance in central Ohio is one of different views held by different people out in the world. If Swan and Jordan were to interview non-Native or non-Kiowa gourd dancers, they would not see their participation in the gourd dance as cultural appropriation. They would offer rich and humane accounts of how the dance came into their lives and what it means to them as an expressive practice. I have been trying to underline the way that cultural appropriation only exists where there is a difference of understanding between the source and the obtaining individuals or communities. Cultural appropriation has to be called into existence by someone taking up a (metacultural) discourse of aggrievement. From the perspective of those whose behavior is in question (or from their allies or ethnographers), such a discourse may seem unfair, overly harsh, or to traffic in essentialisms, but that rebuttal cannot in itself make the discourse to which it responds go away. In small-scale instances where the parties can access one another, respectful mutual dialogue may bring the antagonists together. At larger scales, views may change with time, and the kinds of forgetting that Kroeber noted for diffusion may do their work. As colleagues and I have argued for heritage and innovation, it is possible with time for appropriations to work their way toward normal, unremarkable (unremembered) status (chap. 2, this volume), but under intercultural conditions of inequality and suspicion, this normalization, a kind of "getting over it," can, understandably, be slow (Jackson, Müske, and Zhang 2020). I certainly do not demand or expect injustices to be forgotten. Collective memories can be deep and also a source of power.

Seeing cultural appropriation in terms of metacultural discourse helps situate it alongside rather than in opposition to the constructivist concepts that folklorists (especially performance-oriented ones) regularly use. At the same time, the concerns that Charles Briggs (1996) noted for the literature on the so-called invention of tradition and its destructive impact on Indigenous communities are in play in such discussions of cultural appropriation (Jackson 2013b, 74–85, 216–17). Groups such as the Kiowa do actually prize songs and dances that their ancestors actually did bequeath to them. Given the destructive consequences of cultural appropriation that Native peoples have again and again highlighted, it is not workable for ethnographic disciplines such as folklore studies and ethnology to construct understandings of cultural appropriation unable to attend to these realities and the political circumstances that Indigenous and subaltern communities face. We can (as fields if not as individuals), however, attempt to sympathetically engage those who live on both sides of cultural appropriation contests. If we do our work well, we may help foster more sensitive and respectful forms of intercultural contact and cultural change. The imperative to not cause harm, however, takes precedence over the hope of doing good. Briggs's (1996, 463) reflexive account of scholarly positioning powerfully underlines the stakes in terms that are even more stark now than in 1996 when he published them. "In an environment in which subaltern communities, affirmative action, immigration, and the poor are increasingly targeted in political and economic terms for the perceived woes of the white middle class, it becomes even more important to consider the political-economic distribution of metadiscursive practices that shape the outcome of such contestations, even if researchers can achieve some success in disrupting dominant practices of reading and writing." I cannot do justice to Briggs's account in an excerpt, but a core theme of relevance is the ways that scholars enjoy a privileged vantage point in the sense of access to multiple points of view but also in the sense of comfortable distance from painful lived experiences. Meanwhile, the contests they discuss can have life-or-death, make-or-break consequences for the participants, particularly those whose status remains durably disadvantaged.

I thus do not disagree, per se, with colleagues who would argue that cultural appropriation, as a frame of analysis, risks reimporting risky essentialisms about the dynamics of cultural circulation, the authenticity of some cultural forms relative to the inauthenticity of others, and the boundedness of cultures and societies. For me, that risk is set in tension with its opposite, that all cultural forms are up for grabs in a neoliberal, global commons that offers corporations powerful intellectual property protections but offers the holders of vernacular culture nothing but the opportunity to be disrespected and looted by whoever has the power to pull it off. Thankfully, a perspective that treats cultural appropriation episodes as two-sided contests in which metacultural discourse characterizes on-the-ground realities as seen from both sides need not fully resolve the epistemological and ethical questions at issue. Ethnography can enable us to gain purchase on the specifics at issue by engaging with the people involved. Not all matters characterized by someone as cultural appropriation are equal. Ethnographers can attend to and make sense of the specifics even as they track broader trends and tendencies. At the same time, there is potential for conceptual work that is informed by, but not reducible to, ethnography. I encourage ethnographic investigation of appropriation contests in context. It is hoped that the conceptual framework described here will assist in such work but not determine its outcome.

Conclusion

I do not claim that the framework presented here is novel. It arises out of a lot of important work done by many colleagues. It also relates closely to active discussions in the broader public sphere, and, most importantly, it tracks with and acknowledges the primary work and lived experiences of individuals and groups (Indigenous and otherwise) who have experienced and testified to various forms of cultural appropriation. While it may be too simple a model discussed at too great a length, what I have aimed to do is to consolidate and formalize these streams of experience, reflection, and research into a model or heuristic that we might discuss, use if useful, and ideally improve on in new work. Beyond the specifics of the particular concept under discussion, I have long held that American folklore studies would be stronger if American folklorists devoted more attention to articulating and revisiting the concepts at issue in their work. Ethnology (American, European, and otherwise) tends to devote more attention to this kind of work, but there the problem of relatively disarticulated regional traditions of work also persists as does the shared problem of forgetting relevant work done in earlier eras.

Situating the place of theory in folklore studies, Dorothy Noyes (2008, 40) notes that "humble theory recognizes that all our work is essay, in the etymological sense: a trying-out of interpretation, a provisional framing to see how it looks." Regarding the ongoing revision of such provisional framings, she goes on to note, "In the absence of a better alternative, there is much to be said for the Enlightenment project. Science reduces reality in an effort to understand it but it also properly lays itself open to an ongoing process of collective correction and revision." I hope that this attempt at historicizing, contextualizing, simplifying, synthesizing, and modeling a portion of our literatures related to cultural appropriation will be received as useful concept work in the senses evoked by Noyes. If not useful as a guide, perhaps it will be useful as a provocation for a better account.

As I neared the end of the work of drafting this chapter, I took a break to see what was going on in the lives of my friends and colleagues on Facebook. Of course, there it was. Blowing up in front of me was a new and very painful episode of the sort that is mainly modeled in a sterile, ethnological register in this chapter. Native people I know and admire were again hurting and also debating and sensemaking. An existing law designed to protect them against cultural appropriation was instead weaponized and used as a political instrument in ways that scores of Native people, members of federally recognized tribes, were objecting to as being contrary to both the spirit and the letter of the law. I cannot recount this story directly here, but I evoke it to underline that my dry prose sits on top of the most painful and sometimes life- and livelihood-altering social transformations and contests.

As I have characterized it here, cultural appropriation is a kind of cultural change or movement that is recognizable because it is accompanied by a metacultural discourse in which source communities—as represented by those who take up the role of spokespeople—do not approve of, and are aggrieved by, an unwanted taking of an important cultural practice, cultural form, or body of cultural knowledge. This metacultural response may provoke anything from apologies and restitution to defensive counterarguments, further disrespect, violent reprisal, or further appropriation. While the dynamics can vary greatly, as can the range of factors that come into play, in the model offered here, power differentials of some kind are often important (but see lateral appropriation above). Finally, I have argued that it is heuristically useful to see cultural appropriation alongside but distinct from other modes of cultural change. In actual instances, these ideal-type distinctions will break down and shade into one another. One key purpose of concept work is to better prepare us for such complexities in the worlds in which we live, work, and attempt to be allies.

Notes

1. In support of the proposition that cultural appropriation has received little attention in the English-language, peer-reviewed literature in folklore studies, I prepared a literature review in which I assessed all usages of this term in three key journals—the *Journal of American Folklore*, the *Journal of Folklore Research*, and *Western Folklore*. Rather than include that review in an endnote here or in the body of the text, I have prepared it as a short companion chapter, which has been made persistently available in the IUScholarWorks Repository (see Jackson 2021a). To summarize that effort briefly, I note that the *Journal of American Folklore* had featured (as of fall 2019) seven instances in which the concept of cultural appropriation had appeared. With the exception of Kapchan and Strong (1999), these appearances were relevant to the conceptual discussion here, but incidental. In *Western Folklore*, cultural appropriation is discussed in passing in three articles and one book review, with more detailed engagement occurring in one article and one book review. For the *Journal of Folklore Research*, four articles are relevant. Of these, Bock and Borland (2011) and Swan and Jordan (2015) are discussed in detail in this paper. Because this paper extends into the neighboring field of ethnology, a briefer survey for that field was also undertaken. Two journals were sampled. For *Ethnologia Eurpaea*, cultural appropriation appeared in passing in one article, and for the *American Ethnologist*, it appeared centrally in three articles. Of course, the journals surveyed here represent only a small fraction of the literature in these fields. A line of research in folklore studies related to appropriation of a somewhat different but relevant sort is anchored by Amy Shuman's (2005) treatment of the appropriation of stories within histories of discourse and in relationship to issues of responsibility, evidence, and empathy.

2. This article arises from discussions held with students in an Indiana University graduate course that I taught in the mid-2000s. I thank the participants in two instances of my course Contesting Culture as Property—Curtis Ashton, Zilia Balkansky-Selles, Aditi Deo, Tierza Askren (née Draper), Flory Gingging, Carrie Hertz, Teri Klassen, Wei-Ping Lee, Jiang Lu, Gabriel McGuire, and Tiana Tew in 2004 and Gabrielle Berlinger, Elizabeth Burbach, Jill Hemming Austin, Lanlan Kuang, Rodrigo Pedrosa, and Jeremy Stoll in 2006. For other work derived from this course, see Jackson (2004), American Folklore Society (2005), Gingging (2007), and Klassen (2009).

When students in Contesting Culture as Property chose their research projects, a significant proportion of them chose to focus on issues of cultural appropriation. In this course context and in my thinking since this period (2004–2005), cultural appropriation fits into or is adjacent to themes of cultural heritage and cultural property. In a significant number of instances, cultural appropriation episodes also become entangled in intellectual property regimes such as patent, copyright, trademark, and trade secret and quasiintellectual property frameworks such as geographic indicators. After describing a model of cultural appropriation in the core of this article, I will return briefly to the relationship between cultural appropriation and these neighboring or encompassing metacultural frameworks. These linkages, for me, first emerged from my discussions with students in the Contesting Culture as Property course. I am here trying, after too much delay, to share the general framework that also arose from our discussions. I recount this history in part to acknowledge the impact of these students-turned-colleagues on my thinking and to situate this project in the context out of which it arose.

3. A historical query of the *American Anthropologist* shows *culture change* or *cultural change* being evoked with these terms starting in the 1920s, gaining great prominence starting in the 1930s (e.g., Wissler 1920; Mead 1929; Kroeber 1931; Steward 1932; Mekeel 1932; Redfield 1934; Redfield, Linton, and Herskovits 1936; Strong 1936; Eggan 1937). *Culture change* appears in a 1907 bibliographic review in the *Journal of American Folklore*, but its use became regular in the 1930s and widespread in the 1940s (American Folklore Society 1907). In this period, it was largely the same network of scholars evoking the theme in both flagship journals.

4. Readers wanting to explore the conceptual issues at stake here have a wide vista to explore. Because of the renewed attention that it has been receiving among American folklorists (e.g., Otero 2020, 19–21) and others (Castañeda 2004), one place to begin is with the neighboring concept of transculturation developed by Cuban anthropologist Fernando Ortiz ([1947] 1995, 98) and explored conceptually and empirically in a Native North Americanist context of special relevance to this chapter by A. Irving Hallowell (1963, 523). I also acknowledge the salience of Mary Louise Pratt's (1991) influential, more recent treatment of transculturation in relationship to what she calls *contact zones*.

5. I rely on Kroeber's formulation here rather than that found in the work of his teacher Franz Boas because it is conceptual in character and because it includes aspects of the metacultural arguments that I am exploring here. Examples of Boas's work on diffusion can be found throughout his *Race, Language, and Culture* (1940)—especially within its folklore studies papers.

6. After first using this Swedish example, I discovered that, six months earlier, the Swedish government had made a surprise announcement noting the Turkish origins of the country's meatballs, producing something of a counter story to the appropriation narratives that center this paper. In covering this story, the *New York Times* linked, as I and so many other observers do, the meatballs to IKEA, noting among other things the popularity of IKEA's form of Swedish meatballs in Turkey. For purposes of tracking the place of social media in contemporary cultural appropriation episodes, it is worth noting that by preemptively coming clean about Swedish meatballs on Twitter (the social media platform now known as X), Sweden manufactured diplomatic goodwill rather than derision in Turkey (Yeginsu 2018). I thank Dorothy Noyes for calling this and other mediatized instances discussed in this paper to my attention.

7. Contemporary students focused on diffusion would need to go beyond the folkloristic and ethnological fields to achieve a robust contemporary synthesis. As an example, consider the terminological and conceptual debate in the field of international relations centered on "cultural imperialism" and "cultural transfer" as two different ways of characterizing macrolevel processes of cultural movement (Gienow-Hecht 2004). Cultural transfer reads as somewhat more active than diffusion but is intentionally used as a less power-laden alternative to cultural imperialism.

8. Such problems arising within the use of acculturation theory, manifest in Native North American studies in connection with the related concept of Pan-Indianism, were the focus of a series of my essays (one with Victoria Levine) in which the music and dance practices of Indigenous groups in eastern North America provided an instructive case (Jackson 2003a, 136–38; 2003b, 250–51; 2013b, 176–79; Jackson and Levine 2002, 284–85).

9. For illustrative cases, see Lesser ([1933] 1977), Strong (1936), Spicer (1962), and works summarized and cited in Spicer (1968). For the conceptual problems inherent in acculturation theory, see Jackson (2013b, 176–79).

10. Readers seeking to compare classic social science conceptions of assimilation vis-à-vis acculturation are directed to Spicer (1968) and Simpson (1968). Writing during a period of reactionary social unrest and political change in the United States and Europe, much of it anti-immigrant and antiminority in character, I would note that my take on assimilation is less hopeful than those commonly articulated in the American sociology of the later twentieth century.

11. Beyond George Eaton Simpson (1968), readers will likely find Raymond H. C. Teske Jr. and Bardin H. Nelson's (1974) clarification of the differences between acculturation and assimilation helpful. My account is not in perfect accord with their

more detailed treatment, as my aim is to set up a heuristic for cultural appropriation, but they also attend to the dynamics that I am stressing. A major difference between earlier accounts of assimilation and contemporary reactions to the concept seems to relate to the absence in earlier accounts of adequate treatment of racism and other discriminatory ideologies. These interfere with the outcome of shared identity and common participation in society that classic accounts of assimilation recognized and anticipated. What I am calling classic accounts of assimilation were shaped by the sociology of European immigrants to European-dominant societies.

12. My use of ideal type is methodological and follows from the classic work of German sociologist Max Weber (1949, 89–99). For a current assessment of ideal-type methods, see Swedberg (2017).

13. The best way to find such work is to just go looking for it, but the kinds of work that I have in mind can be illustrated by posts to the *Native Appropriations* blog (Keene 2020) or episodes of the syndicated radio program *Native America Calling* (2020).

14. The distinction between eye-rolling-grade cultural appropriation, often seen, for instance, in simple gestures and excesses of enthusiasm for appreciated foreign practices, and more egregious forms (ethnic fraud, racist mascots, corporate enclosures, etc.) arose in discussion with students in Dorothy Noyes's summer 2019 folklore graduate seminar at Ohio State University. I thank the participants in that seminar for helping me refine and clarify my arguments.

15. Participants in Noyes's graduate seminar (n. 14, above) helped expose this point also. For government contracts based on ethnic fraud as one of my more serious examples, see the *Los Angeles Times* coverage by Paul Pringle and Adam Elmahrek (Pringle and Elmahrek 2019; Elmahrek and Pringle 2019).

16. There are other ways that the current situation with Bavarian dress is complex and changing beyond this evocation of tourism and appropriation. As a detailed *New York Times* story by Katrin Bennhold (2018) noted in detail, young Bavarians are revitalizing such dress, wearing it in new ways in new contexts and, in doing so, evoking different issues of change and insider-outsider status. I appreciate Dorothy Noyes for pointing me to this phenomenon. If we wanted to situate it provisionally in the matrix of kinds of changes, it might be seen in terms of revival or what Sabina Magliocco (2009, 228) has characterized as *reclamation*, "a process by which groups reclaim, re-appropriate and rework elements of their culture previously devalued by a dominant culture."

17. The strength of the German "Indian hobbyist" movement, in which Germans dress as Native Americans and perform Native American life is worth noting in this regard (Eddy 2014; Haircrow 2013; Taylor 1988).

18. The name of the event and its associated dress (*prom*) come from the word *promenade* (*Oxford English Dictionary* 2023). For such dresses as a kind of "ball dress," see Hegland (2010). For ethnographies of the event, see Best (2000) and Zlatunich (2009).

19. The dress style itself is an adaptation of older Manchu dresses and has a complex cultural history in China. That history is about class and other forms of difference in Chinese society, not only majority/minority status (Trower 2010).

20. In addition to Brown (2003), other prominent works relating to cultural appropriation in folklore, ethnology, or adjacent fields include Rosemary Coombe (1998; Coombe and Alywin 2014), Rebecca Tsosie (2002), Sabina Magliocco (2004, 2009), and recently, a public-facing overview by George Nicholas (2018). While Coombe's (1998, chap. 5) primary concern is the appropriation of intellectual properties and other elite assets by subaltern agents, she faces the conundrums of cultural appropriation in the more common sense being discussed here. Nicholas's (2018) views are closely in accord with my own and with the perspective that I offer here.

I particularly highlight Magliocco's work because, while grounded in close, empathetic ethnography with neopagan communities where practices that might be called cultural appropriation are sometimes prominent, she offers a nuanced account of community-internal variation in values and beliefs on this issue. As importantly, she also offers an assessment that has a great deal of sympathy for and understanding of the views of Native American individuals and groups concerned about cultural appropriation (Magliocco 2004, 205–37). Magliocco also conceptualizes another neighboring mode of cultural change, *reclamation* (mentioned in n. 16 above. See also Magliocco 2009).

21. I note in particular the work and publications of the interdisciplinary research group on the "Constitution of Cultural Property" led by Regina Bendix at the Georg-August-Universität Göttingen (Interdisziplinäre Forschungsgruppe zu Cultural Property 2020) and the Intellectual Property Issues in Cultural Heritage project directed by George Nicholas at Simon Fraser University (IPinCH 2016).

22. As a reviewer of this chapter noted, "lateral appropriation" as a work-around for cases like those described by Swan and Jordan may depend on the kind of cultural materials that are in circulation. As argued here, it is the metacultural discourses that do (or do not) arise around the instance of cultural movement that matter, but there may be, across as well as within societies, particular categories of cultural forms that tend to provoke (ceremonies, sacred objects) or not provoke (food) metadiscourses of aggrievement. For a comparable metadiscourse-centered treatment of heritage, see chap. 2, this volume.

4

Toward Wider Framings

World-Systems Analysis and Folklore Studies

Folklore needs to be examined as a part of the political economy of nations and of the world system.
—Gary Alan Fine (2009, 103)

It is always revealing, if sometimes disconcerting, to know how your colleagues in neighboring departments view you.
—Immanuel Wallerstein (2003, 454)

Introduction

While folklorists have cultivated theories and methods of their own, traveling theory and borrowed methods tend to arrive at folklore studies via cultural anthropology or, for some kinds of work, from literary studies.[1] Our friends and key interlocutors in sociology have consistently been influential figures concerned with the interaction order (Goffman 1983) or what sociologist and folklorist Gary Alan Fine (2012) has called "tiny publics." Our favorite sociologies have been social interactional and sociolinguistic. Our preference for the microsociological can be seen, for instance, in the remarkable staying power of Dan Ben-Amos's (1971, 13) formulation characterizing the field's object—folklore—as "artistic communication in small groups." Even more than in cultural anthropology, folklorists have avoided macrosociology, often knowing relatively little about its varied forms. When it comes to history, our preferences have tended toward cultural history (especially in an ethnological mode), oral history, microhistory, and emplaced social histories of relatively narrow spans of space and time. While we appreciated the way that the *Annales* historians cared about continuities in the everyday lives of nonelite people, as well as their interest in worldview and topics such as agriculture and practical technologies, we have tended not to produce or draw much on the kinds of sweeping histories of the *longue durée* that we associate with their most famous works. Even historical work of any kind has grown less common in American folkloristics as the field has continued to shift in ways initiated by its performance and communicative turn of the 1960s and 1970s (Williams 2017).

In this context, one might wonder why I am bothering to consider one of the most macrosociological and sweeping historical perspectives in the social sciences from the vantage point of folklore studies. Few folklorists follow work in world-systems analysis, and fewer still draw on it in their own research.[2] My response to this reasonable query has two aspects. One is broad. As students of the human condition, even if our main concerns are oriented toward diversity rather than commonality and are focused on small groups rather than on the global situation, I think that our work will be stronger if we attend, at least with basic awareness, to the other end of these continua. But my reflection also centers on a specific issue, one in which folklorists need to amend a key discussion in world-systems analysis itself.

This lack needing liquidation concerns the specific place of folklore studies in the historical formation of the social sciences and humanities in Europe in the context of modernization. Because, in a world-systems perspective, the historical rise of the social sciences is closely connected to the development of the modern capitalist world-system; situating folklore studies in its historical European context promises to improve a key understanding in world-systems analysis as developed by its most prominent architect and practitioner, Immanuel Wallerstein (1930–2019). This is not simply a matter of the history of the social sciences because, in Wallerstein's view, not only is the history of these fields part and parcel of the rise of the capitalist world-system, but their status is a fundamental matter of debate for the present and the future. As Wallerstein argued for a significant reconfiguring of these fields, it would be valuable if folklore studies were counted among them, as such a reconfiguration continues to be contemplated.

In this reflection, I proceed in three stages. In the first, I introduce world-systems analysis from a folkloristic perspective. In the second, I evoke the relationship of the human sciences to the rise of the capitalist world-system, as described in Wallerstein's work as a world-systems analyst. This will allow me to situate folklore studies and European ethnology into this historical picture. In a final section, I touch on Wallerstein's case for the reorganization of the social sciences, situating these proposals vis-à-vis folklore studies and ethnology (in its European ethnological form, if not also in its American cultural anthropological one). Through these stages of discussion, my hope is to provide a stepping stone that folklorists can use for further exploration of these issues and themes. As reflected in the first epigraph, I share Fine's view that folklore studies would be well served by giving greater attention to the place of its objects of inquiry in their world-system contexts.[3] The position of folklore studies among the disciplines should also remain a key concern for our field, regardless of the stances that we might occupy. As evoked by the second epigraph, one of the few solutions available to folklore studies to avoid being forgotten and thereby neglected by its scholarly neighbors is to reach out in their direction, something that I also attempt here.

World-Systems Analysis: General Features

I am not a world-systems analyst, although, as should be evident here, I am sympathetic to what the approach can offer. I feel that folklorists should know more about the perspective, even if they choose not to embrace it, incorporate it, or debate it. As an interested outsider to the perspective, there are limits to my ability to be a reliable guide. Thankfully, my task here does not require an elaborate account, as sophisticated-but-accessible introductions to the approach are widely available, as are varied critiques of it. A broad community of scholars working in world-systems analysis exists, and they, as one might expect of work within any research framework, do not all agree on all questions. There are also scholars who share concerns with those who embrace this approach but who do not themselves identify with it. Some of these remain in active dialogue with the approach's advocates, while others work in parallel. Plenty of scholars in the social sciences share with American folklorists a generalized low-level indifference to the perspective—not giving it a whole lot of thought.

In this complexity, it is an oversimplification to use the work of a single scholar to represent a whole collective endeavor. It is a further oversimplification to rely primarily on a single work by a single individual. Recognizing this problem, I propose to go ahead and trade in such a simplification of a simplification. My justifications are as follows. The key work to which I direct readers, and on which I will rely most fully here, is a sophisticated, later-career introduction to world-systems analysis by Immanuel Wallerstein, the scholar who pioneered the approach and is its most well-recognized advocate. This short, book-length introduction draws on more than three decades of work in this field and was written with readers like you and me in mind (Wallerstein 2004, xi–xii). That is, the book—*World-Systems Analysis: An Introduction*—presumes an interest in history and the social sciences, but it does not demand knowledge of its specific topic. Published in 2004, the book has garnered many positive reviews, is widely taught, and has accrued nearly 7,400 citations in the scholarly literature.[4] For my purpose of putting folklore studies into dialogue with world-systems analysis, the volume has many merits beyond its scale, scope, prominence, and the centrality of its author to the perspective. It also includes synthetic discussions of the key matters that I propose to specifically examine here. Readers who wish to go beyond my reflection can find additional sources discussed at the close of the book and, of course, can readily find a much larger and more polyphonic literature on these issues. In addition to this volume (Wallerstein 2004), readers will likely benefit from, and I will draw on, the biographical essay that appears in *The Essential Wallerstein* (Wallerstein 2000).[5]

I will not dwell on Wallerstein's professional biography, but it may help to evoke something of the mood of his work. As many folklorists have brought lived social and political concerns to their own work and have seen their lives and their engagements with the social world in terms of both scholarship about and action within the world, some affinity might be established with words with which Wallerstein (2000, xv) begins his autobiographical account: "My intellectual biography is one long quest for an adequate explanation of contemporary reality that I and others might act upon. The quest is both intellectual and political—I have always felt it could not be one without being at the same time the other—for myself or for anyone."

As a graduate student in sociology at Columbia University, Wallerstein began with a master's degree project on McCarthyism in US political life, followed by many years of work (in and beyond his doctorate) on the sociological study of Africa in colonial and decolonizing contexts. I do not review this history of work specifically on Africa, but it would likely be of interest to many folklorists and ethnologists. As Wallerstein (2004, xvii) describes his concerns retrospectively, he felt that while others centered their concerns in world affairs on the Cold War, the big story, in his estimation, was "the struggle to overcome the control by the western world of the rest of the world."

For my purposes here, the key development in Wallerstein's work from its substantive African studies phase to world-systems analysis was a realization that he describes as having two key elements. One aspect of this shift has to do with the unit of analysis in social research. For folklorists, I note that this is the issue that Dorothy Noyes (1995, 2012, 2016) has explored most influentially in her series of conceptual pieces related to "The Social Base of Folklore." Building particularly on the work of Richard Bauman (1971), Noyes directed our attention to and clarified the different ways that folklorists have thought about the social ground on which the everyday practices and expressive forms of special interest to the field are enacted. Writing in her paper "Group," from the perspective of folkloristics in the United States and Canada, Noyes (1995, 449) notes the ways that folklorists have moved progressively further toward the micro- and away from the macroscale. As she artfully notes throughout these studies, this has to do with a lot of influences and some anxieties that we carry into and forward in our work. Especially since the corruption of our field in Germany before and during World War II, American, Canadian, and Western European folklorists have often been leery of the nation and nationalisms, a social location and an ideology that our field often served since its European birth (Bendix 2012, 365, 371; Abrahams 1993; Bronner 2006). This is a matter to which I will return, but here it is worth noting that folklorists in these regions moved away from the national as a preferred unit of analysis concurrent with a parallel move away from it in the work of Wallerstein and the world-systems analysts who followed his lead. But the shift for North American and some Western European folklorists was toward the interaction order, whereas for the world-systems analysts, the shift was to a larger rather than smaller preferred unit of analysis.[6]

This larger unit of analysis is called a world-system. I want to keep bringing my evocation back to folklore studies. So even before providing Wallerstein's definition of world-system, I would stress that some folklorists already do work in which the modern world-system (whether called such or not) is the "social base" at issue. While we could consider any expressive form or vernacular cultural practice that is in global circulation as a means of seeing this (yoga, for instance, or the drinking of tea), it is most particularly obvious in situations such as the study of global heritage policy, wherein we know that we are studying cultural norms and forms whose primary social location, whose home, so to speak, is marked as "global." This is apparent in a rich body of work from many scholars, but those who have done ethnographic work on cultural heritage and cultural property *within* the bodies of international governance, such as Valdimar Hafstein (United Nations Educational, Scientific and Cultural Organization) and Stefan Groth (World Intellectual Property Organization), offer a particularly obvious and instructive instance (Groth 2012; Hafstein 2018b). In world-systems analysis terms, their work is about the ways that "folklore" becomes not just an object in but an instrument of governance in the "interstate system" that loosely binds nations into the contemporary global social order, that is, into the present world-system. While world-systems analysts have not, to my knowledge, engaged with the global assemblage that is contemporary heritage policy, it might be seen, in Wallerstein's (2004, 93) terms, as part of what he terms *geoculture*, that is, "norms and modes of discourse that are widely accepted as legitimate within the world-system."

Wallerstein (2004, 17) notes that "in 'world-systems' we are dealing with a spatial/temporal zone which cuts across many political and cultural units, one that represents an integrated zone of activity and institutions which obey certain systemic rules." In a glossary to *World-Systems Analysis*, he further observes,

> A world-system is not the system of the world, but a system *that is* a world and which can be, most often has been, located in an area less than the entire globe. World-systems analysis argues that the unities of social reality within which we operate, whose rules constrain us, are for the most part such world-systems (other than the now-extinct, small minisystems that once existed on the earth). World-systems analysis argues that there have been thus far only two varieties of world-systems: world-economies and world-empires. A world-empire (such as the Roman Empire, Han China) is a large bureaucratic structure with a single political center and an axial division of labor, but multiple cultures. A world-economy is a large axial division of labor with multiple political centers and multiple cultures. In English, the hyphen is essential to indicate these concepts. "World system" without a hyphen suggests that there has been only one world-system in the history of the world. (Wallerstein 2004, 99)

In this context, world-systems are a unit of analysis for historical and social research as well as a social aggregation in which I and other people live, with the Roman Empire (a world-empire) or the modern capitalist world-system (a system predicated on the capitalist world-economy) serving as instances. My friends among the Yuchi (Euchee) people of modern Oklahoma, United States, and the Baiku Yao people of Guangxi, China, live in different and varied social structures, social networks, and social frames of reference, operating at a range of scales, but they also share with each other, and with everyone else living today, an encompassing social reality. That common reality has many dimensions, is constantly changing, is experienced differently, and arose under specific historical and social conditions over a long period. World-systems analysis prioritizes its study.

More could be said about the world-system as a unit of analysis, but the other shift in Wallerstein's thinking, which I evoked above, needs to be raised. Alongside a shift of unit of analysis was a shift in methodological understanding. A social science focused on nation-states as the bounded containers for societies was an unhelpful inheritance in Wallerstein's view (cf. Wimmer and Glick Schiller 2003). So, too, were established attitudes about research methods. Viewing the social sciences from a historical perspective, Wallerstein has characterized the division between ideographic (humanistic, interpretive, historical) methods and nomothetic (scientific, generalizing, law-seeking) ones as counterproductive. The division was the result of a series of debates and disagreements, such as the *Methodenstreit* ("methods dispute") in later nineteenth-century German social science, which became routinized, producing both splits into new disciplines and, as in American anthropology during the years of my own graduate training (the 1990s), seemingly unending but fruitless debates within them. Describing his own mature view, Wallerstein (2000, xvii) argues that the social sciences were founded on a false methodological distinction and that to prosper, "all [social] analysis, if it were to grapple seriously with the description and explanation of the real world, had to be simultaneously historic and systemic."

While Wallerstein and other world-system analysts do very different work from most folklorists and ethnologists, such scholars can certainly take comfort in Wallerstein's view, which sees ideographic work (i.e., social research concerned with what is unique [i.e., historically particular] about a given human situation) as a legitimate and integral part of the larger enterprise to which he and his colleagues also contribute. This theme will return in the later sections of this chapter, but for now, the key point is that Wallerstein sees social research as a unified endeavor (the "historical social sciences") advanced with both interpretive or historical methods and scientific or generalizing ones. In terms of our own disciplinary history, Wallerstein is revisiting the issues raised prominently by Franz Boas (1887) in his key early paper "The Study of Geography." In that account, Boas argued for the importance of cosmographic research attending to particulars of the social and natural world alongside, and of course informing, work that develops general systematic understandings.

These two elements—the world-system as unit analysis and an integrative approach to methods that includes historical specifics—are a suitable starting point for my discussion. The range of results of research in world-systems analysis is beyond the scope of this chapter, but some key and widely discussed insights can be raised. It is always awkward to summarize a vast body of complex research in a brief scope. In this case, the matter is made more complex because of the scale of the themes and their deep history and complex and changing present nature.

Perhaps most well known among Wallerstein's (2004, 17) contributions is his characterization of the modern world-economy as being "marked by an axial division of labor between core-like production processes and peripheral production processes, which resulted in unequal exchange favoring those involved in core-like production processes." Wallerstein here is choosing his words of explanation very carefully. He continues, "Since such processes tend to group together in particular countries, one could use a shorthand language by talking of core and peripheral zones (or even core or peripheral states), as long as one remembered that it was the production processes and not the states that were core-like and peripheral" (2004, 17). To the extent that some folklorists have heard of or used this distinction, it seems to manifest most commonly in the simplified form wherein a particular nation-state is characterized as "belonging" to the group of core, semiperipheral, and peripheral states (or "being" such a state). At issue here, though, are kinds of economic activities and their differential effect on different kinds of individuals and groups sharing the larger system. This is most easily seen when we compare nations or regions dominated by raw material extraction and those involved in industrial manufacture or postindustrial "service economies."

This thread in world-systems analysis grows out of earlier work by Latin American political economists and what came to be known as dependency theory. Much work in world-systems analysis accounts for the origin and nature of the unequal economic (and political) relationships that follow from core-periphery patterns. These patterns are dynamic over the run of history. By way of example, in both economic and geopolitical terms, once-powerful imperial nations such as Spain have, in world-systems terms, fallen into semiperipheral patterns and structures, exercising influence on some weaker peripheral nations (former colonies, for instance) but also being influenced by more powerful core nations (and the economic actors based in them), such as the United States.

Often closely allied with specific individuals living culturally rich, if often economically difficult, lives in diverse circumstances around the world, folklorists are often apprehensive about making broad characterizations like "X is a peripheral nation" (although, as Wallerstein notes in the quotation above, this is a risky shorthand). But most folklorists have also indirectly absorbed some of the basic insights of the world-systems understanding of the capitalist world-system, including the interstate system, the global division of labor characterizing the contemporary world, and such features as the dependencies that "developing" nations experience in their relationships with more powerful nations (often former colonial powers) and the corporations based within them. (For a fuller treatment of the modern and contemporary economic order in world-systems terms, see Wallerstein 2004, chap. 2.)

World-Systems Analysis: Illustrative Examples for Folklorists and Ethnologists

I have not provided an adequate sketch of Wallerstein's basic account of the contemporary world-system or even the axial division of labor, which is one of its key features. For folklorists wondering if it offers much of direct relevance to their work beyond providing an account of the largest background level to more local and particular investigations, I highlight the following sample features as points of possible connection and interest. I cite four examples—households, semiproletarian status, national identity, and colonization—but others could be developed with folkloristic interests in mind. These special interests do not, of course, cover the fullness of world-systems analysis, which also includes many concerns (such as long-term cycles of expansion and contraction in the world-economy) to which folklorists have given little or no thought.

Wallerstein (2004, 33) views households (sometimes also recognized as families, sometimes not; sometimes cohabitating, sometimes not) as key social units. Much fruitful ethnographic work by folklorists and ethnologists shares this view, thus attending to the world-systems view of households is a potential point of entry. For Wallerstein (32–35), households pool resources and pursue a mix of productive activities. These go far beyond wage income (which is itself very diverse) and include subsistence activities, petty commodity production, rent, and transfer payments. Viewed from the perspective of the kinds of ethnographic encounters that fieldwork-oriented folklorists and ethnologists have, this is an important list, and world-systems analysts are smart in how they frame these categories. Subsistence activity can include growing or gathering food for one's household or building one's own home from gathered materials—and we have long studied such practices—but it also includes such things as washing dishes or putting together flat-packed DIY furniture (33). These later activities are just the sort of thing that many European ethnologists study today, even if American folkloristics remains focused on more obviously expressive practices (e.g., Damsholt and Jespersen 2014; Ehn and Löfgren 2010; SIEF 2022). Similarly, petty commodity production includes such things as household basket production for local or regional markets or the production of tourist crafts, but also activities such as street vending or freelance work (Wallerstein 2004, 33). For Wallerstein (36–38), households are also prominent as key points of articulation with (socioeconomic) class and with identities and status-group memberships. These modes of social differentiation and their inculcation are part of the bread and butter of much contemporary work in folklore studies.

Households are, of course, hardly the sole concern of world-systems analysts. They are a major focus in social and cultural anthropology, particularly economic anthropology and kinship studies, as well as in many kinds of sociology. Folklorists have contributed in important ways to the study of households also, particularly through their attention to how people live inside vernacular buildings and how households are a locus for the intergenerational transfer of cultural knowledge and artistic repertoires. Those two streams intersect literally when we consider how households entertain themselves inside houses. Consider our field's founding interest in what the Brothers Grimm called *hausmärchen* (household tales) (Grimm and Grimm [1812–14] 1857). I honor these other streams of work, and I evoke Wallerstein's (2004, 32–38) approach to households just as one point of connection for folklorists who share an interest in this node of social life.

Close consideration of the status of households worldwide leads to a number of related topics, one of which can provide another example of common interests between folklore studies and world-systems analysis. On the folklore studies side, consider as an example the work that folklorist Mary Hufford (n.d.) conducted in a coal mining region of West Virginia in the United States. This body of research, public-facing interpretation, and policy activism is rich in many areas of local community as well as scholarly concern. One aspect of it concerns the ways that individuals and their households endeavor to supplement wage labor with additional productive activities. Examples from Hufford's (n.d., 1997, 2002, 2003, 2005, 2006) documentary work (with diverse collaborators) include harvesting ginseng for sale in global markets, gathering mushrooms and ramps (a kind of wild leek) for household and community-wide consumption, and gardening (and preserving) vegetables also for household use. The environmental degradation wrought by mountaintop removal coal mining looms large in Hufford's work, as does local environmental activism aimed at protecting local environments and preserving them as de facto commons that local people can continue to rely on (2002, 2005; Hufford et al. 2011). I only skim the surface of the work of Hufford and her collaborators here. I commend it to you.

I raise the example of Hufford's work here because it so comprehensively articulates a wide range of issues central to world-systems analysis as explicated by Wallerstein (2004). Whether or not the label fits Hufford's interlocutors accurately or exactly, Wallerstein's account of semiproletarian households is an instructive instance. As a heuristic, he posits that a proletarian household is one where 50 percent or more of lifetime household income comes from wage work, and a semiproletarian household as one where total lifetime household income from wages is less than 50 percent. For our purposes here, these calculations can be approximate. The key issue is that "an employer has an advantage in employing those wage-laborers who are in a semiproletarian household" (Wallerstein 2004, 35). In situations in which households pursue the kinds of subsistence activities and petty commodity production activities that Hufford describes so movingly for West Virginia's coal country (a setting where there are also transfer payments [especially forms of government aid] and some rents), employers are able to pay employees less than the absolute minimum wage that would, if it were the only source of household income, ensure household survival. Put more simply, nonwage household income, from gardening or gathering and other ways of "making do," represents a kind of subsidy to employers. Wallerstein has much of interest to say about these kinds of situations, which also loom large in the work of American folklorists, whether they work in rural areas overseas or throughout the United States. In the two regions that have figured in my own ethnographic work (rural and suburban Oklahoma, United States, and rural Guangxi, China), they are profoundly present, even if my own scholarship has not yet stressed them.[7]

Folklore studies has long been entwined with nationalism. This is a larger issue for both our field and world-systems analysts, but in Wallerstein's survey, he highlights three prominent ways that nationalism has historically been promoted—schools, military service, and civic ceremonies. Our field—in the United States, at least—has long attended to the latter, especially through the study of cultural performance events, including civic holidays, but as manifest, for instance, in the massive Veterans History Project (US Library of Congress) and other military-oriented folklore projects, the second of these also figures in our work in important ways. A long stream of work in children's folklore and a robust focus in public folklore practice concerned with folklore and education can also be cited in this context. More broadly, the cultural expressions and social construction of nationalism and nationalist identity are a core concern of both folklore studies and world-systems analysis, a matter that will return in a different guise in the next section (Wallerstein 2004, 54; Bronner 2006).

Colonization can provide a final illustrative point of contact. While the incorporation of peasantries into states in programs of nationalism is the big story behind much folklore studies history, the encompassment of Indigenous populations into colonial empires and settler states is of comparable importance, even if one treats, as I am here, folklore studies and European ethnology (*volkskunde*, etc.) as a distinct disciplinary formation from cultural anthropology (American ethnology), British social anthropology (and its antecedents), German *volkerkunde*, and their closely related disciplinary manifestations. As with nation-building and nationalism, folklore studies was profoundly shaped by its emergence during, and entanglements with, colonization and colonialism (Briggs and Naithani 2012; Naithani 2008; Ó Giolláin 2017). While they have only begun to account for the fuller colonial contexts of their work, folklorists have made important contributions to understanding not only the field's colonial history but also the colonial project and its consequences more broadly. The work of Sadhana Naithani (1997, 2001a, 2001b, 2002, 2008, 2010) provides an important example. In both a specifically Indian and a broad global context, Naithani has charted the scope of the relationships twining folklore studies and colonialism together, pointing as well to changes and possibilities in the present and future. Like Wallerstein, her work shows how disciplinary activity has been shaped by, and how it has helped shape and reshape, the larger global transformations and contexts in which it is situated. It is also noteworthy that Naithani (2010, 1–10) has argued eloquently that the study of folklore in bounded national contexts has impeded its comparative study, including its study at a global scale, as with her work on folklore and folkloristics in the British Empire.[8] The study of folklore history in its colonial (and nationalist) contexts is one area where, despite a widespread disciplinary turn to the microscale and away from historical inquiry, the link to the concerns of world-systems scholars is more immediate and evident.

I have not characterized Wallerstein's approach to understanding colonies, colonization, and decolonization. Going back to Wallerstein's early work on Africa and the postcolonial circumstances of African nations, this has been a significant theme in his work. Colonies and postcolonial regions and states are also fundamental to the history and present of the capitalist world-system and thus feature prominently in Wallerstein's (e.g., [1974] 2011a, [1980] 2011b, [1989] 2011c, 2011d) detailed accounts of it. As noted above, decolonization was what he saw as the crucial transformation in the modern world-system in his own lifetime. Of all that might be said, in a folkloristic context, it might be useful to simply note that from a world-systems analysis perspective, it is through the process of European colonization that those peoples who had long carried on lives outside of any world-system were brought into the changing global order that now (for the present, at least) encompasses all of us. As the long-duration history of the Yuchi people with whom I have collaborated reveals, this does not mean that Indigenous peoples once outside the capitalist world-system were not part of complex social networks. We know that their "pre-Columbian" social world was dizzyingly complex; it just was not a world-system in Wallerstein's sense, even if it was a comprehensive "system of the world" in Marshal Sahlins's (1993, 11; 1999, v) sense (Waselkov with Jackson 2004; Worth 2012; Jackson 2012; Wallerstein 2004, 55–56).

Identities and the concept of identity, social movements (together with national movements constituting "antisystemic movements"), sovereignty, the nature of tradition, and many other issues of shared interest between folklorists and Wallerstein and other world-systems analysts could be flagged. My hope is that I have adequately suggested the value of further exploring such intersections. Having evoked some shared interests, I turn now to the place of folklore studies and European ethnology in the birth of the social sciences.

Folklore Studies and European Ethnology in the Birth of the Social Sciences

While world-systems analysis is best understood in its own terms through engagement with specific research drawing on the approach, through programmatic and introductory works by key practitioners, and through wider debates in and about the approach, one specific gap in world-systems analysis warrants specific engagement by folklorists, even if folklorists as a group do not engage the approach in a general way. As suggested above, Wallerstein's account of the current capitalist world-system is a historical one. Much work in this field focuses, for instance, on the initial rise of capitalism in Europe and, as has been suggested already, its continuing transformations up to the present. In the four volumes on *The Modern World-System* published to date, Wallerstein ([1974] 2011a, [1980] 2011b, [1989] 2011c, 2011d) himself has tracked this history from the sixteenth century into the early twentieth. While these questions have occupied a wide range of scholars, Wallerstein is distinctive, in my view, in his concurrent concern for the rise and role of the social sciences in the context of this larger history. While noteworthy, this interest is not totally unique, of course, and it is reflected in some core works by folklorists. Richard Bauman and Charles Briggs's *Voices of Modernity: Language Ideologies and the Politics of Inequality* (2006) is a significant example that can link folklore studies into my discussion. But Wallerstein's take is distinctive.

A deeper summary of Wallerstein's (2011d, xvi) views would require exploring the impacts that he attributes to the French Revolution and its role in fostering centrist liberalism (in relation to conservatism and radicalism) in the capitalist world-system. In his introductory history of the academic disciplines, he tracks the rise of the modern university and its faculties, placing special emphasis on the fragmentation of philosophy into the modern disciplines that we now possess (2004, 1–22). An early split into the humanities and the sciences proved to have both general and specific significance. (For Wallerstein, it also fostered specific problems.) For the emergent social sciences, a specific effect was to see the emergent disciplines gravitate to one side or the other of the ideographic/nomothetic (humanities/science) divide. But this is not the only way that these fields sorted themselves out. The social worlds that they took account of were also divided up along a different axis—the west/rest one. Finally, there was a topical parsing that was born out of an ideological proposition of that time and place. Referring to economics, political science, and sociology (studying the Western European present) versus the Western European past studied by history, Wallerstein asks, "Why, however would there be *three* disciplines to study the present but only one to study the past?" He answers, "Because the dominant liberal ideology of the nineteenth century insisted that *modernity* was defined by the differentiation of three special spheres: the market, the state, and the civil society" (2004, 6).

Wallerstein provides a rich and nuanced account of the factors that shaped the differentiation of the social science disciplines and their relative alignments with these and other distinctions. History (as a scholarly discipline) was ideographic in orientation, but it shared with the nomothetic social sciences (economics, political science, sociology) a primary (initial, early) concern with the study of the same European societies in which these scholars lived and worked. Sharing with history a more holistic view of social life and an ideographic interest in particulars were two other fields: Oriental studies (concerned with non-Western peoples with writing, imperial histories, and world religions) and anthropology (by which Wallerstein [2004, 4–9] specifically means ethnographically based work pursued in this early period among colonized, non-Western peoples falling outside the purview of the Orientalists). Readers of my summary of his summary history will be left wondering about omissions. I recommend consulting his account directly for more nuance. My purpose is just to set up a system in which folklore studies and (European) ethnology are absent.[9]

Wallerstein tracks the ways that these fields have changed since their formation as modern disciplines in the late nineteenth century, focusing in particular on developments after World War II and then in the wake of 1968. Decolonization, the rise of the concept of "development," and the Cold War–era emergence of area studies fields figure into this story of change. The key point, though, for this part of my account is that all these disciplines arose in a broader European (and North American) context of the rise of centrist liberalism and its alternatives (radicalism, conservativism) and a host of transformations in governance, economics, and cultural life within the world-system. In particular, they arose alongside the formation of modern European (and North American) nation-states of the sort that we now inhabit. They were shaped by, and themselves shaped, both European social transformations and the global transformation in which Europe and European settler societies figured so prominently. In Wallerstein's (2004, xi, 1–16) view, the social sciences were and are an important part of the "knowledge structures" of the capitalist world-system.[10]

A key aspect of Wallerstein's account of the disciplines is what happened in the twentieth century with the rise of area studies and the world changes that it responded to and shaped. There are many facets of this, but one that he stresses is not only how all the disciplines became more muddled and destabilized (and international) but also that Oriental studies and (cultural) anthropology faced particular challenges as the social worlds that they addressed mutated. Regarding this, he writes, "So it [this shift] challenges the logic of the disciplines. Oriental studies give[s] up its name, the scholars join other divisions, they become historians or professors of religion. The cultural anthropologists tried various things. They decided that Europeans and North Americans have tribes too; they would study Swiss mountaineers and people in Chicago slums, and now they decide they'll study, 'culture.' They are in search of a raison d'etre" (Wallerstein 1996, 4, see also 2004, 11).

I do not contest the very macrohistory that Wallerstein recounts in his treatment of the social science disciplines, but, like all such accounts, details can matter and prompt reassessment. Most cultural anthropologists would strongly contest the simplicity of this account. At the very least, details usually matter to those who feel a sense of connection to the specifics. The quotation just given comes from one of Wallerstein's earlier programmatic statements on the refashioning of the social sciences. To arrive at our destination, consider "Swiss mountaineers" as a focus for anthropological research. I suspect that the image Wallerstein had in mind was contemporary, bourgeois outdoors enthusiasts with resources for travel and modern equipment.

For me, though, the image is fortuitous because it could also be taken to refer to people living and working in the mountains of Switzerland. As Regina Bendix (2012) carefully recounts for those unaware of the history of Swiss folklore studies and ethnology (= *volkerkunde* → *vielnamenfach*), the ethnography of Swiss mountaineers in this sense is a long-standing area of research. In keeping with Wallerstein's larger agenda, the formation of the social sciences included an ideographically inclined, ethnographically (and historically) based, holistically oriented, culture-minded field operative in, to use world-systems terms, those European states characterized by core-like economic production and relative strength in the interstate system. Whereas the anthropology that he has in mind (early forms of North American cultural anthropology, the social anthropology of the British Empire, and the volkerkunde of German-speaking and German-influenced areas), the cognate but distinct (national, regional) forms of ethnology and folklore studies found elsewhere in Europe (and North America) are not present in his account, not even in the book-length treatment, *Open the Social Sciences: Report of the Gulbenkian Commission on the Restructuring of the Social Sciences* (Wallerstein et al. 1996), which I discuss more in the next section.[11]

Charles Briggs and Sadhana Naithani stress that folklore studies (folkloristics) has been profoundly shaped (as a whole and on an international basis) by the history and practices of colonialism (what they call the "coloniality of folklore"). They are at pains to demonstrate and explore this point because the dominant histories of the discipline have emphasized its entanglements with the rise of Enlightenment rationalism in northern Europe of the seventeenth and eighteenth centuries and with romantic nationalism in the late eighteenth and nineteenth centuries. I stress Briggs and Naithani's point because it, too, is relevant for engagements with (and by) world-systems analysis but also because, to compensate for the gap in the world-system's treatment of the disciplines, I have to revisit the standard narrative of folklore studies history and, in this specialized context, stress what folklorists largely understand, which is the nationalist genealogy in the history of the field.

For any world-systems analyst who might read these reflections, my task is to stress that there is, basically, a discipline missing from the Wallerstein history of the social sciences. It is not a minor gap either. I do not say this out of chauvinism but because the interpretive concerns of world-systems analysis are so (understandably) concerned with the development of processes and ideas (of global importance) in northern Europe (and North America). Folklore studies and European ethnology are not giant world disciplines, as sociology and economics are, and thus it is understandable how their disciplinary histories might be swept into a larger narrative focused on volkerkunde/ social anthropology/cultural anthropology/non-European ethnology and its colonial engagements.[12] At the same time, the study of the rise of European nation-states has continually emphasized the outsized influence that folklore studies had in these processes. I am not summarizing this work here, but we have extensive literatures on the histories and contexts of nation-making and folklore's disciplinary development for Ireland, Estonia, Greece, Germany, Finland, Sweden, and other parts of Europe.[13] One cannot visit a northern European nation such as Estonia without seeing the historical fingerprints of folklorists and European ethnologists everywhere. In such nations, the ethnography and regional ethnology of the citizenry (particularly the former peasantry) looms large in the polity, in the economy, and in civil society. Scholarship in overseas anthropology (volkerkunde, etc.) in such nations has historically been weak if present at all, whereas folklore studies and (regional, European) ethnology (volkskunde, etc.) have been, over the long haul of disciplinary existence, strong. North America (specifically the United States and Canada as settler colonies) is unique because both forms of scholarship could thrive and hybridize. In ways that accord with Wallerstein's arguments about twentieth-century transformations, still ongoing, these disciplines continue to transform and reorganize in all of these North Atlantic settings. Folklore studies is also now an international discipline, with areas of strength and distinctive practices manifest throughout the world(-system), from Latin America to East Asia (Bendix and Hasan-Rokem 2012a).

Folklore Studies and European Ethnology in the Reorganization of the Social Sciences

While calls for interdisciplinarity are ubiquitous in the scholarly spaces that folklorists and European ethnologists inhabit, Wallerstein has argued prominently for a different reconfiguration of the social sciences, one that he characterizes as unidisciplinary.[14] On the basis of his view that the nineteenth-century division of the social sciences into narrow disciplines atomized what should have been a more holistic endeavor—worldwide in scope, concerned with the full breadth of human activity, and historical and systematic, ideographic and nomothetic, in orientation—Wallerstein has argued for a reconfiguration of the social sciences. The name that he and his collaborators use for this unitary undertaking is *historical social science*.

I will return to the case for a reunified historical social science below, but are political science, sociology, economics, history, geography, anthropology, and others that might be named about to disappear on the basis of wide agreement with Wallerstein's proposals? I do not think so, and I do not raise them because I am eager for folklore studies and ethnology to be recognized fully as a part of this group just in time to join in the abandonment of disciplinary identities. As with my larger reflection, my goal is more basic—to suggest that folklorists and European ethnologists would be well served by engaging with and contemplating the issues that Wallerstein and his colleagues have raised.

As I contemplate such proposals myself, I am mindful that folklorists in the United States and Europe also have some experience of their own with efforts of renaming and reorienting disciplines. In the United States case, proposals (in the 1990s) to decommission the name *folklore* as a disciplinary label (as in *folklore studies* or *folkloristics*) were not realized, although the debate in retrospect was probably therapeutic. The reasons why these proposals were not acted on is too large a topic for this context, but factors relevant to Wallerstein's more ambitious proposals include sunk institutional costs, attachment to distinctive intellectual histories, methods, genealogies, and identities, as well as the nature of collective action problems in general. Individuals, in the US context, could choose to find their own personal paths away from the professional identity of *folklorist*, but, absent an overwhelming consensus to change and the risks associated with putting oneself and one's colleagues out of business, folklore studies in the United States continued onward beyond what, for a moment, seemed like a point of existential crisis (Bendix 1998; Kirshenblatt-Gimblett 1998a; Oring 1998).[15] The way that folklore studies had been established as an autonomous discipline that was largely independent of (American) anthropology (and literature studies) by the 1990s is a factor that needs to be explored in the context of the history of this moment of crisis. The rise and (relative) decline of cultural studies in the English-speaking world is another factor in need of consideration.

The situation in Germany presents a marked contrast. The role of folklore studies during the Nazi era created a situation ripe for collective transformation. The result was significant reflexive consideration of disciplinary pasts and futures and the transformation that Regina Bendix describes as the move "from *Volkskunde* to the 'Field of Many Names.'" While the need to make a break with the past became clear, the choice of what to name the new enterprise was vexing and, ultimately, plural, as Bendix (2012) has chronicled. These are only relatively recent instances of disciplinary renaming and reorganization projects, and many others could be cited, including William Thoms's (1996) coining of the name *folk-lore* itself in 1846.

The history of the social sciences, the consequences of this historical ordering and contemporary practice, and proposals for reorganizing them appear in a number of works by Wallerstein and his collaborators. Most prominent is *Open the Social Sciences: Report of the Gulbenkian Commission on the Restructuring of the Social Sciences* (Wallerstein et al. 1996). The book represents the work of a group of scholars in and beyond the social sciences whose task was to "reflect on the present social sciences and their future" (Calouste Gulbenkian Foundation 1996, x).[16] In a presentation-turned-article for the Social Science Research Council's newsletter *Items*, Wallerstein (1996) offered a short account of the commission's work and its findings. In the 2002 Sydney Mintz lecture, Wallerstein offered a treatment of these issues specifically keyed for an anthropological audience. While that occasion might have prompted a more granular exploration inclusive of European ethnology, if not folkloristics, it presents the core argument in more detail vis-à-vis American-style (overseas) anthropology, without attention to either Americanist anthropology in the mode of Boasian ethnology and folklore studies or European folkloristics/ethnology (Wallerstein 2003). In the context of the book's general overview of his views, Wallerstein also raises the disciplinary questions in *World-Systems Analysis: An Introduction* (2003, chap. 1). Wallerstein shares his thoughts on the work of the commission and elaborates on the issues further in a long interview with Carlos Antonio Aguirre Rojas (2012). These discussions were preceded by a collection of essays that examined various "Limits of Nineteenth-Century Paradigms" in the social sciences (Wallerstein 1991). Wallerstein's colleague Richard Lee (2014) considers these issues from an allied perspective, adding concern for the state of the humanities. The historical factors shaping the social sciences are treated in detail in these works, and I evoked some of them briefly in the previous section. Here, I try to highlight some of the proposals made by Wallerstein and the Gulbenkian Commission in its report (Calouste Gulbenkian Foundation 1996).

The history presented by Wallerstein in his various writings and by the Gulbenkian Commission that he chaired is powerful (although, as I have suggested, it is partial at least with respect to folklore studies and European ethnology). The problems that the structures of knowledge in the social sciences have generated or exacerbated demand the attention that they have been given in this body of work. The final chapter of *Open the Social Sciences* is smart and also realistic in its awareness of what has made the disciplines durable even as they have faltered in changing contexts.

What a reader of the report, especially with the distance provided by more than twenty years since its publication, is likely to think about the recommendations themselves, with which the report closes, is that they are relatively tame in relation to the contexts that provoked them. I attribute this to two factors in particular. One is just the passage of time and the unfolding of the trends that the authors identify and discuss. If the present shares features with the future the commissioners were seeking to reach, some of that can also be attributable to their efforts. The recommendations were read and reflected on by practitioners in the social sciences, even if folklorists did not attend much to their recommendations (which, it is worth noting, happened in the same moment as cognate reassessments in North American folklore studies). But there is also the context of consensus-building attendant to any committee report.

This aspect arises in Wallerstein's interview with Rojas (2012). Asked about *Open the Social Sciences* in relationship to Wallerstein's own aspirations for historical social science, Wallerstein cites the collective nature of that work and the agreements established among the participants about how the work would be pursued. Faced with the choice of developing, weighing, and debating all of the detailed pathways forward that might be constructed, they chose instead to "draw attention to the fundamental problems, inducing and even forcing people to reflect on them" (Rojas 2012, 93). Wallerstein continues, "We didn't want them to discuss a proposed solution but rather to think around a problem, so that each of them might try to look for and elaborate a solution themselves" (Rojas 2012, 93).

Wallerstein notes in this context that having made this choice—that is, to place an emphasis on the context and on provoking wider discussion—the commissioners in turn shaped a different, but related, dynamic. He observes that the commission, in that context, could have been read as identifying a problem but not showing good faith in proposing solutions. This is a reading of such situations that often leads to their dismissal as "not worthwhile" by skeptical colleagues. In response to the conjuncture of the committee dynamic, the desire to promote discussion, and the need to make some suggestions both useful and agreeable to the commissioners, they pursued a "compromise solution," deciding "that it would be best to develop only a few of these small suggestions." Wallerstein personally saw these as "a sort of first step on the path of these possible solutions to our dilemmas" (Rojas 2012, 93). Before returning to Wallerstein's view, we must ask, What were these small suggestions, and what do they look like now, particularly for folklore studies?

Wallerstein clearly wishes that readers of *Open the Social Sciences* (1996) would not (as some have done) skip to the last two pages of the book for the purposes of judging the simple "first step" suggestions out of context, and I do not wish to encourage such readings myself (Rojas 2012, 93). That said, readers of this reflection will want to gain some sense of them. In the commission's first suggestion, they encourage, and provide the rationale for encouraging, programs that bring together scholars "for a year's work" across disciplines for joint research on "specific urgent themes." This suggestion is closely related to the second on "the establishment of integrated research programs within university structures that cut across traditional lines, have specific intellectual objectives, and have funds for a limited period of time (say about five years)" (Wallerstein 1996, 103–104). Bendix, Kilian, and Noyes (2017), from a multidisciplinary vantage point that is centered in folklore studies and European ethnology, have recently described such endeavors in ethnographic, conceptual, and practical terms. In the years since the publication of *Open the Social Sciences*, such work has become common (if not universal) and, for those who work in research universities (a small percentage of active scholars, of course), we now not only confront the impact of such endeavors pursued at scale but are also assessing their costs and consequences, not just their advantages, especially when such activities as "grand challenges" research are given high prioritization by administrators and funding agencies. While not all folklorists have access to opportunities to participate in such work and while the rise of such work has sometimes marginalized those less inclined to join it, we now live in a world in which the commission's first and second recommendations are very present.

The commission's third recommendation, which, like others here, is university-centric, argues for the joint appointment of professors to multiple relevant departments. This practice, at least in American research universities like my own, is certainly more common in one sense now than it was before. The commissioners argue for a strong form of joint appointment, one that goes beyond courtesy appointments to structure the faculty in such a way as to encourage active faculty participation in the work of their multiple home units. The strong form of this practice is perhaps expressed best in condensed form in the suggestion that "we would require that each department have at least 25 percent of its members who did *not* have a degree in that discipline." The commissioners embrace the hope that such an "administrative device" would increase the range of "intellectual debate within each department, the curricula offered, [and] the points of view that were considered plausible or legitimate" (Wallerstein 1996, 104–105). Those university programs where folklore is researched and taught by more than one or two colleagues in relative isolation probably more closely approximated then (Wallerstein 1996), and still more closely approximates now (2024), the goal set by the commissioners than is probably true in any other social science disciplines.

In its more forceful form, such a restructuring is a classic collective action problem, especially when leading research departments with strong disciplinary graduate programs see themselves as having a particular responsibility for the transmission of a disciplinary (as opposed to transdisciplinary) legacy. This disciplinary necessity is even more intensely felt in situations (as with folklore studies and museum ethnology in many locations) wherein such training also ensures continuity in the preservation and use of core national or regional archives or collections.[17] Be that as it may, the field of folklore studies has a long-standing history of (relative) disciplinary openness, both inbound (welcoming scholars not formally trained in the field into full participation) and outbound (folklore scholars finding academic homes in a range of departmental contexts, such as anthropology, English, comparative literature, media studies, history, art history, etc.).

The final "small suggestion" is another one that is probably already familiar to folklorists. The commissioners recommend "joint work for graduate students" by which they mean a graduate curriculum that enables students to study outside their primary field. They are right in noting that this practice is not widespread in the social sciences (ca. 1996), but it is hardly uncommon among folklorists now or when they were writing. Commenting that "only in a few departments in a few universities are students allowed to wander outside," they argue that "we would turn this around too. Why not make it mandatory for students seeking a doctorate in a given discipline to take a certain number of courses, or do a certain amount of research, that is defined as being within the purview of a second department?" (Wallerstein 1996, 105). The largest trainer of folklore doctoral students in the United States, Indiana University has had this norm, as part of a larger campus structure, since long before the Gulbenkian Commission's report. While not all universities have what, at Indiana, is called the "PhD minor field," the structure of most folklore graduate programs within a matrix of disciplinary, interdisciplinary, and cross-disciplinary structures and coursework has ensured that most folklore doctorates have, for decades, gotten the kind of training that the commission proposed. The rise of the double PhD has further extended this characteristic, and the long-standing fact that few folklorists come to graduate training with an undergraduate degree in folklore studies has also contributed to the cross-disciplinary and interdisciplinary nature of the field. This holds true internationally, not solely in the United States.

As noted above, the commissioners saw these four recommendations as modest ones. Their goal was to see to it that "the underlying issues be debated— clearly, openly, intelligently, and urgently" (Wallerstein 1996, 105). I think there is evidence to suggest that they enjoyed at least modest success. Whether they did or did not, there are indications that the world of practice in the social sciences has moved in the direction of their simpler, collective suggestions in the years since 1996. Even though folklorists themselves did not take up the commission's report at the time, the issues discussed in the full report remain important, and current calls by graduate students, folklore studies faculty, and public-facing and applied folklorists to reassess and reorient folklore graduate training for the present and the future would be well served, I think, if they could be articulated and explored in relationship to the report's assessments and arguments.[18]

As suggested by Wallerstein's responses in his interview with Rojas (2012), he has his own personal response to these questions of restructuring. Given the firmness of his historical assessment and the clarity of his arguments about present needs, the softness of his programmatic statements might come as a surprise. It might make sense to understand that his historical work certainly caused him to recognize something of the hubris of earlier predictions and prescriptions for the future. Speaking a number of years after the work of the commission, he notes, "I should say that I don't have a clear view of how to orchestrate this reorganization of the social sciences either" (2012, 93). He continues, "I think that this will be the fruit of a long discussion among all of us, and I can tell you that regarding this point, my position is similar to that which I maintain on the political level: just as I support a plural alternative for the left, so too would I support the construction of a plural schema on the epistemological level for the reorganization of the social sciences" (2012, 93). In this discussion, Wallerstein goes on to suggest that the best that we can do is to experiment ("explore different paths") and then carefully assess the results of those experiments. While this response is mild, the idea of unidisciplinary historical social science introduced above represents Wallerstein taking a firmer personal stance, one that he can occupy as an individual even if he cannot compel the majority of his colleagues in the diverse social sciences to follow suit.

For folklorists, we might benefit not only from engaging with the discussions that I am evoking but also from assessing our own experiments along these lines. For a time, it seemed like cultural heritage or cultural sustainability might, for instance, provide conceptual foci for the reorganization of the discipline in the United States. I am doubtful of this, but what can we learn from those colleagues who embarked on experiments in reorienting in this way?[19] What can we learn not only from the reorganization of German volkskunde but also from the broader reorganization of European ethnology of which it was (and is) an (ongoing) part? For a time, cultural studies as a branded postdisciplinary project seemed like a threat to both cultural anthropology and folkloristics, at least in the United States. That no longer seems to be the case. Similarly, semiotics once loomed large in (American) folklore studies, whereas today, its lessons seem largely (re-)assimilated (back) into the field's canon. What might we learn from revisiting these ebbs and flows, including the rise (and sometimes fall) of neighboring disciplines (e.g., semiotics), paradisciplines (e.g., digital humanities), and interdisciplinary endeavors (e.g., heritage studies)?

While the history and significance of the changing social sciences get more attention than concrete recommendations in *Open the Social Sciences* and associated writings (as was intended), Wallerstein does have his own views as reflected in his discussions of world-systems analysis. I reiterate these in conclusion, using them as a means of rethinking folklore studies as a social science or, if you prefer, as a social science–adjacent humanities field. For anyone considering the status of folklore studies as a field, in itself and in relationship to its neighbors, I feel that attending to Wallerstein's history and assessment of present needs is a valuable resource.

Conclusion

Along the way, I have sought to recruit colleagues in folklore studies and in ethnology to use Wallerstein and his colleagues' views on the world-system and its analysis, including on the nature of the disciplines within it, as a fresh (to them, at least) springboard for rethinking the present and future of work within these linked fields. I do not want to proscribe the uses to which this work might be put, but some implicit aspirations can be offered in conclusion.

One of these concerns the status of history and historical methods and goals in folklore and ethnology. While history remains crucial in some manifestations of these fields, the historical impulse that once was strong in US folklore studies (including Americanist ethnology) and in European folklore studies and European (regional) ethnology have, in many settings, atrophied. With the exception of disciplinary history (which continues to be pursued in a robust way), historical work (in its myriad forms) has been in retreat for many generations. Important exceptions can always be found, but the kinds of historical concerns that animated the work of many folklorists and ethnologists prior to the mid-1970s (especially in the United States) are now scarce. Michael Ann Williams (2017) has written prominently of this, but it is not her view only. While those concerned about the eclipse of historical methods and concerns do not all share the same specific aspirations or remedies, there is a growing conversation among, admittedly, older folklorists about this dynamic and its implications. In engaging with world-systems analysis here, I have tried to frame the folklore and history intersection in a fresh way rather than simply arguing on the basis of the field's past accomplishments in historical work (as much as I respect those). Whatever else world-systems analysts might offer, they are insistent on the importance of "bringing history back in" to social analysis (Goldfrank 1979).

Scale is another dynamic where folklorists would do well to reflexively assess their practices and preferences. While many folklorists (particularly, again, in the United States) have a sound and honorable attachment to the (often convivial) interaction order, we seem (collectively) to think comparatively little about how this world of "artistic communication in small groups" and the "practice of everyday life" articulates with wider social dynamics. As Noyes (2016, 412-16) has argued rather scathingly in her treatment of slogan concepts, even when we work on big, global issues, those we take up are often surrogates for, or derivative of, deeper and more intractable problems that we sometimes avoid engaging directly on their own terms—cultural property rather than colonialism, heritage tourism rather than poverty and inequality, and so on. In no way do I want to sacrifice what makes folklore studies distinctive and compelling—what we are good at—in order to transform ourselves into a discipline like sociology that already exists. But I share what I take to be one of Noyes's points, that folklorists can always do a better job of situating the foci of our work in broader historical and social contexts. This involves attending to scales, including the global one, that are broader than, for instance, performance events and contexts. Some folklorists have been creative in thinking about social scale in folkloristic ways (Mechling 1997 is an example), but an encounter with world-systems analysis can prompt new reflection on scale and the social base of folklore. As suggested here, it also provokes fresh consideration of the serious human issues that our work might address in distinctively folkloristic or ethnological ways.

As a reviewer of this paper suggested, there is also the matter of shared interests linking the two research traditions. I pointed to a series of examples above: specifically, households, nationalism, colonialism, and decolonization, but also identities and movements for social change (e.g., popular resistance, labor rights struggles, antisystemic movements, alter-globalization). In everyday work, such shared interests are the point of intersection most likely to be taken up widely, as reading beyond our fields is less daunting when we find colleagues engaged in empirical research questions or activist scholarship that already overlaps with our concerns. Folklorists and ethnologists can profit from specific studies arising from the world-systems orientation without embracing it comprehensively as a framework. While I value my own disciplinarity, and I think that I share this with my most proximate colleagues, I am also confident that my work and the work of these colleagues would be richer and more nuanced if we could manage more cross-, if not uni-, disciplinary engagement. It is my hope that such engagements would not have to be unidirectional. As Noyes, for instance, has increasingly shown in her own work, even very globally oriented fields such as international relations can be engaged in such a way that folklore studies and European ethnology become inspirational for the work of such less granular fields. Reciprocal engagement does not always work, but it also does not always fail (Becker 2017; The Ohio State University 2022).

Finally, just as Wallerstein and the Gulbenkian commissioners wanted to provoke debate in the social sciences, I am here hoping to provoke discussion and reflection among folklorists and ethnologists. Whether world-systems analysis is the best way to go about it or not, and I am not suggesting that it is, I share Fine's (2009, 103) view, with which I began, "Folklore needs to be examined as a part of the political economy of nations and of the world system." While I cannot be certain I will ever get an audience, on behalf of folklore studies and ethnology, with the core of world-systems analysts, I think also that these small (semiperipheral?) but powerful and distinctive fields warrant their attention, whether in thinking through the bigger story of the rise and status of the capitalist world-system or the smaller but still highly significant story of its changing "knowledge structures."

Notes

1. In this work, I write from the position of a US folklorist and ethnologist. This position shapes my thinking and my way of characterizing the matters under discussion, but as will hopefully be evidenced in my reflections, I have tried to maintain a wide interest in the status and history of these fields around the world. I view both fields (or, in some framings, this common field) as globally networked but provincially situated. I see plurality and differences as valuable to our work, and I am grateful for generous colleagues and collaborators working in various global and disciplinary locations.

2. A December 2018 search in JSTOR of key general, English-language (Anglo-American) folklore journals (*Western Folklore, Folklore, Journal of Folklore Research,* and *Journal of American Folklore*) provides some sense of past levels of engagement by folklorists with world-systems analysis. Of twenty-three works discovered with the terms *world* and *systems* co-occurring, most are passing references and some are not relevant to this discussion. Some of the irrelevant instances deal with issues such as the systematic quality of worldview or lifeworlds (N=4). Some were discovered because they cited a work evoking *world system* or *world-systems analysis* in the cited work's title (N=6). Three such instances involved citation to works on ethnographic methods and writing by George Marcus (1986, 1995), where he evokes *the world system* in his titles. In five articles and two book reviews, authors evoke *the world-system* or *world-systems analysis* in a passing but relevant way (N=7).

(I am the author of one such paper.) Finally, there is a small group of papers where engagement with world-systems issues goes beyond passing mention (N=6). This does not mean that world-systems analysis is a key matter in these works, only that the perspective is recognizable in these works on some level beyond evocation. Of these six, I feel that Hofer (1984), Limón (1983), and Samper (2002) are most relevant, with Strauss (2002), Kenny (2007), and Turgeon and Pastinelli (2002) touching on world-systems analysis mainly as a way of centering discussions of global cultural circulations of broad interest to folklorists.

As an individual named scholar, Immanuel Wallerstein appears on nine occasions in the four general folklore journals examined. Four of these instances fall into the group of works already considered. The remaining five instances break down as follows. On two occasions, authors cited items appearing in volumes edited or coedited by Wallerstein. In one instance, an author cited Wallerstein discussing the nature of ethnic group membership (Ivey 1977). This leaves two cases where folklore authors cited work by Wallerstein in relationship to world-systems issues. Noyes (1995, 463) does so to evoke the complexity of unequal North-South relations, and Feltault (2006, 108) does so to ground a discussion of public folklore work vis-à-vis development discourse and practice in the context of work on globalization.

3. A peer reviewer inquired about Fine's use of *world system* without a hyphen. As evidenced in a quotation given later in this chapter, the hyphen was, for Wallerstein, absolutely crucial, but Fine's usage is widespread nonetheless. Those who write *world system* rather than *world-system* are often, as here, using these words to convey a more general sense that is often cognizant of, but not formally embracing, the world-systems framework. In such usage, the general sense conveyed is of the level of social reality existing at a more encompassing level than that of individual nations viewed in analytic isolation. This is a general answer related to the widespread use of *world system*, and Fine may have specific thoughts on the issue as yet unknown to me.

4. As of July 9, 2024, *World-Systems Analysis: An Introduction* had been cited 7,377 times as calculated by Google Scholar. It was among the texts explored with students in a 2006 folklore studies graduate course on folklore and social/cultural theory that I taught at Indiana University. I here express appreciation to the students, now colleagues, in that course for their engaged participation, from which I benefited.

I need to offer one further note on the book itself. Appearing in 2004, Wallerstein evokes the period in which it was written and published, with terrorism and globalization looming as key global-scale phenomena prominent in both media and general discussions of world affairs in that period. As I write, in 2018–21, and revise, in 2024, globalization has grown still more complicated as a matter of worldwide debate amid the renewal of ethnonationalism, and even fascism, in liberal democracies looms over my own authorial present. Age eighty-eight at the time of my initial writing, Wallerstein then continued his research and writing, including the authoring of public-facing commentaries on world and national affairs. The most comprehensive source for these writings is his website: https://www.iwallerstein .com (accessed December 1, 2018, still accessible July 9, 2024). I mention these facts here to make clear to anyone who turns to *World-Systems Analysis: An Introduction* that the book is very relevant, but, of course, it is not updated in its specifics to the present moment, whereas Wallerstein's writings as a whole are or were. Wallerstein died on August 31, 2019, as this chapter manuscript was first circulating informally among colleagues for comment and discussion (Genzlinger 2019). His most recent book (2021) is the posthumously published volume *The Global Left: Yesterday, Today, Tomorrow*.

5. A version of this autobiographical sketch was also available on the website of the Department of Sociology, Yale University, at the time of my initial writing. No longer online there, it is accessible via the Internet Archive. Note that the two versions differ subtly in wording, including in quotations that I give here. https://sociology.yale.edu/people/immanuel-wallerstein, accessed December 2, 2018. https://web.archive.org/web/20171019093335/http://sociology.yale .edu/people/immanuel-wallerstein, accessed July 9, 2024. As will be seen below, I draw on other works by Wallerstein and his collaborators as are useful to the endeavor. If an interested reader wished to begin with a single work, I recommend Wallerstein (2004).

6. The post–World War II (and also post-Soviet) relationship between folklore studies and nationalism is different in other world regions, with the Baltics and China representing particular cases of special interest to me. I note this to signal my awareness of my positionality on these questions writing from within my own national and provincial context.

7. A generous peer reviewer of this paper queried whether I would be pursuing such questions in my empirical work and, if I did, what would change as a result. I can quickly illustrate these matters with two granular examples that I hope to address in future work. Among Native American peoples in eastern Oklahoma (United States), gathering wild onions for food is a crucial cultural practice that is central to identity and, sometimes, to subsistence. It is also the basis for a petty commodity market based on gathering from de facto commons. The situation there closely follows the West Virginia case documented by Hufford (2005). In southwest China, bamboo basket production and marketing among upland minority nationalities is an extensive petty commodity trade that intersects with the larger political and economic order in ways that are also relevant to the general discussion pursued in this section of this chapter. Colleagues and I working in southwest China have begun writing about these issues there (Zhang et al. 2022). The conceptual work of this chapter is intended, in part, to help my colleagues and I better address the

kinds of situations encountered in our ethnographic and ethnohistorical work, but that work, to this point, does not suggest any modification of the general review undertaken here. In both eastern Oklahoma and southwest China, there is a great deal of "making do," and I aspire to better understand it.

8. Inspired by Naithani's work, but working at a much more modest scale, I began exploring the relationship between folklore studies and colonialism in what is here chapter 1 of this volume (Jackson 2013a).

9. An interesting contrast with folklore studies and world-systems analysis can be found in the case of geography. Geography is also notably absent from the summary account of the social sciences that Wallerstein (2004, 1–12) provides. In contrast to folklorists though, there is evidence of extensive engagements by geographers (political geographers in particular) with the approach. Geographer Colin Flint suggests that deep engagement with world-systems analysis helped strengthen and revitalize political geography in the years since work in world-system analysis began. But the place of the perspective among political geographers has waned as, over time, these scholars engaged more fully with issues of agency and in work concerned more with microscale contexts. Readers interested in this contrastive history of disciplinary engagement can find it in Flint (2017).

10. To the best of my knowledge, Wallerstein does not address Michel Foucault's (1991) notion of governmentality, but my sense is that their interests overlap in concern with the ways that structures of knowledge and the subtle workings of power and governance operate in tandem within social orders that emerge and change over time (see also Huff 2013).

11. European ethnology does actually appear in one passing mention in Wallerstein et al. (1996). In the conclusion of that work, the commissioners mention, in reflecting on the opportunities for restructuring catalyzed by the fall of the Soviet Union, how the history department at Humboldt University "has become the first one in Germany, perhaps in Europe, to create a subdepartment of European ethnology, attempting thereby to give historical anthropology a *droit de cité* inside history" (1996, 100). I do not know the complexities of the histories that the commissioners are evoking here, but a reading of Bendix (2012) suggests that matters in this instance are much more complex than they realize and that, had they known what folklorists and ethnologists know of such matters, their broad arguments about the social sciences as a whole might have been productively enhanced.

12. Just as Briggs and Naithani (2012) stress the coloniality of folkloristics, more can certainly be said about nationalism and its entanglement with the history of ethnologies of overseas, rather than intimate, others.

13. See, for instance, work cited by Briggs and Naithani (2012), Bauman and Briggs (2006), Herzfeld (2012), and Bronner (2006).

14. For interdisciplinarity vis-à-vis folklore studies and ethnology, see Bendix, Bizer, and Noyes (2017). Wallerstein (2004, 98) characterizes unidisciplinarity in this

way: "This term should be clearly distinguished from multi- or trans-disciplinarity. The later terms refer to the now-popular ideas that much research would be better done if the researcher(s) combined the skills of two or more disciplines. Unidisciplinarity refers to the belief, in the social sciences at least, there exists today no sufficient *intellectual* reason to distinguish the separate disciplines at all, and that instead all work should be considered part of a single discipline, sometimes called the historical social sciences." As will be discussed, the emphasis placed on intellectual here seems to acknowledge that there are structural reasons that disciplines persist nonetheless.

15. I cite three prominent position statements associated with the debate in US folklore studies. Others could be included, and not all views in circulation at the time were committed to print. No history of this episode has yet been written, but it is explored thoughtfully by Noyes (2012, 27–32).

16. The Gulbenkian Commission's work was a project (1994–95) of the Calouste Gulbenkian Foundation, a Portuguese philanthropy focused on the arts, the sciences, and education.

17. I thank a generous peer reviewer for reminding me of this key point—one central to my own teaching and curatorial work. As that reviewer aptly noted, "Disciplinary legacies are inseparable from institutional legacies."

18. What I am calling a "current call" for reassessment could be dated and framed in a number of ways. On the one hand, folklore studies is reassessing and rearranging itself on a nearly continuous basis. Graduate departments, for instance, make changes to their curricula almost annually. On the other hand, there are periods of stasis and periods of ferment. The American Folklore Society presidency (2016–17) of Kay Turner saw a series of sustained discussions around such things as curricular review and reform, diversification of course syllabi, and the promotion of engagement by folklorists with scholars in critical race theory and other bodies of scholarship from outside folklore itself. A provocation-rich conference organized in part by graduate students at Indiana University on the "Future of American Folklore," held in Bloomington, Indiana, in May 2017, provided a key moment in what I think of as an ongoing discussion about the structure of the discipline and the training leading into it.

19. For example, what lessons can we derive from the experiences of colleagues and students of the Cultural Sustainability Program that was founded by folklorists at Goucher College or of the Heritage Studies doctoral program founded with significant involvement by folklorists at Arkansas State University?

5

Teaching Concepts in Folklore Studies

FOLK-F 516 Folklore Theory in Practice (3 cr.) An introduction to scholarly practice, developing an integrated idea of folklore as a topic of study and as a way to conduct research.
—**Henry Glassie (new as of the University Graduate School Bulletin, 2004–5)**

Introduction

In his writings and in the accounts of those who knew him, American folklorist Richard M. Dorson (1916–81) appears as a scholarly leader brimming over with confidence. His individual writings and his oeuvre preserve the traces of a folklorist who was unmistakably ambitious, energetic, and quite secure in his opinions while still recognizing that others would have views of their own. Whatever one may think of how things have gone in the wake of his passing over four decades ago, Dorson deeply reshaped the field of folklore studies, disciplining it, and helping make a discipline of it. As the long-serving director of Indiana University Bloomington's Folklore Institute and as a distinguished professor of history and folklore, Dorson built many of the durable institutions that still give space and structure to the discipline, especially at Indiana University and in the United States, but also internationally. While he would certainly be proud of his many books, his greatest enduring impact may be found in the work of the many graduate students whom he trained and in the institutions and curricula that they went on to establish around the world. As one of the inheritors of the scholarly world that Dorson reshaped and expanded, I am thankful for his efforts as a teacher and institution builder even as I know that, had I been in his shoes, I might not have built things in quite the way that he did. While I hopefully would not have made all the same choices that he did, Dorson's record of accomplishment is such that I also know that there is little hope that I could have done all that he did in his too-brief sixty-five years. I am not alone in being puzzled about how he was able to accomplish so much so quickly, so steadily, and so consistently.[1]

Dorson and I share some commonalities, but there are numerous differences between us. One of the commonalities is that I am an inheritor of a key required graduate course that he long taught at Indiana University.[2] I am not the only person other than Dorson to teach it, however. Henry Glassie taught it most consistently after Dorson's time, having taught a parallel graduate course on folklife between 1970 and 1976 when he moved to the University of Pennsylvania ("Penn").[3] He then taught Dorson's old course himself after returning to Indiana in 1988. I began teaching it soon after Glassie's retirement, starting in 2009. At present, I alternate in teaching it with my colleague Ray Cashman. In much of Dorson's time and now, the course has the Indiana University course number FOLK-F 516, where courses numbered 500 and above are intended for graduate students. The name in Dorson's time was "Proseminar in Folklore Theory and Method I: Materials of Folklore." Relatively late in Glassie's time teaching the course (ca. 2004), it was retitled "Folklore Theory in Practice" and was given the description appearing in the epigraph. This remains the name of the course that Cashman and I have taught over the past decade and a half.[4]

While the name and, with it, the focus that the name conjures have shifted, the course retains a key structural role in our department and its graduate program. Then and now, this is the required course taken in common each fall by each new group of graduate students in folklore studies. While they are joined by ethnomusicologists and students studying other fields, the new folklorists have their cohort-building experience together in this course. While some come to the course with previous courses in folklore studies and perhaps even with a bachelor's or master's degree in folklore studies, the course remains, even for such students, a fundamental professional development experience. It is, among other things, a rite of passage. For those like me graced with the privilege to teach such a course, it is both an honor and a serious responsibility.

What does any of this have to do with the work that I have sought to do in the pages of this book? The stuff of folklore, as well as the stuff that Dorson wanted folklorists to dismiss as fakelore, is as wildly popular as ever. How could it not be when, as Dorson's student Alan Dundes (1980, 1–19) argued, we are all the folk. But scholarly discussions for folklorists do not appeal to broad audiences in the same way that enticing foodways, well-told tales, mesmerizing dances, and engaging—but perhaps also corrosive to the health of democracies—internet memes do. The more modest audience for this book, and for the books that inspired me in writing it, is composed of my professional colleagues and, perhaps most importantly, my students and other students like them who are gathering the scholarly tools with which they will do their own work, including their own concept work, as folklorists.

In this context and with this audience in mind, I close the volume with a reflection on the teaching of concepts and concept work to emerging folklorists. I do so in a time of worthy calls to revisit curricula and disciplinary inheritances (and habits) in light of present-day realities and future needs (Fivecoate, Downs, and McGriff 2021; Frandy 2023 in Richardson et al. 2023; González-Martin 2017; Otero and Martínez-Rivera 2021a, 2021b; Prahlad 2021; Roberts 2021; Zhang 2015). While finding value in what our scholarly ancestors bequeathed to us is a reoccurring theme in my work and the studies gathered in this volume, my argument is that they represent a (not the) resource available to us for the work of doing new and necessary things, including the work of identifying and puzzling out new concepts or keywords that will help us understand and perhaps shape social and cultural change. The kind of value that ancestral legacies represent is use value. Folklore studies is not like classical music taught in a conservatory context focused on preserving old repertoire and techniques. What many of my colleagues and I hold to be true about tradition is true of the traditions of folklorists just as much as it is true for other peoples. When Glassie (1995, 409) wrote "tradition is the means for deriving the future from the past" and also characterized it as "volitional, temporal action," he was doing concept work around the concept of tradition, and what he was explicating is just as relevant to folklorists as it is to everyone else. As a field, folklore studies has a past on which it can but need not always draw. The work of the field happens, though, in the present with an eye toward the future. The past is a resource.

In confronting their own present moments through volitional, temporal action, our predecessors also carved paths down which we find ourselves traveling, but we are not trapped unshakably in those groves. As I will show, Dorson's core graduate course was quite different from Glassie's. In part, this difference arose from divergent backgrounds, interests, and goals, but it also arose because, in the early 1970s, there was a division of labor established between their two then-concurrent required graduate courses, with Dorson focusing on folklore and Glassie focusing on folklife, with Dorson focusing on textual methods and Glassie focusing on fieldwork-based and contextual methods.

When Glassie took up Dorson's own course in the 1980s, it was retooled to reflect his experiences in the field and the interdisciplinary and performance-oriented Penn milieu. Throughout, Glassie's purpose in these linked courses, as with his core courses at Penn, was to prepare students conceptually and by way of exemplary examples for context-attentive field research.

While the course that Cashman and I teach is more like Glassie's than Dorson's, it is different from both. At the same time, those earlier courses were shaped by their departmental and disciplinary contexts just as they also shaped those contexts. While it may seem that I am just talking about one course in one university, the discussion is actually broader because Dorson's course shaped the creation of related courses in multiple other universities. Later, Glassie's version of the course in turn reshaped many of those related courses at other institutions. And, to an extent, the same thing has happened again as newer students have moved through these courses and taken up the work of refashioning the present out of their own pasts.

These are some of the contexts in which I want to update the story of the required, first-year graduate course in folklore studies at Indiana University. I say update because one of Dorson's (1983c) last published writings was an accounting of his own motives and strategies in teaching this course. That work is a posthumously published chapter in a posthumously published book for which Dorson (1983a) was the primary editor, the monumental *Handbook of American Folklore* published by Indiana University Press in 1983. Through the contributions of many scholars, some young, others old, that book summarized what was, at the time, the status of the field that Dorson had presided over in the United States during the 1970s while also outlining the newer directions that the field was already well along in taking into the 1980s. In this context, reading Dorson's account of his course alone creates an inappropriate sense of the field as it already was in the 1980s. At the same time, reading the whole volume offers a fresher and broader horizon. The book is like a delta into which multiple rivers—some long, wide, and slow moving, others shorter and moving more rapidly—have converged. I urge readers here to (re)visit the collection for its own sake but also to avoid mistaking its nature in light of my own focus on Dorson's "Proseminar" chapter. For me here, that chapter is simply a rare and instructive instance of an influential practitioner reflecting on his own pedagogy in a keystone course.

The full name of Dorson's chapter is "Teaching Folklore to Graduate Students: The Introductory Proseminar." Where I began my chapter with a good bit of scholarly metacommentary and a sprinkle of hedging, Dorson dove right into the task at hand. In the opening of a single paragraph, he sets the stage and declares his problem. He notes that folklore graduate students come from diverse disciplinary backgrounds and will need to be oriented to the field. English departments teach bibliography, and history departments teach historiography. Pioneering for folklore studies, Dorson and his colleagues in the American folklore studies graduate programs were then (i.e., in his time leading the Indiana University program) seeking to work out the equivalent kind of introductory course for folklore studies. In the remainder of his chapter, he lays out the topics of his seminar in the order that he taught them. Along the way, he provides descriptions of one or two paragraphs in which he not only discusses what he is trying to teach but also reveals how. While presented in a very narrative form, the chapter is the present-day equivalent of a detailed syllabus annotated for other teachers of folklore studies (Dorson 1983c, 463). More briefly, I will characterize Dorson's topics as a prelude to comparing and contrasting with the present course and its cognates.

Dorson (1983c, 463) writes of having a "baker's dozen" (i.e., thirteen) of course topics in his introductory paragraph, but there are only twelve subtitled sections in his narrative. Readers can consult Dorson for an account of his course sessions on each of the following topics. I number them so that I can refer to them in discussing my own course. His topics, in his course and chapter order, are:

1. Distinguishing Folklore from Fakelore
2. Fieldwork
3. Terminology
4. Bibliographic Expertise
5. Library Uses
6. Use of Folklore Archives
7. Annotation
8. Material Culture Research
9. Interdisciplinary Knowledge
10. History of Folklore Studies
11. International Communications in Folklore
12. Folklore in the Mass Media

I was aware of Dorson's account of his course when I constructed my own, but I did not much emulate him vis-à-vis topics.[5] To help my own students sort out continuity and change in their field and in the course, I have sometimes assigned Dorson's chapter, and, whether assigned or not, I have consistently pointed students to it, providing them with a physical copy or easy access to a digital copy of it. While I did not embrace Dorson specific course model as my own, I see the still-considerable value inherent in doing it his way. Something that I share to a degree with him but where he significantly exceeds me is his approach to assignments. This is an area where Dorson's approach is aligned with present-day pedagogical best practices in being rich in practical doing. Students did not complete one large term paper but instead were given several smaller assignments designed to give them firsthand experience doing the work of a folklorist in the library, in the local community, in the museum, and in the archive. Students were tasked with documenting expressive culture, annotating it contextually and comparatively, and, finally, interpreting it. While I have multiple exploratory assignments, the agenda is not nearly so broad. In part, this has to do with the richness of other departmental course offerings. Indiana University students, like peers elsewhere now, experience a range of fieldwork exercises in independent courses on ethnographic methods, and, for instance, Dorson's assignment to study and contextualize a museum object is quite like an assignment in my own graduate course on museum methods.

Before getting to the specific topics in my own course, I want to appreciate how Dorson, while primarily an Americanist and a scholar of the North Atlantic world, was also highly internationalist in orientation. He is overt about how his course included students from around the world, and he makes clear that he expected all his students to cultivate a cosmopolitan and multilingual outlook and folklore studies practice. This is another of the virtues evident across the course as described and remembered in disciplinary oral history.

Preparation

The basic nature of most of Dorson's course topics, as listed above, is probably evident from his headings, but durable debates about Dorson's concern for what he polemically called fakelore obscure that his first substantive course meeting (1) is basically about what the word *folklore* refers to. This is an essential theme across the run of my own course, and it is central to the substance of the first course session where I entwine consideration of folklore as a scholarly object with a discussion of the course structure and purposes. It is difficult to expect students to complete detailed readings before day one of a course, but I have had success assigning short, sophisticated treatments of folklore as phenomenon, concept, and discipline (Bauman 1992b; Klein

2001; Noyes 2004). The main difference between Dorson and the present, as reflected in my course and the courses of those colleague-interlocutors who teach the same (Ray Cashman) or closely analogous (e.g., Patricia Sawin, Gabrielle Berlinger, Dorothy Noyes, Michael Ann Williams) courses, is that current discussions emphasize folklore's status as a metacultural category entangled with social histories and current predicaments. While Dorson was working to define folklore in a way that would be typologically clear and that would underwrite disciplinarity, I (and I think my colleagues) am not fighting that battle, even as we are welcoming our students into the community of folklorists. While this can be framed as discontinuity, Dorson's battle against fakelore illustrates a point that often arises when discussing folklore as a field. Put in the form of a quip, a folklorist is a person who finds value in debating the definition of folklore. To the extent that I am tracking the concept work done in the field and in my course, I share with Dorson a sense, then, that the place that a graduate introduction in folklore studies should begin is with a critical consideration of what folklore and, by extension, folklore studies is. My course section headings are far too telegraphic, but we do this work of scoping folklore amid scouting out the course under the banner Preparation.

Ancestors

Under the heading Ancestors, I try to evoke disciplinary history in a presentist rather than historicist way (after Stocking 1965, 2010, 89). A separate required course at Indiana University Bloomington deals with the fuller run of disciplinary history (FOLK-F 517 History of Folklore Study). In the introductory course, my purpose is to evoke the history of the field in a way that is simultaneously manageable and accessible while also nuanced, suggestive of complexity, and useful for the present and the future. In particular, I am trying to convey my sense that disciplinary history is a resource for living and doing the work. In my most recent version of the course, I did this by assigning and discussing Zora Neale Hurston's (2018) *Barracoon: The Story of the Last "Black Cargo"* together with Franz Boas's (1887) "The Study of Geography." In my experience, both of these works offer much to sustain rich and complex discussions, and students and I return to them repeatedly over the semester. In particular, they help me place the Americanist tradition in which I work into a global, particularly Atlantic world and world-historical, context (Darnell 2001, 2021). As with the chapters at the heart of this book, these readings, especially Hurston's book, help us think at different scales, from the intimacy of the small tale told quietly between two humans sitting alone and the terrors and transformations of the formation of the modern world-system, including the horrors of the middle passage and the linked global rise of the plantation and the "feral proliferations" that it in turn produces (Hurston 2018; Tsing, Mathews, and Bubandt 2019).

While my sense is that some acknowledgment of history is required at the start of my course, Dorson attended to disciplinary history late in his own (10). In his defense, it seems to me that his students—like my own—would be better prepared to make sense of that history after they had learned their way around the field. But this is not an either-or question. A bit of history, but not too much, works, I think, in a context in which a fuller history is available in a second course that is required of folklore studies master's and doctoral students at Indiana University. To me, first encountering a discipline without an initial glimpse of the epistemological and world-historical contexts that birthed it would seem like an artificial bracketing out of something essential.

Inheritances

A problem that must be addressed in my course and that is present in Dorson's course as described is the relationship between named theories and the work of the course. The course is currently named Folklore Theory in Practice. That post-Dorson name implies that theory and its use will center the course. In practice, I think that what I have been calling concepts and concept work, and the ways that these concepts are used in practice, is the actual center of gravity. Concepts relate closely to broader theories, but my course and the courses of my interlocutors are not built as a parade in which floats labeled social evolutionism, culture history, functionalism, structuralism, Marxism, Freudianism, feminism, poststructuralism, posthumanism, and so on pass us by as onlookers. Those broad orientations reoccur repeatedly in the course, but they are not how the course is partitioned. But I feel a need to introduce the concept of social and cultural theories and the concept of theory in general, and I do this overtly but very gently in my third session under the heading Inheritances. To introduce some of the relevant theories overtly in a case suitable for students still getting their first taste of the discipline—and this includes students pursuing degrees in other disciplines and not solely new folklore studies graduate students—I assign and discuss Glassie's (1975) *All Silver and No Brass: An Irish Christmas Mumming*. I do this because it remains compelling to students as ethnography and history—they tell me so—and also because it shows how classic social theories play out through interpretation in a grounded case of folkloristic interest.[6] Because I do not embrace any theoretical perspective as orthodoxy and because I want students to at least begin their careers as theoretical pragmatists and pluralists, this book helps show the ways that multiple perspectives can offer illumination. I wish that we had more and newer ethnographic cases that similarly were overt in using multiple theoretical lenses to address the same folkloristic phenomenon.

Dorson (1983b) had a theoretical orientation of his own, presented in the *Handbook of American Folklore* as "A Historical Theory for American Folklore," but theory definitely takes a back seat to methods and folkloristic (disciplinary) ethos in his course plan. While *theory* is present in his course title, it is otherwise covertly present throughout. As Harrah-Johnson (2020; also Briggs 2008) documents, the degree to which theory was left in the background is a part of Dorson's legacy.[7] While my own course does not suggest that theory is the most important matter, of course, the place of theory is diagnostic. As we will see, concepts and case studies center my course, with theory overtly and steadily present but not dominant. Disciplinarity, rigorous methods, and a conception of folklore itself centered Dorson's late-career course.

Genre(s)

Dorson and I share an interest in making sure that students are oriented to recognizing a full range of folklore forms and genres. I was impressed, for instance, by Dorson giving a full week to material culture studies and museum-based object research (8). While he expected all of his students to master the vast apparatus of working with oral and entextualized folk narrative (especially 2, 4, 6, 7), some of his assignments gave students free rein to explore customs, objects, and performances. At the same time, his focus was consistently on the methods that distinguish and thereby professionalize a folklorist. The folktale and, beyond that, other verbal genres were certainly centered.

For me and my course, concepts of genre and the recognition of the ways that different approaches to genre are used in scholarship and in diverse social settings are a foundational matter that is front-loaded so that they can be explored repeatedly across different weeks and works. Later in the semester, I overtly introduce students to a series of book-length cases that treat specific instances of verbal art, material culture, and cultural performance events, as well as the extrageneric domains of cosmology and worldview, but four weeks into the course, I introduce genre in a conceptual way that attends to the different, layered ways that folklorists think about genre (cf. Barker 2022; Bauman 1999; Ben-Amos 1976a, 1976b; Briggs and Bauman 1992; Cashman 2016a; Honko 2005; Stewart 1991). While given considerable attention in my course, genre and a broad sample of genres are the focus of an additional required course in the Indiana University graduate curriculum (Barker 2022).

Society

I came to folklore studies from sociology and cultural anthropology. Dorson came to the field from history and American studies. His professional identity was formed prior to the integration of interactionist sociology and the reintegration of anthropological linguistics/linguistic anthropology into folklore studies work in a North American context. At the time when he was writing about his course and editing the *Handbook*, he was aware of these trends and their manifestation in a changing field that was making a performance, communications, and contextual turn, but they were not centered in his own course, even as significant space was given to them in the *Handbook* (e.g., Abrahams 1983; Bauman 1983; Glassie 1983; Green 1983; Kirshenblatt-Gimblett 1983).

My course—framed after Dundes's (1980, 1–19) "Who Are the Folk?," Bauman's (1971) "Social Base," and with the benefit of Dorothy Noyes's synthesis in and after "Group"—tries to situate the conceptual issues around the social base of folklore as of fundamental importance (Mechling 1997; Noyes 1995, 2012; Shuman 1993). In a very introductory way, genre is "about" the lore in folklore, and discussing what I label *society* is "about" the folk in folklore. As is, I hope, suggested by chapter 4 (this volume), I do not think that there is only one workable framing of the social in and for folklore studies, but I do think that folklorists need to give serious thought to the social worlds in which their work unfolds and to join the work of puzzling out the best concepts with which to move forward in varied contexts for varied purposes. Thus, as with genre, my consideration, with the students, of society focuses on generative conceptual essays. While in recent versions of the course, I have centered the discussion on Dundes's, Bauman's, and Noyes's contributions, I have discussed chapter 4 (this volume) fruitfully in this context as a means of looking beyond the small-group contexts that are central in the field in my own period.[8]

Space-Time

The following may seem surprising, but I think that I appreciate historic-geographic methods more than Dorson does. While it pays homage to Stith

Thompson and leans in on the apparatus of comparative folk narrative research, paying particular attention to the importance of annotating new texts comparatively using the full run of disciplinary tools, Dorson's course summary does not suggest much engagement with the cultural-historical ends to which the fuller set of historic-geographic methods, including in their anthropological, specifically Boasian, forms could take (Boas 1891; Dundes 1995; Kniffen and Glassie 1966; Kroeber 1948, 538–71; Thompson 1965; von Sydow 1999). Historical concerns run through Dorson's course, but they are the concerns of a historian and not those of the historical ethnologist. In older versions of my own course, I addressed the neighboring sets of historic-geographic methods (Americanist anthropological, European ethnological, cultural geographic, Europeanist folk narrative–focused) more fully. More recently, for reasons of space within the course and student interest, I have treated these matters more briefly together within a broader discussion that includes considerations of other space-time relationships. It is in this context that questions of the construction of place through narrative (Basso 1984), the coloniality of folklore (Briggs and Naithani 2012; Jackson, chap. 1, this volume), and the concept of chronotope (Blommaert 2015) and of history (Williams 2017) are also considered. To make the historic-geographic methods vivid and contemporary, I introduce students to contemporary work on innovation diffusion, including in its business world contexts.

Texts

By this point in my course and in this recounting of it, we are at the halfway point. It is probably apparent that while skills drove Dorson's course, core concepts—particularly those familiar to readers of core works such as *Eight Words for the Study of Expressive Culture* (Feintuch 2003) and *A Companion to Folklore* (Bendix and Hasan-Rokem 2012)—drive my course. Text is the next core concept that my students and I tackle. After several article-driven weeks, we change course and do this through deep engagement with Américo Paredes's (1958) *"With His Pistol in His Hand": A Border Ballad and Its Hero*, supplemented by very brief discussions of the Boasian conception of text (Boas 1974) and a glance at oral formulaic theory (Lord 1965). As with genre and society, the goal is to start gathering multiple approaches to, and understandings of, text as well as to begin cultivating awareness of some of the ways that texts are made and studied toward different ends, including the ways that people, and not just folklorists, make and remake texts through techniques of inter- and intratextuality.

Texts and concepts of text are on one level ubiquitous in Dorson's course, but I think that it may be with the conceptualization of text (but not with the importance of texts and care in their production and use) where the outlook embedded in Dorson's course and my own are most divergent. This is obvious when it comes to developments found in the field since his work, but it is perhaps also evident in my own loyalty to, and engagement with, ancestral approaches to texts. I have in mind not only those pioneered by Boas but also those found in the work of older generations of literary folklorists. These orientations to texts differentiate us and our courses.

Thought

Under the heading Thought lives my treatment of psychological, psychoanalytic, formalist, structuralist, and other pattern-attentive approaches to work in folklore. As my course is not a history of folklore and it is also not a history of theory in the social sciences, my approach is again presentist and focused on usable pasts for present and future purposes. While needing to give a range of older thinkers their due, my core purpose is to cultivate student interest in, and capacity to pursue the enduring task of, seeking formal patterns and doing what might be called morphological work as a prerequisite to doing interpretive work. To the extent that students encounter a range of classic grand theories in this week, my goal is to cultivate appreciation rather than dismissiveness. My aim in this is to strengthen scholarly "muscles" and habits of work, as well as develop the historical understanding of the field, necessary for concept work and for the interpretation of expressive culture and everyday practices.[9]

While the *Handbook* points to such work as it was in and before the early 1980s, Dorson's course makes no allusion to theories and concepts of the type I am evoking in this part of my course. That said, surely he was minimally morphological in that he clearly needed to make sure that his students could distinguish motifs and tales in the context of comparative folk narrative research and its toolbox. (For the atheoretical nature of Dorson's own folkloristics, see Briggs 2008.)

Doing

While Thought covers a wide range of pattern-attentive theories and methods, I use Doing as the cover term for dealing directly with performance- and practice-oriented approaches in folklore studies. Relative to performance, I deal with both the cultural performance event-centered approach that tackles such phenomena as festival, ritual, and theater and the more linguistically oriented study of verbal art in performance contexts. As these orientations are integrated into a communications-centered, context-minded paradigm that has been a hallmark of my home department over the period since Dorson's death, it is here that my students and I reach the heart of the concerns that have brought most of them into our program. Relative to practice, my goal is as much to draw connections and parallels as it is to stake out boundaries and frame differences. As always, these two neighboring-but-not-the-same approaches would benefit from more time and attention and their own space to breathe, but it is helpful also to treat them more briefly and together. In part, this is because this session (my ninth of fourteen sessions in 2023) concludes one phase of the course and precedes a new one. Over the four sessions that follow it, my students and I engage closely with a series of exemplary monograph studies in which the concepts and theories explored to this point in the course are examined in a rich empirical context. Those four works, which have varied over instances of the course, were selected because of the genres that center them, but they all share alignment with the theories discussed, particularly with work on performance and practice.

While Dorson's course did not preclude students from taking up documentary or interpretive work in what was then the emergent performance or practice ways, these approaches or theoretical orientations were not his special concern. But, as noted previously, his selection of topics and authors for the *Handbook*, along with his own introductions to various sections in the book, indicate that he was aware of such approaches and their then-emergence (Dorson 1983a).

Speaking, Things, Performances, Worldviews

Here I treat the penultimate four sections of my 2023 course together. As in earlier instances, my students and I spent a month together at the end of the course working through exemplary ethnographies and histories chosen not only for their capacity to illuminate and extend themes and concepts woven through the course but also because they could speak to one of four broad macrogeneric categories. Under the heading Speaking, we consider a book-length work on verbal art studied in context. In the second of these four weeks, the focus is on material culture and a study of people and objects pursued in communicative- and context-centered ways. This is followed, in a week on Performances, by a contextual study of cultural performance events. In the final week of four, the focus is a book-length study of issues of worldview that build on but go beyond a genre-centered approach to deal with matters of interest to folklorists that escape the generic frame. Students appreciate these encounters with present-day studies from current practitioners. When possible, the authors of these works visit the course for discussion with the students. This is much easier in the era of video-conferencing applications.

While I know that the work my students do with these works and authors would be perfectly legible to Dorson, nothing quite like this is found in his account of his course. Part of the issue has to do with the relationship between reading and his course. He discusses using his important 1972 edited volume *Folklore and Folklife* as his course textbook. That was a reasonable choice for the time, and I find much of value in that earlier work myself, but his account of his course indicates that students are expected to do a great deal of independent work, particularly in the library. As suggested above, that work seems meritorious to me, but it does not leave much time for the joint reading of works by practicing folklorists. This difference in our courses is most evident in the four-case-studies phase of my course.

Concepts

In the final week of my 2023 course, my students and I read and discussed a range of works that—along the lines of this book—deal with emerging rather than established concepts in and for folklore studies (and in and for adjacent fields and interdisciplinary endeavors). In my syllabus, I described this phase of the course as follows:

> Research methods (ethnographic, historical, comparative, philological etc.) and theories (whether grand or humble) both play key roles in the work of folklore studies, but much of the field's intellectual work can be seen as being organized around an ever-growing body of concepts. Some concepts are both commonly used and persistently debated among folklorists. Examples of these include concepts such as context, tradition, creativity, community, and identity. The field of folklore studies also regularly takes up new concepts. These sometimes arise from within the field and in other instances they are carried into disciplinary conversations from wider contexts. In such instances, the field often aims to contribute back to those broader discussions. Recent concept work in, or of relevance to, folklore studies will be illustrated by a selection of readings. We will discuss these but in

conversation we will also try to identify and at least name a wider selection
of concepts of possible interest to our group.

While I see my course as organized around most of the enduring eight keywords central to much work in North American folklore studies: *group, art,
text, genre, performance, context, tradition,* and *identity* (Feintuch 2003), I want
my students to see this list as a starting point and not an end point. In 2023,
the concepts that we discussed at the conclusion of the course could be boiled
down to the following keywords: *decolonization* (Tuck and Yang 2012), *resilience*
(Noyes 2016, 410–37), *Anthropocene* (Tsing, Mathews, and Bubandt 2019), *cultural appropriation* (chap. 3, this volume), and *community love* (Morales and
Alvarez 2022), with *porous social orders* (Gershon 2019), *heritage* (Kirshenblatt-
Gimblett 1995; Noyes 2014b), *globalization* (Tsing 2000), *the sensory* (Bendix
2021), and *nostalgia* (Cashman 2006) represented by supplemental readings.
I mention my full list, including those only evoked and discussed briefly via
optional readings because this final week is the crux of the matter at the intersection of the course and the work of this volume and this chapter.

This final session is a high point for me, and I think also for my students.
Why? I cannot speak for them, but I think that it derives from the sequential
pedagogical experience of moving from a state of grappling with a field that
seems established, characterized by a sense of "getting up to speed" but then
arriving, at the last moment or so, at a place where the field is being more
actively constructed and feeling, on arrival, that some of what is being discussed in a real-time present is now understandable and that there are new
discussions that one is invited to join, with encouragement to contribute to
emerging work.

Did Dorson's course work the same way? I was not there, and I cannot answer conclusively. I have the sense that Dorson very much recruited his students to his own version of the project of making the discipline on solid, rigorous ground. In this respect, they were certainly not recipients of a completed
work but were expected to be contributors to it. At the same time, my sense that
concepts are central to the task of being oriented into and getting underway
as a folklorist does not seem to be reflected in Dorson's course. Methods and
an attitude of disciplined rigor were his overt center. I appreciate those things
too, but as the curriculum at Indiana University Bloomington has matured
and diversified, other courses and other colleagues have taken up some of that
work. Of course, students then and now typically take more than one course
per semester, and they take more than one semester of coursework. Both ver-

sions of FOLK-F 516 operated or operate in a wider departmental and disciplinary context. They were or are elements in a larger disciplinary assemblage. It is obvious that the older concepts of concern to me and to my peers teaching this or cognate courses were present, if in older forms, in the US folklore studies graduate programs of the 1970s and 1980s. My focus here has been on highlighting the growing place of concepts and what in this volume I call concept work.

What about Public and Applied Work?

Dorson does not give any special attention to public and applied work in his version of FOLK-F 516, and this is unlikely to come as a surprise to anyone who has studied the history of the field in the United States as it relates to the rise of public and applied folklore work in the twentieth century vis-à-vis Dorson's concerns and priorities, particularly his concern to build up folklore studies as a legitimatized, professionalized academic discipline centered in colleges and universities (Briggs 2008; Harrah-Johnson 2020; Kirshenblatt-Gimblett 1988). But what about me—do I also neglect such work in my own introduction to the field? No, but context is important here too. I did not mention public and applied work above in my march through my topics culminating in the final session on emerging concepts. In 2023, the most recent version of my course, which I have used for illustrative purposes, was scheduled such that a university holiday made my normal fifteen-week semester a fourteen-week one. Contrary to my normal practice, I removed a week devoted to public and applied work. On that occasion, I directed students to Timothy Lloyd's (2021) important edited collection *What Folklorists Do: Professional Possibilities in Folklore Studies,* to which I contributed an essay on the work of folklorists as museum directors (see also Jackson 2021b). I also urged them to watch a video recording of Lloyd and colleagues discussing the book and their own roles in the field (Indiana University Press 2021). The book and video are great resources, but they are less than a full seminar session based on having read the book. This was a one-time compromise. I feel that it is vitally important that incoming students—incoming to campus or to the discipline from across campus—gain a full sense of the range of contexts in which folklorists work. A seminar session built around Lloyd's book is a proven way to begin such exploration. As with all the other sessions in my course, it is a beginning and not an end. In 2009, I created and twice taught a different graduate course at Indiana University, FOLK-F 532 Public Practice in Folklore and Ethnomusicology. This introduction to public and applied folklore (and ethnomusicology) is now ably and regularly taught by my colleague Jon Kay.

That course is just one of a range of public and applied courses that are offered in our home department. My regular graduate course on Curatorship (FOLK-F 731) is another. It is perhaps the regular offering of a wide range of public and applied courses of this type that most differentiates the Folklore Institute of the 1970s and 1980s from the Department of Folklore and Ethnomusicology in the twenty-first century.

But I have one more thing to offer on this point, which is that it has been important to me that folklorists being trained at the graduate level be fully fluent in the field's methodological, theoretical, empirical, and, for my purposes here, conceptual literatures and repertoire. I want folklorists who land in academe to be fully knowledgeable about the scope and substance of public and applied folklore studies, and I want future public and applied folklorists to be fully and well trained in the field in general.

Cashman vis-à-vis Jackson

My real purpose here was to narrate my course topics with Dorson's earlier version in mind, but I can briefly make a roughly synchronic comparison to my friend Ray Cashman's version of Folklore Theory in Practice. In a nutshell, our versions share a great deal, which is no big surprise because he and I share a great deal, including access to my own version of the course, which preceded his. We also were shaped, as I note below, by Glassie's version of the course. Our students read many works in common. In the 2021 version of his course, he combined the substance of my Society and Genre discussions into one combined Folk+Lore session with readings common between us. Doing these together speeds him and his students on to a larger collection of book-length case studies. For instance, this allows for two book-length studies of material culture, more attention to literary folkloristics, and a case focused on folklore and social problems. Different auditors would judge differently, but from a syllabus topics perspective, our two courses are similar garments cut from similar, if not the same, cloth. While that similarity might be seen as a problem, we also share the same community of students with similar interests working within the same larger scholarly ecology with the same set of course offerings and requirements and the same set of diverse and interesting colleagues.

Cashman and Jackson vis-à-vis Glassie

Cashman and I both had the opportunity to take versions of FOLK-F 516 from Glassie. That course was transformative for both of us. Do our courses look like his did? At present, no. When I began teaching FOLK-F 516 and his course was fresh in the minds of all around me, my course was more closely modeled on Glassie's. This was most obvious in the way in which that course was scheduled within the day of its teaching. It featured a late-afternoon session heavy on the lecture-based presentation of case material and concepts, followed by a dinner break and a return to campus for an hour-long discussion. That discussion usually would begin over dinner and continue back in the classroom. Having done this as a student, I cannot capture how rich, immersive, and generative Glassie's approach was. Having done it both as a student and then as a teacher, it was also enjoyable—especially the dinners and evening discussions. I hope that my version in this format (in 2009) retained some of the magic that Glassie cast over the proceedings. I know that I lack many of the ingredients and spells that Glassie brought to the task. Going into my second year with the course, bureaucratic questions were raised about the number of contact hours vis-à-vis the number of credits (this was not in sync with university norms), and the financial implications of weekly restaurant or campus cafeteria visits were discussed when that had largely been accepted earlier. After doing it once under the old timing, I reverted to the standard two-and-a-half-hour format typical of graduate courses in our department. As with so many practices documented by folklorists, the old way now lives mostly in the memory of those who saw it firsthand. There can be little doubt that the new way is more equitable but far less rich as a social and learning experience. As Glassie's Irish interlocutor Hugh Nolan noted regarding change in human affairs, things often get better *and* they get worse concurrently (Glassie 2011, 7). Cashman inherited this change already made.

But what of substance? The spirit of my course, Cashman's course, and Glassie's course shared much, but Glassie's course framework was distinctive separate from the weekly format. I have two syllabus documents to supplement my memories of Glassie's course and our discussions of it over the years. I treasure a reading list from my own experience as a student in 1991. It contains a listing of books spread over eleven sessions. For each of these sessions, there is a book at the top of the list that is the primary text followed by a series of other books that constitute a supplemental reading list. Written in my own hand next to these lists are keywords or catchphrases that capture a sense of the themes uniting the books in the group. I cannot be certain that I recorded these just as Glassie intended, but I have the following topics. For each, I cite the primary text to better illustrate the topic intended.[10]

1. Professionalized Travel (Synge, *The Aran Islands* [1992])
2. Folklife (Evans, *Irish Folk Ways* [1957])
3. Folklore Collecting (Dorson, *Bloodstoppers and Bearwalkers* [1952])
4. Field Study of Literary Practice (Dégh, *Folktales and Society* [1989])
5. Study of the Individual (Ives, *Lawrence Doyle* [1971])
6. Dynamics of Consciousness (Lévi-Strauss, *The Way of the Masks* [1982])
7. Compositional Dynamics (Lord, *The Singer of Tales* [1960])
8. Theory and Interpretation (Dundes, *Interpreting Folklore* [1980])
9. Neo-Literary (Abrahams, *Deep Down in the Jungle* [1970])
10. Neo-Folklife (Glassie, *Passing the Time in Ballymenone* [1982])
11. Neo-Philological (Bauman, *Story, Performance, and Event* [1986])

The course that I took, as represented by the preceding list of topics and monographs, was one of the greatest intellectual adventures of my life, and I will always treasure the memory of it and the many lessons learned from it. While on the faculty of the University of Oklahoma, I taught an elective graduate seminar on theory and practice in folklore studies in the Department of Anthropology that was closely modeled on this version of Glassie's course. That was a rich experience that built to a high point of devoting three weeks to reading and discussing Glassie's *Passing the Time in Ballymenone* (1982). Former students, now colleagues, in that early version of the course continue to reminisce with me about it and to share my sense of appreciation for the path that Glassie set for us in it. While my version of FOLK-F 516 is now different—and not built only around book-length works—much that I learned with Glassie and with my own earlier students continues in my present course.

In a later undated syllabus from FOLK-F 516, preserved in my files, Glassie ([ca. 2006]) simplified his topics to six broad themes that were discussed, on the basis of multiple subtopics and historical and ethnographic instances from Glassie's own research, over multiple sessions. These higher-level groupings were:

1. Folklore as Cultural Creation
2. Folklore as Political Stance and Academic Act
3. Form and Meaning: Structure
4. Form and Meaning: Genre
5. Culture
6. History

Subtopics were grouped as follows: part 1 encompassed issues of text, tradition, performance, communication, culture, and history, with bibliographic resources for performance, fieldwork, and the individual provided. Part 2 encompassed "Affirmation and Critique in Romanticism" as well as "Situation and Change in Disciplinary History," and associated bibliographic sources related to general theory in folklore and disciplinary history were provided. Part 3 dealt with structure and included a reading list for this topic. Part 3 also dealt with genre and included separate reading lists for genre theory, oral literature, music, and material culture. Part 4, "The Cause and Consequence of Form and Meaning," included a reading list of key interpretive books from across the field, past and present. Part 5, on history, included subsections on historic-geographic studies (with readings) and on "alternative histories" (also with a readings list). Not experiencing it as a student, I do not have firsthand knowledge of this version of Glassie's ([ca. 2006]) course. My sense is that the wider six-part schema, with its subtopics, allowed for a more streamlined overview and, in the doing, a less historical approach (in the sense of chronological development of ideas, concepts, and practices in the discipline presented on a week-by-week basis). Broad categories containing multiple topics would seem to have allowed for a more fluid and holistic presentation.

The recent versions of the course offered by Cashman and me depart from Glassie's versions in that they are not built (seminar experience–wise) so heavily around our own research. This is a logical outgrowth of our research work being frankly more limited (than Glassie's) in geographic and sociocultural scope as well as in sheer quantity and quality. We are different people with different life histories and different careers, and we are at a different stage in those careers. Cashman's course and mine in some ways share more with the earlier version of Henry's class where there were more discrete topics and a greater reliance on more readings. A full analysis is beyond the scope of this chapter, but Cashman and I (and I have consulted with him on this) share the sense that our courses structurally differ significantly from Glassie's (just as our students and their interests differ also from his students then), but they are closely aligned in spirit, and they share much of the same content or, to use a biological metaphor with caution, DNA. As suggested above, Glassie is with me in my mind and memory each time I teach this course. He is also literally present in the readings and in my explication of not only his own writings but the writings of other folklorists. His understanding of the eight keywords is largely my own, modified by time and the accumulation of new disciplinary insights (Feintuch 2003). Just as he and his peers defined or redefined those keywords, my generation and those that it has taught aspire to keep the conversation moving in linear time and not simply circling around recursively.

Assignments

My focus here has been the place of concepts in teaching the graduate introduction to folklore studies. Readers are welcome to consult my 2023 syllabus to see the specifics and to consider the assignments in detail (Jackson 2023b). In summary, students in that year completed four modest assignments that shared the purpose of orienting participants to the field and its past and current practitioners. One of these related to broad (perhaps "grand") theories in or relevant to folklore studies (complementing the concept-focus of the course). One dealt in a Dorson-like way with getting to know the journals in the field. Two relate to profiling scholars in the field, one deceased and one living. The course concludes with a final exam. The choice of a final exam rather than a concluding paper is to allow time for keeping up with the sizable reading load and to allow space for the smaller exploratory projects. In this, the purpose is quite close to what Dorson described in his chapter. He leveraged smaller projects to make room for students to explore and read/study independently in the library, the archive, the museum, and the community. I leverage smaller projects and an exam to make space for significant amounts of reading done in common. But we share an approach to smaller assignments aimed at fostering self-discovery within the space of the field.

Conclusion

Dorson described his approach to a single graduate course at a single university as it was during the later phase of his own career. There were obviously other ways to teach the same topics in his own time, and there were other topics that someone introducing graduate students to folklore studies would want to, and in some cases did, teach. During Dorson's lifetime, there were other major world centers of research and training in folklore studies. Other teachers surely did other things. At the same time, Dorson trained folklorists who would carry their experiences in his seminar rooms with them in their work as folklorists, and some of these folklorists would in turn train other folklorists at the undergraduate and graduate level. In sociological terms, the field has, throughout the periods in question, continued to reproduce itself. I have been fortunate to be a part of that process, which I see as being like other responsibility-heavy instances of handing on an always-changing but also continuity-aware tradition (Noyes 2009). Social reproduction is not stasis. As in other domains studied by folklorists, studying the history of any long-standing course such as Folklore Theory in Practice will almost always reveal continuities and changes.

In the theoretical orientation that is most prominent in my own version of this course, performance is understood to involve performers assuming responsibility toward both a shared expressive practice of concern and an audience who will knowledgeably judge the performance for competence, creating a feedback loop with the performer and within the community assembled around the performance and around those who preceded and will follow it (Bauman 2012, passim). A performer often understands themselves to be in a vulnerable position, making themselves and their efforts open to critique. In university teaching, this happens in manifold everyday ways, including bored rather than engaged facial expressions, postcourse survey–style student evaluations, and class visits for evaluation by campus peers. Here, by making my more relevant (to the purposes of this book) course legible to colleagues and students, I have opened this space further. I have done so for what I hope are good purposes. Just as I hope to continue thinking about and trying to do useful work related to the study of folklore and the advancement of folklore studies, I hope that any future versions of this course or my other courses are better (in some practical sense) than those that came before. To do that will involve keeping up with and participating in disciplinary and interdisciplinary discussions and tracking social realities that continue to reshape the worlds we live, work, and study in. I accept responsibility for the choices inherent in the courses that I have taught, and I have little trouble imagining a host of criticisms that could be leveled against the course that I have described here. I know that great versions of this and similar courses can be conceived of, and have been conceived of, very differently. I know that the reading lists that I have made and modified over the years reflect biases that I am only partially aware of. Every version of a course is an experiment, and I hope to continue experimenting. While my engagements with Native American nations lead me to more of a landback conception of decolonization (Tuck and Yang 2012), I have ears for those (DeMallie 1993) who see decolonization as something done to syllabi and curricula.[11] I am eager for suggestions on how to make the course discussed here—and all of my courses—better in ways that pedagogy reform activists call for (Muldoon 2019). Teaching and concept work, like humble theory, are provisional (Noyes 2008, 40).

My purpose in this chapter has not been to advocate for my way of teaching this course or similar courses over other existing or possible approaches. It has been to illustrate the way that one concept-centered approach to teaching the field works now. If there is advocacy, it is at a higher level, with advocacy for the matter of concept-centrism more broadly. While areas of professional practice (i.e., *What Folklorists Do* [Lloyd 2021] in colleges, universities, research centers, museums, archives, arts agencies, parks, libraries, social service agencies, technology firms, etc.), research methods (comparative, archival, historical, computational, ethnographic, literary, artifactual, etc.), generic and formal interests (memes, festivals, foodways, legend, body art, oral history, etc.), ethics, and theoretical inspiration (posthumanism, Freudianism, structuralism, feminism, rational-choice theory, symbolic interactionism, etc.) all matter greatly and need evocation in our courses and curricula, I think that concepts, both iterative discussion of established concepts viewed in new or more refined ways (tradition, genre, text, context, history, etc.) and new ones for addressing new needs and interests (intersectionality, indigeneity, repair, resilience, authoritarianism, the Anthropocene, etc.), center our practice today. It is not destructive to the continued construction of folkloristic professional identities that such concepts (just as with text and genre and history, etc.) are relevant to other fields to which we can contribute and from which we can draw. Folkloristic professional identities are configurational, not singular. Many shared motifs combine to make our unique tales. Our field, like other fields, is an assemblage.

My students have generally been open to, and see the value in, learning about theory writ large. But for all but a few exceptions, this is not their driving purpose. I say this after having taught and mentored graduate students since the start of the current century and having explored through this and other courses, as well as through theses, dissertations, and public-facing projects, a nearly full range of phenomena and approaches found on the ideal-type continuum between the most academic and the most public and applied folklore work. When younger folklorists show disinterest in building folklore-specific (grand, or grander) theory (Oring 2019a, 2019b; Dorst 2019; Baron 2019; Noyes 2019), this is not, I think, because they are only interested in the empirical or applied details of their own work. It is because, in part, the kinds of theory wars characteristic of the academic social sciences and humanities in the later twentieth century do not seem like the most crucial matter for them. Gathering intellectual and scholarly tools and ideas—resources with which to confront reality as scholars, scholar-practitioners, scholar-citizens, or scholar-activists—*is* a key motivation for them. The concept of humble theory, as articulated by Noyes (2008), is relevant here as a broad characterization for the many more-than-idiosyncratic, less-than-all-encompassing intellectual and intellectual-practical projects that they wish to pursue. A full accounting of the intellectual and scholarly life of folklore studies today is way beyond my remit, but I hope to have suggested—for further iterative discussion and debate—that concepts in particular and humble theory, as Noyes character-izes the enterprise as a broader whole, are a sensible center for pedagogical work in the actually existing world that folklore studies faculty teach actually existing students in. This is a proposition that has not been studied earnestly here, but it is one that could be studied in a project designed for this purpose. While the world in which I live and write often challenges hope, my students are a steady source of inspiration for the future. Each of the essays presented in this volume arose out of discussions unfolding in conversations with stu-dents and students-turned-colleagues, and each responds in its own way not only to that inspiration but also, more importantly, to the world-engaged and world-engaging questions that they have foregrounded as emerging or now-emerged folklorists.

Notes

1. For an overview of the history of the present-day Department of Folklore and Ethnomusicology at Indiana University Bloomington, one that centers on Dorson's outsized impact between his arrival on campus in 1957 and his death in 1981, see Harrah-Johnson (2020). For a sense of how my orientation (and that of my more immediate teachers and senior colleagues) differs from Dorson's, see Briggs (2008). For consideration of how structural racism is manifest in Dorson's work and career, with a focus on a period prior to the one that is my own focus, see Roberts (2021).

2. Reviewing the history of FOLK-F 516 has reminded me of the ways that docu-mentary history and oral history grounded in individual experiences can diverge. Richard Bauman (personal communication, July 24, 2024) has noted for me that during his own master's studies in folklore in the early 1960s, the proseminar that Dorson would go on to teach and write about was not yet established (Dorson 1983b). According to Bauman, the only required course at that time was a seminar in which different Indiana University or visiting scholars presented their work in a succession of individual, disconnected sessions. The kind of course that Bauman described is like a different course, no longer required, that was required when I was a student: FOLK-F 501 Colloquy in Folklore. Reviewing the university's Schedule of Classes and Bulletins in the Indiana University Archives confirms the broad truth of Bauman's account—during the time of his studies, the program was built around eclectic and heterogenous elective courses—but also reveals how coming

and going from a program at a single moment can miss a broader trend. In the time of his own master's work, Bauman did get a chance to take FOLK-F 831/FOLK-F 517, Proseminar in Folklore Theory and Techniques II (3 cr.) in which "Fellows of the Folklore Institute and other specialists lecture on approaches to the study of folklore." But through hit-or-miss factors of scheduling, he missed out on FOLK-F 830/F516. It was offered regularly, but not each and every year, going back to 1952. In reflecting on Bauman's relationship to the course, I note that he would later—as a Folklore Institute director and department chair—play a significant role in maintaining and updating the required curriculum. He was most associated with teaching FOLK-F 517 in its Proseminar II version (see n. 3).

3. While FOLK-F 517 has been a required History of Folklore Course during my own time on the faculty, it was for many decades a second proseminar course—a part-two companion to the course FOLK-F 516, which is my focus here. Its most common name was Proseminar in Folklore Theory and Method II: Basic Concepts. It is this course that Glassie discussed with me and that he taught during his first period on the IU faculty. Other teachers of this course have included Richard Bauman, Sandy Dolby, John McDowell, Mary Ellen Brown, and Warren Roberts. An earlier version of F517 was taught as FOLK-F 831 with the title Seminar in Folklore Theory and Technique 2. Dorson taught this course in the 1950s and 1960s. Stith Thompson taught it for the last time in the spring of 1955, as reflected by the Schedule of Classes in the Indiana University Archives.

4. For the historical record, I note that Henry Glassie last taught F516 in 2007. While he was the primary teacher of the course after his return to Bloomington, the published IU Bloomington Schedule of Classes shows Sandy Dolby teaching the course in 1997. The schedule also shows her teaching it twice before Glassie began teaching it (in 1987 and 1988), and she taught it for the final time in 2008. I began teaching it in the fall of 2009. I taught it again in 2010, 2011, and 2012. My duties as director of the then-Mathers Museum of World Cultures began in 2013, and my teaching of it became intermittent. John McDowell taught F516 in the fall of 2013. I taught it in 2014 and 2015. Ray Cashman taught the course each fall between 2016 and 2021. I returned to teaching it in 2022 and 2023. Ray is slated to teach it again in the fall of 2024. In addition to Dolby, two others who taught the course in the gap between Dorson and Glassie are Hasan El-Shamy (1984, 1985) and John Johnson (1982, 1983). The earliest version of FOLK-F 516 found in the IU Bloomington Schedule of Classes was with Dorson in the fall of 1967. Between that year and his death, Dorson was the main teacher of the course, but Warren Roberts taught it in the spring of 1968 and the fall of 1971. Not evident from the published schedule of classes, Linda Dégh stepped in to teach the course in 1981 due to Dorson's hospitalization and passing that semester (Moira Marsh, personal communication, August 6, 2024). A folklorist unknown to me with the family name Baghban taught it in the fall of 1978.

I believe that a predecessor course to FOLK-F 516 was FOLK-F 830, Seminar in Folklore Theory and Technique 1, taught by Dorson in the late 1950s and early 1960s and by others prior to that period. A study of university bulletins in the Indiana University Archives makes clear, based on course descriptions, that F830 was a direct precursor to F516 (as F831 was to F517, although these two courses were colloquiums with a rotating schedule of presenters and were thus more like FOLK-F 501 in later periods). As for F516, the bulletins suggest that an initial version of this course was present on the books in the first year for which folklore is listed as a bulletin topic (1949). The most ancient version is thus Folklore 360, Seminar in Folklore Theory and Techniques, for which Stith Thompson or George Herzog were the linked instructors (Indiana University 1949).

5. I base the explication in this chapter primarily on Dorson's published account of his course, but I have in my files his syllabus for Fall 1979. In order of presentation, that document announced the following topics with primary headings and associated readings. The readings draw extensively from the journal literature. The letters given here are my own additions. I use letters to help differentiate relative to the numbered topics given in the published account and above. A. The Battle of Folklore and Fakelore, B. Terminology, C. Bibliography, D. Archiving, E. Indexes, F. Printed Sources, G. Folklore in Literature, H. Folklore and Anthropology, I. Folklore and History, J. Aesthetics of Oral Style, K. Folklife and Material Culture, L. History of Folkloristics, M. International Relations in Folklore, N. Folklore in the Mass Media. There are some direct matches here between the two lists, and some sections on the more extensive syllabus list are clearly subsections, as with G–I (and perhaps J) all relating to topic 9, Interdisciplinary Knowledge (Dorson 1979). Perhaps J (Aesthetics of Oral Style) is the missing thirteenth topic from Dorson's "baker's dozen."

6. For readers who do not know Glassie's study, I note here briefly that it is an ethnographic and historical account of rural Irish mumming centered in one particular rural townland in Northern Ireland but engaging expansively and comparatively with the island as a whole and with the wider European and Atlantic world context. Of special relevance here, the author finds interpretive utility in the use of survivalist, historic-geographic, performance, interpretive, and functionalist frameworks, critiquing each in turn as well. The study also centers on the words, experiences, and interpretations of five key local cultural experts who were Glassie's interlocutors (Glassie 1975).

7. During Glassie's first period on the Indiana University faculty, it is clear that Dorson tasked him with teaching contemporary and emerging theories, particularly those from anthropology and other social science fields in his parallel course on folklife (i.e., then FOLK-F 517 [personal communication, July 31, 2024]).

8. Scrutinizing my course in a new way in this context has prompted a realization that iterative revisions of the course have diminished the attention given to the concept of culture and to debates about it. While the concept of culture is introduced early, in connection with the initial engagement with the history of the field in a (mostly) Boasian context, and is discussed repeatedly in various contexts, I think that a focused discussion that involves a wider range of perspectives, including those that argue against using the culture concept, would be useful in future versions of the course. In connection to, or just before or after, the concept of society would be appropriate for this.

9. In 2023, my students and I read a large number of excerpts and shorter works. Rather than cite the full list here, see the course syllabus (Jackson 2023b). Authors for this week included Boas on alternating sounds (anticipating metaculture and metacultural awareness), Pravina Shukla on part-whole relations in dress and adornment as assemblage, James Frazier on magic, Arnold van Gennep on rites of passage, Claude Lévi-Strauss on structures in food systems, and Dundes's Freudian account of antisemitism.

10. In a July 31, 2024, discussion with me, Glassie confirmed my topic captions and reflected on his objectives in his version of the course. Whereas Dorson might have emphasized disciplinarity and I speak of useful concepts, Glassie stressed to me that his goal was to prepare students with the frameworks and examples needed to successfully undertake contextual and performance-informed ethnographic fieldwork. My own view is that his framework and book choices succeeded admirably in this and were well calibrated to the 1990s context in which I was a student at Indiana University.

11. I postpone any broad discussion of decolonization in general or for folklore studies, but I am aware of the major lines of discussion and practice. Sometimes scholars may align with one or more of these, but decolonization labels things in the world, including things that a scholar of the social-world-that-is has to confront but may very much not wish to embrace. Decolonization can now be a more diverse reading list engendering a broader, more empathetic outlook on the world. Decolonization can be the Miami Tribe of Oklahoma purchasing land in present-day Indiana and thereby reconnecting with and stewarding more of their homeland. Decolonization can be the same Nation restoring its ancestral language to everyday use. But decolonization can also still be an improvised bomb claiming the lives of innocent children on the way to school. And those are just four evocations of a broader range. All those who take up decolonization as a program, and not just a description of what is, have hard thinking to do and should think hard about what is sometimes called semantic bleaching, as when a word loses its power and significance through wider and wider extension and use in more and more contexts. In English, "The withdrawal of a colonizing state" usage dates to 1836. "The process of eliminating the effects of colonization or colonialism on the attitudes,

assumptions . . . etc. of a people . . ." dates to 1963. Both meanings center on the production or reorganization of independent, postcolonial *states*. Neither of these two varieties recognized by the *Oxford English Dictionary* (2023) capture either the more complicated and mixed programs now underway among Indigenous peoples and polities within settler colonies such as the United States or the ways that non-Indigenous peoples in settler colonies (and elsewhere) are engaging in diffuse and diverse projects, including curricular reform, under the banner of decolonization.

REFERENCES CITED

Aarne, Antti, and Stith Thompson. 1981. *The Types of the Folktale: A Classification and Bibliography*. FF Communications 184. Helsinki: Suomalainen Tiedeakatemia.

Abrahams, Roger D. 1970. *Deep Down in the Jungle: Negro Narrative Folklore from the Streets of Philadelphia*. Chicago: Aldine.

Abrahams, Roger D. 1983. "Interpreting Folklore Ethnographically and Sociologically." In *Handbook of American Folklore*, edited by Richard M. Dorson, 345–50. Bloomington: Indiana University Press.

Abrahams, Roger D. 1993. "Phantoms of Romantic Nationalism in Folkloristics." *Journal of American Folklore* 106 (419): 3–37. https://doi.org/10.2307/541344.

Aldred, Lisa. 2000. "Plastic Shamans and Astroturf Sun Dances: New Age Commercialization of Native American Spirituality." *American Indian Quarterly* 24 (3): 329–52. https://doi.org/10.1353/aiq.2000.0001.

American Folklore Society. 1907. "Record of American Folk-Lore." *Journal of American Folklore* 20 (76): 76–83. http://www.jstor.org/stable/534731.

American Folklore Society. 2005. *2005 Annual Meeting* [Program]. Colubus, OH: American Folklore Society. http://hdl.handle.net/2022/13116.

An Deming and Yang Lihui. 2015. "Chinese Folklore since the Late 1970s: Achievements, Difficulties, and Challenges." *Asian Ethnology* 74 (2): 273–90. https://www.jstor.org/stable/43799241.

Anderson, Jane, and Kimberly Christen. 2013. "'Chuck a Copyright on It': Dilemmas of Digital Return and the Possibilities for Traditional Knowledge Licenses and Labels." *Museum Anthropology Review* 7 (1–2): 105–26. https://scholarworks.iu.edu/journals/index.php/mar/article/view/2169.

Anonymous. 1938. "Dr. W. C. Willoughby." *Nature* 142 (3589): 282. https://doi.org/10.1038/142282a0.

Arbousset, Thomas, and Francois Daumas. 1842. *Relation d'un voyage d'exploration au nord-est de la colonie du Cap de Bonne-Espérance*. Paris: Arthus Bertrand.

Arbousset, Thomas, and Francois Daumas. 1846. *Narrative of an Exploratory Tour to the North-east of the Colony of the Cape Good Hope by the Revs. T. Arbousset and F. Daumas of the Paris Missionary Society*, translated by John Croumbie Brown.

Cape Town: A. S. Robertson, Heerengracht, Saul Solomon. http://hdl.handle
.net/2027/nyp.33433082327390.

Bacchilega, Cristina, and Sadhana Naithani. 2018. "Colonialism, Postcolonialism,
and Decolonization." In *The Routledge Companion to Media and Fairy-Tale Cultures*, edited by Pauline Greenhill, Jill Terry Rudy, Naomi Hamer, and Lauren
Bosc, 83–90. New York: Routledge.

Bahr, Donald. 2001. "Bad News: The Predicament of Native American Mythology."
Ethnohistory 48 (4): 587–612. https://doi.org/10.1215/00141801-48-4-587.

Bain, Christina. 2018. "Christina Fallin: 'Appropriate Culturation?'" *Ethics Un-
wrapped*. https://ethicsunwrapped.utexas.edu/case-study/christina-fallin
-appropriate-culturation.

Barbeau, Marius. 1915. *Huron and Wyandot Mythology*. Canada Department of Mines,
Geological Survey Memoir 80, Anthropological Series 11. Ottawa: Government
Printing Bureau. http://hdl.handle.net/2027/uc1.32106000740347.

Barbeau, Marius. 1960. *Huron-Wyandot Traditional Narratives, in Translations and
Native Texts*. National Museum of Canada, Bulletin 165, Anthropological Series
47. Ottawa: Queen's Printer.

Barbeau, Marius. 2006. *Marius Barbeau: A Canadian Hero and His Era, 1883–1969*.
http://www.civilization.ca/tresors/barbeau/index_e.html.

Bareither, Christoph, Alexander Harder, and Dennis Eckhardt. 2023. "Special Issue: Digital Truth-Making: Anthropological Perspectives on Right-Wing Politics and Social Media in 'Post-Truth' Societies." *Ethnologia Europaea* 53 (2):
1–20. https://doi.org/10.16995/ee.9594.

Barker, Brandon. 2022. *Syllabus: F512 Survey of Folklore-Genres and Genre Theories*. Bloomington: Department of Folklore and Ethnomusicology, Indiana
University.

Baron, Robert. 2019. "Public Folklore: Theory of/in Practice (A Response to Elliott
Oring)." *Journal of American Folklore* 132 (524): 163–74. https://doi.org/10.5406
/jamerfolk.132.524.0163.

Barth, Fredrik. 1969. "Introduction." In *Ethnic Groups and Boundaries: The Social
Organization of Cultural Difference*, edited by Fredrik Barth, 9–38. New York:
Little, Brown.

Basso, Ellen B. 1990. "The Last Cannibal." *Journal of Folklore Research* 27 (1–2):
133–73. http://www.jstor.org/stable/3814462.

Basso, Keith H. 1979. *Portraits of "The Whiteman": Linguistic Play and Cultural Sym-
bols among the Western Apache*. New York: Cambridge University Press.

Basso, Keith H. 1984. "'Stalking with Stories': Names, Places, and Moral Narratives among the Western Apache." In *Text, Play, and Story: The Construction
and Reconstruction of Self and Society*, edited by Edward M. Bruner, 19–55. Proceedings of the American Ethnological Society. Washington, DC: American
Ethnological Society.

Baughman, Ernest Warren. 1966. *Type and Motif-Index of the Folktales of England and North America*. Indiana University Folklore Series 20. The Hague: Mouton.

Bauman, Richard. 1971. "Differential Identity and the Social Base of Folklore." *Journal of American Folklore* 84 (331): 31–41. https://doi.org/10.2307/539731.

Bauman, Richard. 1975. "Verbal Art as Performance." *American Anthropologist* 77 (2): 290–311. https://doi.org/10.1525/aa.1975.77.2.02a00030.

Bauman, Richard. 1983. "The Field Study of Folklore in Context." In *Handbook of American Folklore*, edited by Richard M. Dorson, 362–68. Bloomington: Indiana University Press.

Bauman, Richard. 1986. *Story, Performance, and Event: Contextual Studies of Oral Narrative*. New York: Cambridge University Press.

Bauman, Richard. 1992a. "Contextualization, Tradition, and the Dialogue of Contexts: Icelandic Legends of the Kraftaskald." In *Rethinking Context: Language as an Interactive Phenomenon*, edited by Alessandro Duranti and Charles Goodwin, 125–46. New York: Cambridge University Press.

Bauman, Richard. 1992b. "Folklore." In *Folklore, Cultural Performances, and Popular Entertainments: A Communications-Centered Handbook*, edited by Richard Bauman, 29–40. New York: Oxford University Press.

Bauman, Richard. 1999. "Genre." *Journal of Linguistic Anthropology* 9 (1–2): 84–87. https://doi.org/10.1525/jlin.1999.9.1-2.84.

Bauman, Richard. 2012. "Performance." In *A Companion to Folklore*, edited by Regina Bendix and Galit Hasan-Rokem, 94–118. Malden, MA: Blackwell.

Bauman, Richard, and Charles L. Briggs. 2006. *Voices of Modernity: Language Ideologies and the Politics of Inequality*. New York: Cambridge University Press.

Becker, Cathy. 2017. "Do Folklore and Security Studies Mix? Mershon Affiliate Says Yes." Mershon Center for International Security Studies News, April. https://kb.osu.edu/handle/1811/87953.

Ben-Amos, Dan. 1971. "Toward a Definition of Folklore in Context." *Journal of American Folklore* 84 (331): 3–15. http://www.jstor.org/stable/539729.

Ben-Amos, Dan. 1976a. "Analytic Categories and Ethnic Genres." In *Folklore Genres*, edited by Dan Ben-Amos, 215–42. Austin: University of Texas Press. https://doi.org/10.7560/724150-013.

Ben-Amos, Dan. 1976b. "Introduction." In *Folklore Genres*, edited by Dan Ben-Amos, ix–xlv. Publications of the American Folklore Society 26. Austin: University of Texas Press. https://doi.org/10.7560/724150-002.

Ben-Amos, Dan. 2020. *Folklore Concepts: Histories and Critiques*. Edited by Elliott Oring and Henry Glassie. Bloomington: Indiana University Press. https://muse.jhu.edu/book/85749.

Bendix, Regina F. 1998. "Of Names, Professional Identities, and Disciplinary Futures." *Journal of American Folklore* 111 (441): 235–46. https://doi.org/10.2307/541309.

Bendix, Regina F. 2003. "Translating between European Ethnologies." In *Times—Places—Passages: Ethnological Approaches to the New Millennium*, edited by Attila Paládi-Kovacs, Gyorgyi Csukas, Reka Kiss, Ildiko Kristof, Ilona Nagy, and Zsuzsa Szarvas, 371–80. Budapest: Akademiai Kiado.

Bendix, Regina F. 2009. "Inheritances: Possession, Ownership and Responsibility." *Traditiones* 38 (2): 181–99. https://doi.org/10.3986/Traditio2009380212.

Bendix, Regina F. 2012. "From *Volkskunde* to the 'Field of Many Names': Folklore Studies in German-Speaking Europe since 1945." In *A Companion to Folklore*, edited by Regina F. Bendix and Galit Hasan-Rokem, 364–90. Malden, MA: Wiley-Blackwell. https://doi.org/10.1002/9781118379936.ch19.

Bendix, Regina F. 2018. *Culture and Value: Tourism, Heritage, and Property*. Bloomington: Indiana University Press.

Bendix, Regina F. 2021. "Life Itself: An Essay on the Sensory and the (Potential) End of Heritage Making." *Traditiones* 50 (1): 43–51. https://doi.org/10.3986/Traditio2021500104.

Bendix, Regina F., Kilian Bizer, and Dorothy Noyes. 2017. *Sustaining Interdisciplinary Collaboration: A Guide for the Academy*. Champaign: University of Illinois Press. https://muse.jhu.edu/book/51744.

Bendix, Regina F., Aditya Eggert, and Arnika Peselmann, eds. 2013. *Heritage Regimes and the State*. Göttingen Studies in Cultural Property, 6. Göttingen: Universitätsverlag Göttingen. http://resolver.sub.uni-goettingen.de/purl?isbn-978-3-86395-122-1.

Bendix, Regina F., and Galit Hasan-Rokem, eds. 2012a. *A Companion to Folklore*. Malden, MA: Wiley-Blackwell.

Bendix, Regina F., and Galit Hasan-Rokem. 2012b. "Introduction." In *A Companion to Folklore*, edited by Regina F. Bendix and Galit Hasan-Rokem, 1–6. Malden, MA: Wiley-Blackwell.

Bennett, Tony, Lawrence Grossberg, and Meaghan Morris, eds. 2005. *New Keywords: A Revised Vocabulary of Culture and Society*. Malden, MA: Blackwell.

Bennhold, Katrin. 2018. "Bavarian Millennials Embrace Tradition (Dirndls, Lederhosen and All)." *New York Times*, October 10, 2018. https://www.nytimes.com/2018/10/10/world/europe/germany-bavaria-dirndl-lederhosen.html.

Best, Amy L. 2000. *Prom Night: Youth, Schools, and Popular Culture*. New York: Routledge.

Bierhorst, John. 1995. *Mythology of the Lenape: Guide and Texts*. Tucson: University of Arizona Press.

Blank, Trevor, ed. 2008. *Folklore and the Internet: Vernacular Expression in a Digital World*. Logan: Utah State University Press. https://digitalcommons.usu.edu/usupress_pubs/35.

Blommaert, Jan. 2015. "Chronotopes, Scales, and Complexity in the Study of Language in Society." *Annual Review of Anthropology* 44:105–16. https://doi .org/10.1146/annurev-anthro-102214-014035.

Boas, Franz. 1887. "The Study of Geography." *Science*, n.s., 9 (210): 137–41. https:// doi.org/10.1126/science.ns-9.210S.137.

Boas, Franz. 1891. "Dissemination of Tales among the Natives of North America." *Journal of American Folklore* 4 (12): 13–20. https://doi.org/10.2307/532927.

Boas, Franz. 1911. "Introduction." In *Handbook of American Indian Languages*, vol. 1, 1–84. Bureau of American Ethnology Bulletin 40. Washington, DC: Government Printing Office.

Boas, Franz. 1940. *Race, Language, and Culture*. New York: Macmillan.

Boas, Franz. 1974. "Documentary Function of the Text." In *The Shaping of American Anthropology, 1883–1911: A Franz Boas Reader*, edited by George W. Stocking, 122–23. New York: Basic Books.

Bock, Sheila, and Katherine Borland. 2011. "Exotic Identities: Dance, Difference, and Self-Fashioning." *Journal of Folklore Research* 48 (1): 1–36. https://doi .org/10.2979/jfolkrese.48.1.1.

Boon, James A. 1977. *The Anthropological Romance of Bali, 1597–1972: Dynamic Perspectives in Marriage and Caste, Politics and Religion*. New York: Cambridge University Press.

Bourdieu, Pierre. 1994. "Structures, Habitus, Power: Basis for a Theory of Symbolic Power." In *Culture/Power/History: A Reader in Contemporary Social Theory*, edited by Nicholas B. Dirks, Geoff Eley, and Sherry B. Ortner, 155–99. Princeton, NJ: Princeton University Press.

Brandes, Stanley. 1979. "Ethnographic Autobiographies in American Anthropology." *Central Issues in Anthropology* 1 (2): 1–17. https://doi.org/10.1525 /cia.1979.1.2.1.

Briggs, Charles. 1996. "The Politics of Discursive Authority in Research on the 'Invention of Tradition.'" *Cultural Anthropology* 11 (4): 435–69. https://www .jstor.org/stable/656664.

Briggs, Charles L. 2008. "Disciplining Folkloristics." *Journal of Folklore Research* 45 (1): 91–105. https://www.jstor.org/stable/40206968.

Briggs, Charles L. 2012. "What We Should Have Learned from Américo Paredes: The Politics of Communicability and the Making of Folkloristics." *Journal of American Folklore* 125 (495): 91–110. https://doi.org/10.5406 /jamerfolk.125.495.0091.

Briggs, Charles L., and Richard Bauman. 1992. "Genre, Intertextuality and Social Power." *Journal of Linguistic Anthropology* 2 (2): 131–72. https://doi.org/10.1525 /jlin.1992.2.2.131.

Briggs, Charles L., and Sadhana Naithani. 2012. "The Coloniality of Folklore: Towards a Multi-Genealogical Practice of Folkloristics." *Studies in History* 28 (2): 231–70. https://doi.org/10.1177/0257643013482404.

Bronner, Simon. 2006. "Nationalism." In *The Greenwood Encyclopedia of World Folklore and Folklife*, edited by William Clements, 60–64. Westport, CT: Greenwood.

Brown, Michael F. 2003. *Who Owns Native Culture?* Cambridge, MA: Harvard University Press.

Bruyneel, Kevin. 2016. "Race, Colonialism, and the Politics of Indian Sports Names and Mascots: The Washington Football Team Case." *Native American and Indigenous Studies* 3 (2): 1–24. https://www.muse.jhu.edu/article/643780.

Buettner, Joe. 2018. "Gov. Mary Fallin Named Least Popular US Governor, Per Report." *Fox 25 News*, July 25, 2018. https://okcfox.com/news/local/gov-mary-fallin-owns-lowest-approval-rating-in-us-per-report.

Burkholder, Mabel. 1923. *Before the White Man Came: Indian Legends and Stories*. Toronto: McClelland and Stewart.

Calouste Gulbenkian Foundation. 1996. "Foreword." In *Open the Social Sciences: Report of the Gulbenkian Commission on the Restructuring of the Social Sciences*, Immanuel Wallerstein, Calestous Juma, Evelyn Fox Keller, Jürgen Kocka, Dominique Lecourt, V. Y. Mudimbe, Kinhide Mushakoji, Ilya Prigogine, Peter J. Taylor, and Michel-Ralph Troullot, ix–xi. Stanford, CA: Stanford University Press.

Cantwell, Robert. 1996. *When We Were Good: The Folk Revival*. Cambridge, MA: Harvard University Press.

Casagrande, Joseph B., ed. 1960. *In the Company of Man: Twenty Portraits by Anthropologists*. New York: Harper and Brothers.

Cashman, Ray. 2006. "Critical Nostalgia and Material Culture in Northern Ireland." *Journal of American Folklore* 119 (472): 137–60. https://www.jstor.org/stable/4137921.

Cashman, Ray. 2016a. "Genre as Ideology-Shaping Form: Storytelling and Parading in Northern Ireland." In *Genre, Text, Interpretation: Multidisciplinary Perspectives on Folklore and Beyond*, edited by Kaarina Koski and Frog, 381–402. Helsinki: Studia Fennica Folkloristics. https://library.oapen.org/handle/20.500.12657/31124.

Cashman, Ray. 2016b. *Packy Jim: Folklore and Worldview on the Irish Border*. Madison: University of Wisconsin Press.

Cashman, Ray, Tom Mould, and Pravina Shukla. 2011. "Introduction: The Individual and Tradition." In *The Individual and Tradition: Folkloristic Perspectives*, edited by Ray Cashman, Tom Mould, and Pravina Shukla, 1–26. Special Publications of the Folklore Institute. Bloomington: Indiana University Press.

Castañeda, Quetzil E. 2004. "Art-Writing in the Modern Maya Art World of Chichén Itzá: Transcultural Ethnography and Experimental Fieldwork." *American Ethnologist* 31 (1): 21–42. http://www.jstor.org/stable/3805302.

Chakrabarty, Dipesh. 2000. *Provincializing Europe: Postcolonial Thought and Historical Difference.* Princeton, NJ: Princeton University Press.

China Made. 2019. "China Made / CEKP Workshop." *China Made* (blog), July 21, 2019. https://chinamadeproject.net/china-made-cekp-workshop/.

Clark, Raymond J. 1970. "A Classical Foundation-Legend from Newfoundland." *Folklore* 81 (3): 182–84. https://doi.org/10.1080/0015587X.1970.9716680.

Clements, William. 1997. "Oikotype/Oicotype." In *Folklore: An Encyclopedia of Beliefs, Customs, Tales, Music, and Art,* edited by Thomas A. Green, 604–605. Santa Barbara, CA: ABC-CLIO.

Coombe, Rosemary J. 1998. *The Cultural Life of Intellectual Properties: Authorship, Appropriation, and the Law.* Durham, NC: Duke University Press.

Coombe, Rosemary J., and Nicole S. Aylwin. 2014. "The Evolution of Cultural Heritage Ethics via Human Rights Norms." In *Dynamic Fair Dealing: Creating Canadian Culture Online,* edited by Rosemary J. Coombe, Darren Wershler, and Martin Zeilinger, 201–12. Toronto: University of Toronto Press. https://ssrn.com/abstract=2644457.

Cosse, Sebastien. 2015. "Aventador Oakley Design." Flickr. https://www.flickr.com/photos/seb77181/20062211400/.

Crisco 1492. 2015. "Plastic Comb." *Wikimedia Commons.* https://commons.wikimedia.org/wiki/File:Plastic_comb,_2015-06-07.jpg.

Damsholt, Tine, and Astrid Pernille Jespersen. 2014. "Innovation, Resistance or Tinkering: Rearticulating Everyday Life in an Ethnological Perspective." *Ethnologia Europaea* 44 (2): 17–30. https://doi.org/10.16995/ee.1124.

Darnell, Regna. 1973. "American Anthropology and the Development of Folklore Scholarship: 1890–1920." *Journal of the Folklore Institute* 10 (1–2): 23–39. https://doi.org/10.2307/3813878.

Darnell, Regna. 2001. *Invisible Genealogies: A History of Americanist Anthropology.* Lincoln: University of Nebraska Press.

Darnell, Regna. 2021. *The History of Anthropology: A Critical Window on the Discipline in North America.* Critical Studies in the History of Anthropology. Lincoln: University of Nebraska Press.

Dégh, Linda. 1989. *Folktales and Society: Story-Telling in a Hungarian Peasant Community: A Reissue with an Afterword.* Bloomington: Indiana University Press.

Deloria, Ella Cara. 1988. *Waterlily.* Lincoln: University of Nebraska Press.

Deloria, Ella Cara. 1998. *Speaking of Indians.* Lincoln: University of Nebraska Press.

DeMallie, Raymond J. 1993. "'These Have No Ears': Narrative and the Ethnohistorical Method." *Ethnohistory* 40 (4): 515–38. https://doi.org/10.2307/482586.

DeMallie, Raymond J. 1998. "Kinship: The Foundation for Native American Society." In *Studying Native America: Problems and Prospects,* edited by Russell Thornton, 306–56. Madison: University of Wisconsin Press.

Deutsche Forschungsgemeinschaft (DFG) Interdisciplinary Research Group on Cultural Property. 2018. "Publikationen." http://cultural-property.uni-goettingen.de /publikationen/.

Diaz, Juan. 2014. "Tron Cars Are the Latest Fad in China." Gizmodo, January 31, 2014. https://sploid.gizmodo.com/tron-cars-are-the-latest-fad-in-china-1513161453.

Dinwoodie, David. 2006. "Time and the Individual in Native North America." In *New Perspectives on Native North America: Cultures, Histories, and Representations,* edited by Sergei A. Kan and Pauline Turner Strong, 327–48. Lincoln: University of Nebraska Press.

Dixon, R. B. 1915. "Dr. Dixon's Reply." *American Anthropologist,* n.s., 17 (3): 599–600. https://www.jstor.org/stable/660516.

Dorson, Richard M. 1946. "Comic Indian Anecdotes." *Southern Folklore Quarterly* 10 (2): 113–28.

Dorson, Richard M. 1952. *Bloodstoppers and Bearwalkers: Folk Traditions of the Upper Peninsula.* Cambridge, MA: Harvard University Press.

Dorson, Richard M., ed. 1972. *Folklore and Folklife: An Introduction.* Chicago: University of Chicago Press.

Dorson, Richard M. 1979. *Syllabus, F516, Proseminar in Folklore Theory and Techniques.* Bloomington: Department of Folklore and Ethnomusicology, Indiana University. https://scholarworks.iu.edu/dspace /items/19d148d1-3285-434e-9313-98f2d1967f1d.

Dorson, Richard M., ed. 1983a. *Handbook of American Folklore.* Bloomington: Indiana University Press.

Dorson, Richard M. 1983b. "A Historical Theory for American Folklore." In *Handbook of American Folklore,* edited by Richard M. Dorson, 326–37. Bloomington: Indiana University Press.

Dorson, Richard M. 1983c. "Teaching Folklore to Graduate Students: The Introductory Proseminar." In *Handbook of American Folklore,* edited by Richard M. Dorson, 463–69. Bloomington: Indiana University Press.

Dorst, John D. 2019. "Aliens: The Perils of Ignoring 'Outside' Theory (A Response to Elliott Oring)." *Journal of American Folklore* 132 (524): 157–62. https://doi .org/10.5406/jamerfolk.132.524.0157.

Dowd, Gregory Evans. 1993. *A Spirited Resistance: The North American Indian Struggle for Unity, 1745–1815.* Baltimore: Johns Hopkins University Press.

Dowd, Gregory Evans. 2004. *War under Heaven: Pontiac, the Indian Nations, and the British Empire.* Baltimore: Johns Hopkins University Press.

Dundes, Alan. 1963. "Review of *Indian Tales of North America* by Tristan P. Coffin." *Journal of American Folklore* 76 (299): 69–71. https://doi.org/10.2307/538079.

Dundes, Alan. 1980. *Interpreting Folklore*. Bloomington: Indiana University Press.

Dundes, Alan, ed. 1984. *Sacred Narrative: Readings in the Theory of Myth*. Berkeley: University of California Press.

Dundes, Alan. 1993. "Preface." In *Contemporary Legend*, edited by Paul Smith and Gillian Bennett, ix–xiii. New York: Garland.

Dundes, Alan. 1995. "How Indic Parallels to the Ballad of the 'Walled-Up Wife' Reveal the Pitfalls of Parochial Nationalistic Folkloristics." *Journal of American Folklore* 108 (427): 38–53. https://doi.org/10.2307/541733.

Dundes, Alan, ed. 1999. *International Folkloristics: Classic Contributions by the Founders of Folklore*. Landham, MD: Rowman & Littlefield.

Dundes, Alan, ed. 2005. *Folklore: Critical Concepts in Literary and Cultural Studies*. New York: Routledge.

Eaton, Kristi. 2014. "Gov. Fallin's Daughter Defends Headdress Photo." *Tulsa World*, March 7, 2014. https://www.tulsaworld.com/news/state/gov-fallin-s-daughter-defends-headdress-photo/article_93965ac6-a60b-11e3-97d5-0017a43b2370.html.

Eck, Rutger van. 1880. "Schetsen van het eiland Bali" [Sketches of the Island of Bali]. *Tijdschrift voor Nederlandsch Indië* 9 (1): 1–39.

Eddy, Melissa. 2014. "Lost in Translation: Germany's Fascination with the American Old West." *New York Times*, August 17, 2014. https://www.nytimes.com/2014/08/18/world/europe/germanys-fascination-with-american-old-west-native-american-scalps-human-remains.html.

Edmunds, R. David. 1983. *The Shawnee Prophet*. Lincoln: University of Nebraska Press.

Eggan, Fred. 1937. "Historical Changes in the Choctaw Kinship System." *American Anthropologist*, n.s., 39 (1): 34–52. http://www.jstor.org/stable/662072.

Eggan, Fred. 1967. "From History to Myth: A Hopi Example." In *Studies in Southwestern Ethnolinguistics*, edited by Dell Hymes, 33–53. The Hague: Mouton.

Ehn, Billy, and Orvar Löfgren. 2010. *The Secret World of Doing Nothing*. Berkeley: University of California Press.

Ellmann, Richard. 1983. *James Joyce*. Rev. ed. New York: Oxford University Press.

Elmahrek, Adam, and Paul Pringle. 2019. "Claiming to be Cherokee, Contractors with White Ancestry Got $300 Million." *Los Angeles Times*, July 2, 2019. https://www.latimes.com/local/lanow/la-na-cherokee-minority-contracts-20190626-story.html.

El-Shamy, Hasan M. 1995. *Folk Traditions of the Arab World: A Guide to Motif Classification*. Vol. 1. Bloomington: Indiana University Press.

El-Shamy, Hasan M. 1997. "Psychologically-Based Criteria for Classification by Motif and Tale Type." *Journal of Folklore Research* 34 (3): 233–43. https://www.jstor.org/stable/3814890.

Evans, E. Estyn. 1957. *Irish Folkways*. London: Routledge & Kegan Paul.

Evans-Pritchard, Deirdre. 1987. "The Portal Case: Authenticity, Tourism, Traditions, and the Law." *Journal of American Folklore* 100 (397): 287–96. https://doi.org/10.2307/540325.

Faubion, James D., Jane I. Guyer, Tom Boellstorff, Marilyn Strathern, Clémentine Deliss, Frédéric Keck, and Terry Smith. 2016. "On the Anthropology of the Contemporary: Addressing Concepts, Designs, and Practices." *HAU: Journal of Ethnographic Theory* 6 (1): 371–402. https://doi.org/10.14318/hau6.1.020.

Feintuch, Burt. 1995. "Introduction: Words in Common." *Journal of American Folklore* 108 (430): 391–94. https://www.jstor.org/stable/541652.

Feintuch, Burt, ed. 2003. *Eight Words for the Study of Expressive Culture.* Urbana: University of Illinois Press.

Fei Xiaotong, Gary G. Hamilton, and Wang Zheng. 1992. *From the Soil: The Foundations of Chinese Society.* Berkeley: University of California Press.

Feltault, Kelly. 2006. "Development Folklife: Human Security and Cultural Conservation." *Journal of American Folklore* 119 (471): 90–110. http://www.jstor.org/stable/4137785.

Fenton, William N. 1998. *The Great Law and the Longhouse: A Political History of the Iroquois Confederacy.* Norman: University of Oklahoma Press.

Fine, Gary Alan. 2009. "Review of *Once Upon a Virus: AIDS Legends and Vernacular Risk Perception,* by Diane E. Goldstein." *Journal of American Folklore* 122 (483): 102–103. https://www.jstor.org/stable/20487657.

Fine, Gary Alan. 2012. *Tiny Publics: A Theory of Group Action and Culture.* New York: Russell Sage Foundation. http://www.jstor.org/stable/10.7758/9781610447744.

Fivecoate, Jesse A., Kristina Downs, and Meredith A. E. McGriff, eds. 2021. *Advancing Folkloristics.* Bloomington: Indiana University Press.

Fixico, Donald L. 2003. *The American Indian Mind in a Linear World: American Indian Studies and Traditional Knowledge.* New York: Taylor and Francis.

Flint, Colin. 2017. "Geographic Perspectives on World-Systems Theory." In *Oxford Research Encyclopedia of International Studies.* https://doi.org/10.1093/acrefore/9780190846626.013.196.

Fogelson, Raymond D. 1984. "Who Were the Aní-Kutánî? An Excursion into Cherokee Historical Thought." *Ethnohistory* 31 (4): 255–63. https://doi.org/10.2307/482712.

Fogelson, Raymond D. 1989. "The Ethnohistory of Events and Nonevents." *Ethnohistory* 36 (2): 133–47. https://doi.org/10.2307/482275.

Foster, Michael Dylan. 2017. "The Challenges of Bridging Metacultural and Esocultural Perspectives on Intangible Cultural Heritage." In *Glocal Perspectives on Intangible Cultural Heritage: Local Communities, Researchers, States and UNESCO,* edited by

Tomiyuki Uesugi and Mari Shiba, 73–88. Tokyo: Center for Glocal Studies, Seijo University.

Foster, Michael Dylan, and Lisa Gilman, eds. 2015. *UNESCO on the Ground: Local Perspectives on Intangible Cultural Heritage*. Bloomington: Indiana University Press.

Foucault, Michel. 1991. "Governmentality." In *The Foucault Effect: Studies in Governmentality*, edited by Graham Burchell, Colin Gordon, and Peter Miller, 87–104. Chicago: University of Chicago Press.

Frazer, James G. 1888. "Hide-Measured Lands." *Classical Review* 2 (10): 322. http://www.jstor.org/stable/691214.

Frazer, James G. 1935. *The Golden Bough: A Study in Magic and Religion*. Part 4, *Adonis Attis Osiris*. Vol. 2. 3rd ed. New York: Macmillan.

Garfinkel, Harold. 1991. *Studies in Ethnomethodology*. Boston: Polity.

Genzlinger, Neil. 2019. "Immanuel Wallerstein, Sociologist with a Global View, Dies at 88." *New York Times*, September 10, 2019. https://www.nytimes.com/2019/09/10/books/immanuel-wallerstein-dead.html.

Gershon, Ilana. 2019. "Porous Social Orders." *American Ethnologist* 46 (4): 404–16. https://doi.org/10.1111/amet.12829.

Gienow-Hecht, Jessica C. E. 2004. "Cultural Transfer." In *Explaining the History of American Foreign Relations*, 2nd ed., edited by Michael J. Hogan and Thomas G. Patterson, 253–78. New York: Cambridge University Press.

Gingging, Flory Ann Mansor. 2007. "'I Lost My Head in Borneo': Tourism and the Refashioning of the Headhunting Narrative in Sabah, Malaysia." *Cultural Analysis* 6:1–29. https://www.ocf.berkeley.edu/~culturalanalysis/volume6/vol6_article1.html.

Gisling. 2007. "Fujian Tulou (Earth Buildings) at Tianluokeng (Snail Pit Village) in Southwestern Fujian Province." *Wikimedia Commons*. https://commons.wikimedia.org/wiki/File:Snail_pit_tulou.jpg.

Gladwell, Malcolm. 2002. *The Tipping Point: How Little Things Can Make a Big Difference*. Boston: Back Bay Books.

Glassie, Henry. 1975. *All Silver and No Brass: An Irish Christmas Mumming*. Bloomington: Indiana University Press.

Glassie, Henry. 1982. *Passing the Time in Ballymenone: Culture and History of an Ulster Community*. Philadelphia: University of Pennsylvania Press.

Glassie, Henry. 1983. "Folkloristic Study of the American Artifact: Objects and Objectives." In *Handbook of American Folklore*, edited by Richard M. Dorson, 376–83. Bloomington: Indiana University Press.

Glassie, Henry. 1991. "20th Century Folklore Scholarship" [Syllabus: FOLK-F 516 Folklore Theory and Practice]. Bloomington: Department of Folklore and Ethnomusicology, Indiana University.

Glassie, Henry. 1995. "Tradition." *Journal of American Folklore* 108 (430): 395–412. https://doi.org/10.2307/541653.

Glassie, Henry. ca 2006. "Folklore" [Syllabus: FOLK-F 516 Folklore Theory and Practice]. Bloomington: Department of Folklore and Ethnomusicology, Indiana University.

Glassie, Henry. 2011. *A Life in Learning: Henry Glassie.* Charles Homer Haskins Prize Lecture for 2011. ACLS Occasional Paper, 68. New York: American Council of Learned Societies. https://www.acls.org/resources/the-2011-charles-homer-haskins-prize-lecture/.

Goddard, Ives. 1978. "Delaware." In *Handbook of North American Indians.* Vol. 15, *Northeast,* edited by Bruce Trigger, 213–39. Washington, DC: Smithsonian Institution.

Goel, Vindu. 2018. "Ikea Opens First India Store, Tweaking Products but Not the Vibe." *New York Times,* August 7, 2018. https://www.nytimes.com/2018/08/07/business/ikea-first-india-store.html.

Goffman, Erving. 1963. *Behavior in Public Places.* New York: Free Press.

Goffman, Erving. 1971. *Relations in Public: Microstudies of the Public Order.* New York: Basic Books.

Goffman, Erving. 1974. *Frame Analysis: An Essay on the Organization of Experience.* New York: Harper & Row.

Goffman, Erving. 1983. "The Interaction Order: American Sociological Association, 1982 Presidential Address." *American Sociological Review* 48 (1): 1–17. https://doi.org/10.2307/2095141.

Goldenweiser, A. A. 1915. "The Heuristic Value of Traditional Records." *American Anthropologist,* n.s., 17 (4): 763–64. http://www.jstor.org/stable/660000.

Goldfrank, Walter L. 1979. "Introduction: Bringing History Back In." In *The World-System of Capitalism: Past and Present,* edited by Walter L. Goldfrank, 9–17. Beverly Hills, CA: Sage.

González-Martin, Rachel V. 2017. "A Latinx Folklorist's Love Letter to American Folkloristics: Academic Disenchantment and Ambivalent Disciplinary Futures." *Chiricú Journal: Latina/o Literatures, Arts, and Cultures* 2 (1): 19–39. https://doi.org/10.2979/chiricu.2.1.04.

Green, Archie. 1983. "Interpreting Folklore Ideologically." In *Handbook of American Folklore,* edited by Richard M. Dorson, 351–58. Bloomington: Indiana University Press.

Grimm, Jacob. 1881. *Deutsche Rechtsalterthümer.* 3rd ed. Göttingen: Dieterich.

Grimm, Jakob, and Wilhelm Grimm. (1812–14) 1857. *Kinder und Hausmärchen.* 2 vols. 7th ed. Göttingen: Verlag der Dieterichschen Buchhandlung.

Groth, Stefan. 2012. *Negotiating Tradition: The Pragmatics of International Deliberations on Cultural Property.* Göttingen Studies in Cultural Property, 4. Göttingen: Universitätsverlag Göttingen. http://resolver.sub.uni-goettingen.de/purl?isbn-978-3-86395-100-9.

Grumet, Robert S. 1995. *Historic Contact: Indian People and Colonists in Today's Northeastern United States in the Sixteenth through Eighteenth Centuries*. Norman: University of Oklahoma Press.

Guardian. 2018. "Oktoberfest Dirndl: Is It Ever OK to Wear 'Sexy' Versions of Traditional Dress?" September 10, 2018. https://www.theguardian.com/world/2018/sep/10/oktoberfest-dirndl-is-it-ever-ok-to-wear-sexy-versions-of-traditional-dress.

Haase, Donald. 2010. "Decolonizing Fairy-Tale Studies." *Marvels and Tales* 24 (1): 17–38. http://www.jstor.org/stable/41389024.

Hafstein, Valdimar Tr. 2012. "Cultural Heritage." In *A Companion to Folklore*, edited by Regina Bendix and Galit Hasan-Rokem, 500–19. Malden, MA: Blackwell.

Hafstein, Valdimar Tr. 2018a. "Intangible Heritage as a Festival; Or, Folklorization Revisited." *Journal of American Folklore* 131 (520): 127–49. http://www.jstor.org/stable/10.5406/jamerfolk.131.520.0127.

Hafstein, Valdimar Tr. 2018b. *Making Intangible Heritage: El Condor Pasa and Other Stories from UNESCO*. Bloomington: Indiana University Press. https://doi.org/10.2307/j.ctv4v3086.

Haircrow, Red. 2013. "Germany's Obsession with American Indians Is Touching—And Occasionally Surreal." *Indian Country Today*, March 24, 2013. https://web.archive.org/web/20170512060910/https://indiancountrymedianetwork.com/news/indigenous-peoples/germanys-obsession-with-american-indians-is-touchingand-occasionally-surreal/.

Hallowell, A. Irving. 1942. "Some Psychological Aspects of Measurement among the Saulteaux." *American Anthropologist*, n.s., 44 (1): 62–77. http://www.jstor.org/stable/662829.

Hallowell, A. Irving. 1963. "American Indians, White and Black: The Phenomenon of Transculturalization." *Current Anthropology* 4 (5): 519–31. http://www.jstor.org/stable/2739653.

Hannerz, Ulf. 1989. "The Global Ecumene." *Public Culture* 1 (2): 66–75. https://doi.org/10.1215/08992363-1-2-66.

Hansen, Stephen A., and Justin W. VanFleet. 2003. *Traditional Knowledge and Intellectual Property: A Handbook on Issues and Options for Traditional Knowledge Holders in Protecting Their Intellectual Property and Maintaining Biodiversity*. Washington, DC: American Association for the Advancement of Science.

Harkin, Michael E., ed. 2007. *Reassessing Revitalization Movements: Perspectives from North America and the Pacific Islands*. Lincoln: University of Nebraska Press.

Harrah-Johnson, Jeanne. 2020. "The Jewel in the Crown: Hallmarks of Success in Indiana University's Folklore Program." In *Folklore in the United States and Canada: An Institutional History*, edited by Patricia Sawin and Rosemary Lévy Zumwalt, 76–87. Bloomington: Indiana University Press. https://doi.org/10.2307/j.ctv16h2ngc.9.

Hegland, Jane E. 2010. "Ball Dress." In *The Berg Companion to Fashion*, edited by Valerie Steele. Oxford: Bloomsbury Academic. http://dx.doi.org/10.5040/978 1474264716.0001080.

Heidenreich, Conrad E. 1978. "Huron." In *Handbook of North Americas*. Vol. 15, *Northeast*, edited by Bruce Trigger, 368–88. Washington, DC: Smithsonian Institution.

Herzfeld, Michael. 2012. "Nationalism." In *Oxford Bibliographies: Anthropology*. https://doi.org/10.1093/obo/9780199766567-0017.

Hilleary, Cecily. 2017. "Native Americans Decry Appropriation of Their History, Culture." Voice of America, May 4, 2017. https://www.voanews.com/a/native -americans-decry-appropriation-of-their-hist/3837209.html.

Hofer, Tamás. 1984. "The Perception of Tradition in European Ethnology." *Journal of Folklore Research* 21 (2–3): 133–47. http://www.jstor.org/stable/3814549.

Honko, Lauri. 2005. "Folkloristic Theories of Genre." In *Folklore: Critical Concepts in Literary and Cultural Studies*. Vol. 3, *The Genres of Folkore*, edited by Alan Dundes, 3:4–25. New York: Routledge.

Huff, Richard. 2013. "Governmentality." In *Encyclopedia Britannica Online*. London: Encyclopedia Britannica. https://www.britannica.com/topic/governmentality.

Hufford, Mary. n.d. *Tending the Commons: Folklife and Landscape in Southern West Virginia*. Digital Collection, Library of Congress. Accessed December 5, 2018. https://www.loc.gov/collections/folklife-and-landscape-in-southern-west-virginia /about-this-collection/.

Hufford, Mary. 1997. "American Ginseng and the Idea of the Commons." *Folklife Center News* 19 (1–2): 3–18.

Hufford, Mary. 2002. "Reclaiming the Commons: Narratives of Progress, Preservation, and Ginseng." In *Culture, Environment and Conservation in the Appalachian South*, edited by Benita J. Howell, 100–20. Urbana: University of Illinois Press.

Hufford, Mary. 2003. "Knowing Ginseng: The Social Life of an Appalachian Root." *Cahiers de littérature orale* 53–54:265–94.

Hufford, Mary. 2005. "Ramp Suppers, Biodiversity, and the Integrity of "The Mountains"" In *Cornbread Nation III: The Best of Writing about Foods of the Mountain South*, edited by Ronni Lundy, 108–16. Chapel Hill: University of North Carolina Press.

Hufford, Mary. 2006. "Molly Mooching on Bradley Mountain: The Aesthetic Ecology of Appalachian Morels." *Gastronomica: The Journal of Critical Food Studies* 6 (2): 49–56. https://doi.org/10.1525/gfc.2006.6.2.49.

Hufford, Mary, with Dianne Bady, Janet Keating, Laura Forman, and Corinna McMackin. 2011. *Waging Democracy in the Kingdom of Coal: OVEC [Ohio Valley Environmental Coalition] and the Movement for Social and Environmental Justice in Central Appalachia*. Rev. ed. Philadelphia: Mid-Atlantic Ecology Project, Center for Folklore and Ethnography, University of Pennsylvania.

Hurston, Zora Neale. 2018. *Barracoon: The Story of the Last "Black Cargo."* Edited by Deborah G. Plant. New York: Amistad.

Hymes, Dell H. 1974. *Foundations in Sociolinguistics: An Ethnographic Approach.* Philadelphia: University of Pennsylvania Press.

Indiana University. 1949. *Indiana University Bulletin.* Bloomington: Indiana University. [Available in the Indiana University Archives on the Bloomington campus.]

Indiana University Press. 2021. "What Folklorists Do—Book Launch." https://www.youtube.com/watch?v=sjeAo-Csz-8&t=3s.

Interdisziplinäre Forschungsgruppe zu Cultural Property. 2020. "Willkommen /Welcome." http://cultural-property.uni-goettingen.de/.

IPinCH. 2016. "Intellectual Property Issues in Cultural Heritage: Theory, Practice, Policy, Ethics." https://www.sfu.ca/ipinch/.

IRRI Photos. 2009. "A Bowl of Rice." Flickr. https://www.flickr.com/photos /ricephotos/4763103718.

Irvine, Judith T. 2012. "Language Ideology." In *Oxford Bibliographies.* New York: Oxford University Press. https://doi.org/10.1093/OBO/9780199766567-0012.

Ives, Edward D. 1971. *Lawrence Doyle: The Farmer-Poet of Prince Edward Island: A Study in Local Songmaking.* University of Maine Studies, 92. Orono: University of Maine Press.

Ivey, Saundra Keyes. 1977. "Ascribed Ethnicity and the Ethnic Display Event: The Melungeons of Hancock County, Tennessee." *Western Folklore* 36 (1): 85–107. https://doi.org/10.2307/1498216.

Jääts, Indrek. 2019. "Favourite Research Topics of Estonian Ethnographers under Soviet Rule." *Journal of Ethnology and Folkloristics* 13 (2): 1–15. https://doi.org/10.2478/jef-2019-0010.

Jackson, Jason Baird. 1998. "Architecture and Hospitality: Ceremonial Ground Camps and Foodways of the Yuchi Indians." *Chronicles of Oklahoma* 76 (2): 172–89.

Jackson, Jason Baird. 1999. "Indian Territory as a Model of Woodland Social History." Paper presented at the American Society for Ethnohistory Meetings, Mashantucket, CT, October 20–23, 1999.

Jackson, Jason Baird. 2000. "Franz Boas." In *Dictionary of Modern Philosophers*, edited by John R. Shook, 274–76. Bristol: Thoemmes.

Jackson, Jason Baird. 2003a. "The Opposite of Powwow: Ignoring and Incorporating the Intertribal War Dance in the Oklahoma Stomp Dance Community." *Plains Anthropologist* 48 (187): 237–53. http://www.jstor.org /stable/25669843.

Jackson, Jason Baird. 2003b. *Yuchi Ceremonial Life: Performance, Meaning, and Tradition in a Contemporary Native American Community.* Lincoln: University of Nebraska Press.

Jackson, Jason Baird. 2004. "Contesting Culture as Property: Introductory Comments to the Symposium." Digital Library of the Commons. http://hdl.handle.net/10535/562.

Jackson, Jason Baird. 2006a. "Diaspora." In *The Greenwood Encyclopedia of World Folklore*, edited by William M. Clements, 18–22. Westport, CT: Greenwood.

Jackson, Jason Baird. 2006b. "Review of *Who Owns Native Culture?*, by Michael F. Brown." *Journal of American Folklore* 119 (474): 492–93. http://www.jstor.org/stable/4137654.

Jackson, Jason Baird. 2006c. "Tracing the Distribution of a Folktale Motif." *SSILA Newsletter* 24 (4): 3.

Jackson, Jason Baird. 2007. "The Paradoxical Power of Endangerment: Traditional Native American Dance and Music in Eastern Oklahoma." *World Literature Today* 81 (5): 37–41.

Jackson, Jason Baird. 2010. "Boasian Ethnography and Contemporary Intellectual Property Debates." *Proceedings of the American Philosophical Society* 154 (1): 40–49. http://www.jstor.org/stable/20721526.

Jackson, Jason Baird, ed. 2012. *Yuchi Indian Histories Before the Removal Era*. Lincoln: University of Nebraska Press. https://doi.org/10.2307/j.ctt1d9nqx5.

Jackson, Jason Baird. 2013a. "The Story of Colonialism, or Rethinking the Ox-Hide Purchase in Native North America and Beyond." *Journal of American Folklore* 126 (499): 31–54. https://doi.org/10.5406/jamerfolk.126.499.0031.

Jackson, Jason Baird. 2013b. *Yuchi Folklore: Cultural Expression in a Southeastern Native American Community*. Norman: University of Oklahoma Press.

Jackson, Jason Baird. 2014. "Seminole Histories of the Calusa: Dance, Narrative, and Historical Consciousness." *Native South* 7:122–42. https://doi.org/10.1353/nso.2014.0000.

Jackson, Jason Baird. 2018. "Lessons from a Partnership Linking a Network of Chinese and American Museums of Ethnography." Paper presented at the International Committee of Museums and Collections of Ethnography Meetings, Estonian National Museum, Tartu, Estonia, October 9, 2018.

Jackson, Jason Baird. 2019. "At Home and Abroad: Reflections on Collaborative Museum Ethnography at the Mathers Museum of World Cultures." *Museum Anthropology* 42 (2): 62–70. https://doi.org/10.1111/muan.12210.

Jackson, Jason Baird. 2021a. *Cultural Appropriation: A Review of the Literature in US Folklore Studies*. Bloomington, IN: IUScholarWorks Open. https://doi.org/10.5967/y6f5-5x88.

Jackson, Jason Baird. 2021b. "Directing a Museum." In *What Folklorists Do: Professional Possibilities in Folklore Studies*, edited by Timothy Lloyd, 92–95. Bloomington: Indiana University Press.

Jackson, Jason Baird. 2023a. "Collaborative Work in Museum Folklore and Heritage Studies: An Initiative of the American Folklore Society and Its Partners in China and the United States." *Journal of American Folklore* 136 (539): 48–74. https://doi.org/10.5406/15351882.136.539.03.

Jackson, Jason Baird. 2023b. *Syllabus: F516 Folklore Theory in Practice*. Bloomington: Department of Folklore and Ethnomusicology, Indiana University. https://hdl .handle.net/2022/30028.

Jackson, Jason Baird, and Raymond D. Fogelson. 2004. "Introduction." In *Handbook of North American Indians*. Vol. 14, *Southeast*, edited by Raymond D. Fogelson, 1–13. Washington, DC: Smithsonian Institution.

Jackson, Jason Baird, and Victoria Lindsay Levine. 2002. "Singing for Garfish: Music and Woodland Communities in Eastern Oklahoma." *Ethnomusicology* 46 (2): 284–306. https://doi.org/10.2307/852783.

Jackson, Jason Baird, Johannes Müske, and Lijun Zhang. 2020. "Innovation, Habitus, and Heritage: Modeling the Careers of Cultural Forms through Time." *Journal of Folklore Research* 57 (1): 111–36. https://doi.org/10.2979/jfolkrese.57.1.04.

Jacobs, Melville. 1966. "A Look Ahead in Oral Literature Research." *Journal of American Folklore* 79 (313): 413–27. https://doi.org/10.2307/537506.

Jakobson, Roman. 1944. "Franz Boas' Approach to Language." *International Journal of American Linguistics* 10 (4): 188–95. http://www.jstor.org/stable/1262788.

Jakobson, Roman. 1960. "Closing Statement: Linguistics and Poetics." In *Style in Language*, edited by Thomas A. Sebeok, 350–77. Cambridge, MA: MIT Press.

Jakobson, Roman. 1980. "Metalanguage as a Linguistic Problem." In *The Framework of Language*, 81–92. Ann Arbor: Graduate School, University of Michigan.

Jessup, Lynda, Andrew Nurse, and Gordon E. Smith, eds. 2008. *Around and About Marius Barbeau: Modeling Twentieth-Century Culture*. Mercury Series, Cultural Studies Paper 83. Gatineau, QC: Canadian Museum of Civilization.

Johnston, James J. 1976. "Jayhawker Stories: Historical Lore in the Arkansas Ozarks." *Mid-South Folklore* 4:3–10.

Jordan, Michael Paul, and Daniel C. Swan. 2014. "Painting a New Battle Tipi: Public Art, Intellectual Property, and Heritage Construction in a Contemporary Native American Community." *Plains Anthropologist* 56 (219): 195–213. https://doi.org/10.1179/pan.2011.017.

Justice, Daniel Heath. 2016. "A Better World Becoming: Placing Critical Indigenous Studies." In *Critical Indigenous Studies: Engagements in First World Locations*, edited by Aileen Moreton-Robinson, 19–32. Tucson: University of Arizona Press.

Kan, Sergei A., and Pauline Turner Strong, eds. 2006. *New Perspectives on Native North America: Cultures, Histories, and Representations*. Lincoln: University of Nebraska Press.

Kapchan, Deborah A., and Pauline Turner Strong. 1999. "Theorizing the Hybrid." *Journal of American Folklore* 112 (445): 239–53. https://doi.org/doi:10.2307/541360.

Keene, Adrienne. 2014. "Dear Christina Fallin." *Native Appropriations*, March 7, 2014. http://nativeappropriations.com/2014/03/dear-christina-fallin.html.

Keene, Adrienne. 2020. *Native Appropriations*. http://nativeappropriations.com/.

Kelty, Chris. 2006. "Universal Internets: Hubs and Routers of Encounter across Difference." Paper presented at the 2006 American Anthropological Association Annual Meeting, San Jose, CA, November 14–19, 2006. https://kelty.org/or/papers/unpublishable/Kelty_Tsing-AAA06.pdf.

Kenny, Erin. 2007. "Bellydance in the Town Square: Leaking Peace through Tribal Style Identity." *Western Folklore* 66 (3–4): 301–27. http://www.jstor.org/stable/25474870.

Kirshenblatt-Gimblett, Barbara. 1983. "Studying Immigrant and Ethnic Folklore." In *Handbook of American Folklore*, edited by Richard M. Dorson, 39–47. Bloomington: Indiana University Press.

Kirshenblatt-Gimblett, Barbara. 1988. "Mistaken Dichotomies." *Journal of American Folklore* 101 (400): 140–55. https://doi.org/10.2307/540105.

Kirshenblatt-Gimblett, Barbara. 1995. "Theorizing Heritage." *Ethnomusicology* 39 (3): 367–80. https://doi.org/10.2307/924627.

Kirshenblatt-Gimblett, Barbara. 1998a. "Folklore's Crisis." *Journal of American Folklore* 111 (441): 281–327. https://doi.org/10.2307/541312.

Kirshenblatt-Gimblett, Barbara. 1998b. "Sounds of Sensibility." *Judaism* 47 (1): 49–78.

Kirshenblatt-Gimblett, Barbara. 2004. "Intangible Heritage as Metacultural Production." *Museum International* 56 (1–2): 52–65. http://dx.doi.org/10.1111/j.1350-0775.2004.00458.x.

Kirshenblatt-Gimblett, Barbara. 2006. "World Heritage and Cultural Economics." In *Museum Frictions: Public Cultures/Global Transformations*, edited by Ivan Karp, Corinne A. Kratz, Lynn Szwaja, and Tomas Ybarra-Frausto, 161–202. Durham, NC: Duke University Press.

Klassen, Teri. 2009. "Representations of African American Quiltmaking: From Omission to High Art." *Journal of American Folklore* 122 (485): 297–334. http://www.jstor.org/stable/40390070.

Klein, Barbro. 2001. "Folklore." In *International Encyclopedia of the Social and Behavioral Sciences*, 5711–15. New York: Elsevier.

Kniffen, Fred, and Henry Glassie. 1966. "Building in Wood in the Eastern United States: A Time-Place Perspective." *Geographical Review* 56 (1): 40–66. https://doi.org/10.2307/212734.

Köhler, Reinhold. 1864. "Sagen von Landerwerbung durch zershnittene Häute." *Orient und Occident* 3:185–87.

Köhler, Reinhold. 1900. *Kleinere Schriften von Reinhold Köhler*. Vol. 2. Edited by Johannes Bolte. Weimar: Verlag von Emil Felber.

Kraft, Herbert C. 1986. *The Lenape: Archaeology, History and Ethnography*. Newark: New Jersey Historical Society.

Kroeber, A. L. 1931. "Review of *Tepoztlan: A Mexican Village*, by Robert Redfield." *American Anthropologist*, n.s., 33 (2): 236–38. http://www.jstor.org/stable/660844.

Kroeber, Alfred L. 1948. *Anthropology: Race, Language, Culture, Psychology, Prehistory*. Rev. ed. New York: Harcourt, Brace.

Kuhn, Thomas S. 1996. *The Structure of Scientific Revolutions*. 3rd ed. Chicago: University of Chicago Press.

Kuutma, Kristin. 2013. "Between Arbitration and Engineering: Concepts and Contingencies in the Shaping of Heritage Regimes." In *Heritage Regimes and the State*, edited by Regna Bendix, Aditya Eggert, and Arnika Peselmann, 21–36. Göttingen Studies in Cultural Property, 6. Göttingen: Universitätsverlag Göttingen. http://resolver.sub.uni-goettingen.de/purl?isbn-978-3-86395-122-1.

Kuutma, Kristin. 2016. "From Folklore to Intangible Cultural Heritage." In *A Companion to Heritage Studies*, edited by William Logan, Máiréad Nic Craith, and Ullrich Kockel, 41–54. Malden, MA: Wiley.

Laudun, John. 2006. "Oikotypification." In *Encyclopedia of World Folklore and Folklife*, edited by William Clements, 67–68. London: Greenwood.

Lee, Richard E. 2014. "Disciplines and the University." *Review* 37 (1): 61–80. https://www.jstor.org/stable/90007843.

Lesser, Alexander. (1933) 1977. *The Pawnee Ghost Dance Hand Game: Ghost Dance Revival and Ethnic Identity*. Madison: University of Wisconsin Press.

Lesser, Alexander. 1985. *History, Evolution, and the Concept of Culture: Selected Papers of Alexander Lesser*. Edited by Sidney W. Mintz. New York: Cambridge University Press.

Lévi-Strauss, Claude. 1969. *The Raw and the Cooked*. Translated by John and Doreen Weightman. New York: Harper & Row.

Lévi-Strauss, Claude. 1973. *From Honey to Ashes*. Translated by John and Doreen Weightman. New York: Harper & Row.

Lévi-Strauss, Claude. 1978. *The Origin of Table Manners*. Translated by John and Doreen Weightman. New York: Harper & Row.

Lévi-Strauss, Claude. 1981. *The Naked Man*. Translated by John and Doreen Weightman. New York: Harper & Row.

Lévi-Strauss, Claude. 1982. *The Way of the Masks*. Translated by Sylvia Modelski. Seattle: University of Washington Press.

Limón, José E. 1983. "Western Marxism and Folklore: A Critical Introduction." *Journal of American Folklore* 96 (379): 34–52. https://doi.org/10.2307/539833.

Linn, Mary S., and Jason Baird Jackson. 2004. "Yuchi Trickster Tales." In *Voices from Four Directions: Contemporary Translations of the Native Literatures of North America*, edited by Brian Swann, 368–82. Lincoln: University of Nebraska Press.

Lloyd, Timothy, ed. 2021. *What Folklorists Do: Professional Possibilities in Folklore Studies*. Bloomington: Indiana University Press.

Löfgren, Orvar, and Richard Wilk, eds. 2006. *Off the Edge: Experiments in Cultural Analysis*. Copenhagen: Museum Tusculanum Press.

Lord, Albert. 1960. *The Singer of Tales*. Harvard Studies in Comparative Literature, 24. Cambridge, MA: Harvard University Press.

Lord, Albert. 1965. "Yugoslav Epic Folk Poetry." In *The Study of Folklore*, edited by Alan Dundes, 265–68. Englewood Cliffs, NJ: Prentice Hall.

Lowie, Robert. 1915. "Oral Tradition and History." *American Anthropologist*, n.s., 17 (3): 597–99. http://www.jstor.org/stable/660515.

Lowie, Robert. 1917. "Oral Tradition and History." *Journal of American Folklore* 30 (116): 161–67. https://doi.org/10.2307/534336.

Lowie, Robert H. 1928. "Incorporeal Property in Primitive Society." *Yale Law Journal* 37 (5): 551–63. https://doi.org/10.2307/790747.

Lowie, Robert H. 1940. *An Introduction to Cultural Anthropology*. 2nd ed. New York: Farrar & Rinehart.

Luo Yu. 2018a. "Alternative Indigeneity in China? The Paradox of the Buyi in the Age of Ethnic Branding." *Verge: Studies in Global Asias* 4 (2): 107–34.

Luo Yu. 2018b. "An Alternative to the 'Indigenous' in Early Twenty-First-Century China: Guizhou's Branding of Yuanshengtai." *Modern China* 44 (1): 68–102.

Lynskey, Dorian. 2014. "This Means War: Why the Fashion Headdress Must Be Stopped." *Guardian*, July 30, 2014. https://www.theguardian.com/fashion/2014/jul/30/why-the-fashion-headdress-must-be-stopped.

Maags, Christina, and Marina Svensson, eds. 2018. *Chinese Cultural Heritage in the Making: Experiences, Negotiations, and Contestations*. Amsterdam: Amsterdam University Press.

MacDowell, Marsha, and Lijun Zhang, eds. 2016. *Quilts of Southwest China*. Nanning: Guangxi Museum of Nationalities. [Distributed by Bloomington: Indiana University Press.]

Magliocco, Sabina. 2004. *Witching Culture: Folklore and Neo-Paganism in America*. Philadelphia: University of Pennsylvania Press.

Magliocco, Sabina. 2009. "Reclamation, Appropriation and the Ecstatic Imagination in Modern Pagan Ritual." In *Handbook of Contemporary Paganism*, edited by Murphy Pizza and James R. Lewis, 223–40. Leiden: Brill.

Marcus, George E. 1986. "Ethnography in the Modern World System." In *Writing Culture: The Poetics and Politics of Ethnography*, edited by James Clifford and George E. Marcus, 165–93. Berkeley: University of California Press.

Marcus, George E. 1995. "Ethnography in/of the World System: The Emergence of Multi-Sited Ethnography." *Annual Review of Anthropology* 24:95–117. https://doi.org/10.1146/annurev.an.24.100195.000523.

Mauss, Marcel. 1979. "Body Techniques." In *Psychology and Sociology*, translated by Ben Brewster, 97–123. London: Routledge & Kegan Paul.

May, Sarah, Katia Laura Sidali, Achim Spiller, and Bernhard Tschofen, eds. 2017. *Taste—Power—Tradition: Geographical Indications as Cultural Property.*

Göttingen Studies in Cultural Property, 10. Göttingen: Universitätsverlag Göttingen. http://library.oapen.org/handle/20.500.12657/31866.

Mayor, Adrienne. 1995. "The Nessus Shirt in the New World: Smallpox Blankets in History and Legend." *Journal of American Folklore* 108 (427): 54–77. https://doi.org/10.2307/541734.

McCartney, Eugene S. 1927. "Popular Methods of Measuring." *Classical Journal* 22 (5): 325–44. http://www.jstor.org/stable/3288475.

McConnell, Michael N. 1992. *A Country Between: The Upper Ohio Valley and Its Peoples, 1724–1774.* Lincoln: University of Nebraska Press.

McDowell, John H. 2010. "Rethinking Folklorization in Ecuador: Multivocality in the Expressive Contact Zone." *Western Folklore* 69 (2): 181–209. http://www.jstor.org/stable/27896341.

Mead, Margaret. 1929. "Review of *Orokaiva Magic*, by F. E. Williams." *American Anthropologist*, n.s., 31 (3): 528–31. http://www.jstor.org/stable/661284.

Mechling, Jay. 1997. "Folklore and the Civil Sphere." *Western Folklore* 56 (2): 113–37. https://doi.org/10.2307/1500202.

Mekeel, Scudder. 1932. "A Discussion of Culture Change as Illustrated by Material from a Teton-Dakota Community." *American Anthropologist*, n.s., 34 (2): 274–85. http://www.jstor.org/stable/661656.

Mendoza, Zoila S. 2000. *Shaping Society through Dance: Mestizo Ritual Performance in the Peruvian Andes.* Chicago: University of Chicago Press.

Merrell, James H. 1999. *Into the American Woods: Negotiators on the Pennsylvania Frontier.* New York: W. W. Norton.

Merriam-Webster. 2018. "Model." *Merriam-Webster.com.* https://www.merriam-webster.com/dictionary/model.

Miller, Jay. 1975. "Kwulakan: The Delaware Side of Their Movement West." *Pennsylvania Archaeologist* 45 (4): 45–46.

Mintz, Sidney W. 1985a. "Introduction to Part II." In *History, Evolution, and the Concept of Culture: Selected Papers of Alexander Lesser,* edited by Sidney W. Mintz, 45–52. New York: Cambridge University Press.

Mintz, Sidney W. 1985b. *Sweetness and Power: The Place of Sugar in Modern World History.* New York: Penguin.

Moon, Louise. 2018. "Chinese Dress at US Prom Wins Support in China after Internet Backlash." *South China Morning Post*, May 1, 2018. https://www.scmp.com/news/china/society/article/2144207/qipao-us-prom-wins-support-china-after-internet-backlash.

Moore, Robert E. 1999. "Endangered." *Journal of Linguistic Anthropology* 9 (1–2): 65–68.

Morales, Selina, and Maribel Alvarez. 2022. "10 Lessons in Community Love." *Journal of American Folklore* 135 (536): 164–79. https://doi.org/10.5406/153518 82.135.536.04.

Moreton-Robinson, Aileen. 2017. "Relationality: A Key Presupposition of an Indigenous Social Research Paradigm." In *Sources and Methods in Indigenous Studies*, edited by Chris Andersen and Jean M. O'Brien, 69–77. New York: Routledge.

Morissonneau, Christian. 1978. "Huron of Lorette." In *Handbook of North Americas.* Vol. 15, *Northeast*, edited by Bruce Trigger, 389–93. Washington, DC: Smithsonian Institution.

Mould, Tom. 2003. *Choctaw Prophecy: A Legacy for the Future.* Tuscaloosa: University of Alabama Press.

Muldoon, James. 2019. "Academics: It's Time to Get Behind Decolonising the Curriculum." *Guardian*, March 20, 2019. https://www.theguardian.com/education/2019/mar/20/academics-its-time-to-get-behind-decolonising-the-curriculum.

Murg, Wilhelm. 2014. "Christina Fallin, in Her Own Words: 'I'm Tired of the Misinformation.'" *Indian Country Today*, May 2, 2014. https://web.archive.org/web/20170909062821/https://indiancountrymedianetwork.com/culture/arts-entertainment/christina-fallin-in-her-own-words-im-tired-of-themis information/.

Müske, Johannes. 2015. *Klänge als Cultural Property: Technik und die kulturelle Aneignung der Klangwelt* [Sounds as Cultural Property: Technology and the Cultural Appropriation of the Soundworld]. Zürich: Chronos. https://doi.org/10.5167/uzh-111069.

Nabokov, Peter. 2002. *A Forest of Time: American Indian Ways of History.* New York: Cambridge University Press.

Naithani, Sadhana. 1997. "The Colonizer-Folklorist." *Journal of Folklore Research* 34 (1): 1–14. http://www.jstor.org/stable/3814697.

Naithani, Sadhana. 2001a. "An Axis Jump: British Colonialism in the Oral Folk Narratives of Nineteenth-Century India." *Folklore* 112 (2): 183–88. http://www.jstor.org/stable/1260831.

Naithani, Sadhana. 2001b. "Prefaced Space: Tales of the Colonial British Collectors of Indian Folklore." In *Imagined States: Nationalism, Utopia, and Longing in Oral Cultures*, edited by Luisa Del Giudice and Gerald Porter, 64–79. Logan: Utah State University Press. https://digitalcommons.usu.edu/usupress_pubs/60/.

Naithani, Sadhana. 2002. "To Tell a Tale Untold: Two Folklorists in Colonial India." *Journal of Folklore Research* 39 (2–3): 201–16. http://www.jstor.org/stable/3814691.

Naithani, Sadhana. 2004. [Excerpt from] Colonial Hegemony and Oral Discourse. *Indian Folklife* 3 (2): 10. https://indianfolklore.org/index.php/if/issue/view/17/17.

Naithani, Sadhana. 2006. "Colonial Hegemony and Oral Discourse." In *Folklore as Discourse*, edited by M. D. Muthukumaraswamy, 50–60. Chennai: National Folklore Support Centre.

Naithani, Sadhana. 2008. "Colonialism." In *The Greenwood Encyclopedia of Folktales and Fairy Tales*, edited by Donald Haase, 222–26. Westport, CT: Greenwood.

Naithani, Sadhana. 2010. *The Story-Time of the British Empire: Colonial and Post-colonial Folkloristics*. Jackson: University Press of Mississippi. https://muse.jhu.edu/book/1328/.

Narayan, Kirin. 1993. "Banana Republics and V. I. Degrees: Rethinking Indian Folklore in a Postcolonial World." *Asian Folklore Studies* 52 (1): 177–204. https://doi.org/10.2307/1178456.

Native America Calling. 2020. "Search Results for Appropriation." Archive. https://nativeamericacalling.com/?s=cultural+appropriation.

Nicholas, George. 2018. "Confronting the Specter of Cultural Appropriation." *Sapiens*, October 5. https://www.sapiens.org/culture/cultural-appropriation-halloween/.

Nowry, Laurence. 1998. *Man of Mana: Marius Barbeau, a Biography*. Toronto: NC Press.

Noyes, Dorothy. 1995. "Group." *Journal of American Folklore* 108 (430): 449–78. https://doi.org/10.2307/541656.

Noyes, Dorothy. 2003. *Fire on the Plaça: Catalan Festival Politics after Franco*. Philadelphia: University of Pennsylvania Press.

Noyes, Dorothy. 2004. "Folklore." In *The Social Science Encyclopedia*, edited by Adam Kuper and Jessica Kuper, 375–78. New York: Routledge.

Noyes, Dorothy. 2006. "Colonization and Narrative Migrations." [Conference prospectus for an event held May 12, 2006, at The Ohio State University under the sponsorship of the Center for Folklore Studies at The Ohio State University.] http://cfs.osu.edu/activities/conferences/fy2006/colonization_narrative.

Noyes, Dorothy. 2007. "Voice in the Provinces: Submission, Recognition, and the Making of Heritage." In *Prädikat "Heritage": Wertschöpfungen aus kulturellen Ressourcen*, edited by Dorothee Hemme, Markus Tauschek, and Regina Bendix, 33–52. Berlin: Lit Verlag.

Noyes, Dorothy. 2008. "Humble Theory." *Journal of Folklore Research* 45 (1): 37–43. https://www.jstor.org/stable/40206962.

Noyes, Dorothy. 2009. "Tradition: Three Traditions." *Journal of Folklore Research* 46 (3): 233–68. https://doi.org/10.2979/jfr.2009.46.3.233.

Noyes, Dorothy. 2012. "The Social Base of Folklore." In *A Companion to Folklore*, edited by Regina F. Bendix and Galit Hasan-Rokem, 13–39. Malden, MA: Wiley-Blackwell. https://doi.org/10.1002/9781118379936.ch1.

Noyes, Dorothy. 2014a. "From Heritage to Sustainability to Resilience: Compromised Concepts in Rising Waters." Paper presented at the colloquium "Sustainable Pluralism: Linguistic and Cultural Resilience in Multiethnic Societies." Mershon Center for International Security Studies, The Ohio State University, September 5, 2014.

Noyes, Dorothy. 2014b. "Heritage, Legacy, Zombie: How to Bury the Undead Past." In *Cultural Heritage in Transit: Intangible Rights as Human Rights,* edited by Deborah A. Kapchan, 58–86. Philadelphia: University of Pennsylvania Press. https://doi.org/10.9783/9780812209464.58.

Noyes, Dorothy. 2016. *Humble Theory: Folklore's Grasp on Social Life.* Bloomington: Indiana University Press. https://doi.org/10.2307/j.ctt1zxz0bs.

Noyes, Dorothy. 2019. "'Incalculably Diffusive': Revisiting the Disciplinary Deficit (A Response to Elliott Oring)." *Journal of American Folklore* 132 (524): 175–84. https://doi.org/10.5406/jamerfolk.132.524.0175.

Noyes, Dorothy, and David Staley. 2024. "Dorothy Noyes: Folklore, Exemplarity and Politics." *Voices of Excellence* (blog), May 14, 2024. https://podcast.osu.edu/voices-of-excellence/dorothy-noyes-folklore-exemplarity-and-politics/.

Nurse, Andrew. 2001. "'But Now Things Have Changed': Marius Barbeau and the Politics of Amerindian Identity." *Ethnohistory* 48 (3): 433–72. https://www.muse.jhu.edu/article/11742.

Ó Giolláin, Diarmuid. 2017. "Province, Nation and Empire: The Remit of Folklore Studies." In *Mapping the History of Folklore Studies: Centres, Borderlands and Shared Spaces,* edited by Dace Bula and Sandis Laime, 207–22. Newcastle-upon-Tyne: Cambridge Scholars Publishing.

The Ohio State University. 2022. "Noyes Named Director of Mershon Center." College News, March 25, 2022. https://web.archive.org/web/20220629152841/https://artsandsciences.osu.edu/news/noyes-director-mershon-center.

Oring, Elliott. 1998. "Anti Anti-'Folklore.'" *Journal of American Folklore* 111 (441): 328–38. https://doi.org/10.2307/541313.

Oring, Elliott. 2019a. "Back to the Future: Questions for Theory in the Twenty-First Century." *Journal of American Folklore* 132 (524): 137–56. https://doi.org/10.5406/jamerfolk.132.524.0137.

Oring, Elliott. 2019b. "Questions about Questions: A Response to Robert Baron, Dorothy Noyes, and John D. Dorst." *Journal of American Folklore* 132 (524): 185–94. https://doi.org/10.5406/jamerfolk.132.524.0185.

Ortiz, Fernando. (1947) 1995. *Cuban Counterpoint: Tobacco and Sugar.* Durham, NC: Duke University Press.

Otero, Solimar. 2020. *Archives of Conjure: Stories of the Dead in Afrolatinx Cultures.* New York: Columbia University Press.

Otero, Solimar, and Mintzi Auanda Martínez-Rivera. 2021a. "Introduction: How Does Folklore Find Its Voice in the Twenty-First Century?" In *Theorizing Folklore from the Margins: Critical and Ethical Approaches,* edited by Solimar Otero and Mintzi Auanda Martínez-Rivera, 3–21. Bloomington: Indiana University Press.

Otero, Solimar, and Mintzi Auanda Martínez-Rivera, eds. 2021b. *Theorizing Folklore from the Margins: Critical and Ethical Approaches.* Bloomington: Indiana University Press.

Oxford English Dictionary Online. 1989. 2nd ed. Oxford: Oxford University Press.

Oxford English Dictionary Online. 2023. Oxford: Oxford University Press.

Paredes, Américo. 1958. *"With His Pistol in His Hand": A Border Ballad and Its Hero.* Austin: University of Texas Press.

Paredes, Américo. (1973) 1993. "José Mosqueda and the Folklorization of Actual Events." In *Folklore and Culture on the Texas-Mexican Border,* edited by Richard Bauman, 177–214. Austin: University of Texas Press.

Parsley, Jon Keith. 1993. "Regulation of Counterfeit Indian Arts and Crafts: An Analysis of the Indian Arts and Crafts Act of 1990." *American Indian Law Review* 18 (2): 487–514. https://doi.org/10.2307/20068750.

Powell, J. U. 1933. "Byrsa, the Bull's Hide, at Carthage, and Some Parallels." *Folklore* 44 (3): 310–15. http://www.jstor.org/stable/1256435.

Prahlad, Anand. 2021. "Tearing Down Monuments: Missed Opportunities, Silences, and Absences—A Radical Look at Race in American Folklore Studies." *Journal of American Folklore* 134 (533): 258–64. https://doi.org/10.5406/jamerfolk.134.533.0258.

Pratt, Mary Louise. 1991. "Arts of the Contact Zone." *Profession* (1991): 33–40. http://www.jstor.org/stable/25595469.

Primiano, Leonard Norman. 1995. "Vernacular Religion and the Search for Method in Religious Folklife." *Western Folklore* 54 (1): 37–56. https://doi.org/10.2307/1499910.

Pringle, Paul, and Adam Elmahrek. 2019. "Native American Minority Contracts Are Under Scrutiny as Officials Vow Strict Enforcement." *Los Angeles Times,* July 2, 2019. https://www.latimes.com/local/lanow/la-me-ln-native-american-minority-contracts-cherokee-20190702-story.html.

Qin, Amy. 2018. "Teenager's Prom Dress Stirs Furor in U.S.—But Not in China." *New York Times,* May 2, 2018. https://www.nytimes.com/2018/05/02/world/asia/chinese-prom-dress.html.

Rabinow, Paul. 2008. "Concept Work." In *Biosocialities, Genetics and the Social Sciences: Making Biologies and Identities,* edited by Sahra Gibbon and Carlos Novas, 188–92. New York: Routledge.

Rabinow, Paul. 2018. "Apologia of a Crucible of Experience and Experimentation: Chronicle of the Anthropology of the Contemporary 2004–2018." *SNAFU.* https://web.archive.org/web/20220706201329/https://www.snafu.dog/arc-a-chronicle/.

Rabinow, Paul, and George Marcus with James D. Faubion and Tobias Rees. 2008. *Designs for an Anthropology of the Contemporary.* Durham, NC: Duke University Press.

Rabinow, Paul, and Anthony Stavrianakis. 2016. "Movement Space: Putting Anthropological Theory, Concepts, and Cases to the Test." *HAU: Journal of Ethnographic Theory* 6 (1): 403–31. https://doi.org/10.14318/hau6.1.021.

Radcliffe-Brown, A. R. 1952. *Structure and Function in Primitive Society: Essays and Addresses*. Glencoe, IL: Free Press.

Radin, Paul. 1956. *The Trickster: A Study of Native American Mythology*. New York: Philosophical Library. http://hdl.handle.net/2027/inu.30000118310030.

Redfield, Robert. 1934. "Culture Changes in Yucatan." *American Anthropologist*, n.s., 36 (1): 57–69. http://www.jstor.org/stable/661757.

Redfield, Robert, Ralph Linton, and Melville J. Herskovits. 1936. "Memorandum for the Study of Acculturation." *American Anthropologist*, n.s., 38 (1): 149–52. http://www.jstor.org/stable/662563.

Rees, Tobias. 2007. "Concept Work and Collaboration in the Anthropology of the Contemporary." *ARC Exchange* 1. https://web.archive.org/web/20170705054539/http://anthropos-lab.net/wp/publications/2007/08/exchangeno1.pdf. [For the remains of the ARC website in the Internet Archive, see https://web.archive.org/web/20240000000000*/http://anthropos-lab.net/.]

Rementer, Jim. 2005. "The Arrival of the Whites." In *Algonquian Spirit: Contemporary Translations of the Algonquian Literatures of North America*, edited by Brian Swann, 49–61. Lincoln: University of Nebraska Press.

Richardson, Thomas Grant, Jon Kay, Maida Owens, and Tim Frandy. 2023. "'Urgencies' in the Field: Three Perspectives." *Journal of American Folklore* 136 (540): 181–98. https://doi.org/10.5406/15351882.136.540.03.

Roberts, John W. 2021. "Systemic Racism in American Folkloristics." *Journal of American Folklore* 134 (533): 265–71. https://doi.org/10.5406/jamerfolk.134.533.0265.

Rodgers, Susan. 2003. "Folklore with a Vengeance: A Sumatran Literature of Resistance in the Colonial Indies and New Order Indonesia." *Journal of American Folklore* 116 (460): 129–58. http://www.jstor.org/stable/4137895.

Rogers, Everett M. 2003. *Diffusion of Innovations*. 5th ed. New York: Free Press.

Rojas, Carlos Antonio Aguirre. 2012. "The World-Systems Analysis Perspective: An Interview with Immanuel Wallerstein." In *Uncertain Worlds: World-Systems Analysis in Changing Times*, edited by Immanuel Wallerstein, Carlos Antonio Aguirre Rojas, and Charles Lemert, 1–100. Boulder: Paradigm.

Rose, H. J. 1929. *A Handbook of Greek Mythology, Including Its Extension to Rome*. New York: E. P. Dutton.

Rossman, Sean. 2018a. "Chinese Are OK with Utah Teen's Controversial Cheongsam Prom Dress." *USA Today*, May 4, 2018. https://www.usatoday.com/story/news/nation-now/2018/05/04/chinese-ok-utah-teens-controversial-cheongsam-prom-dress/580062002/.

Rossman, Sean. 2018b. "Chinese Prom Dress Draws Rage, but Utah Student Said She Meant No Harm." *USA Today*, May 2, 2018. https://www.usatoday.com/story/news/nation-now/2018/05/01/chinese-prom-dress-draws-rage-but-utah-studentsaid-she-meant-no-harm/567846002/.

Sacks, Howard L. 1997. "Review of *When We Were Good: The Folk Revival*, by Robert Cantwell." *Journal of American Folklore* 110 (435): 103–105. https://www.jstor.org/stable/541598.

Sahlins, Marshall. 1993. "Goodby to Tristes Tropes: Ethnography in the Context of Modern World History." *Journal of Modern History* 65 (1): 1–25. http://www.jstor.org/stable/2124813.

Sahlins, Marshall. 1999. "What Is Anthropological Enlightenment? Some Lessons of the Twentieth Century." *Annual Review of Anthropology* 28:i–xxiii. https://doi.org/10.1146/annurev.anthro.28.1.0.

Sahlins, Marshall. 2000. "Cosmologies of Capitalism: The Trans-Pacific Sector of 'The World System.'" In *Culture in Practice: Selected Essays*, 415–69. New York: Zone Books.

Samper, David. 2002. "Cannibalizing Kids: Rumor and Resistance in Latin America." *Journal of Folklore Research* 39 (1): 1–32. http://www.jstor.org/stable/3814829.

Schieffelin, Edward L., and Robert Crittenden. 1991. *Like People You See in a Dream: First Contact in Six Papuan Societies*. Stanford, CA: Stanford University Press.

Schmidt, Samantha. 2018. "'It's Just a Dress': Teen's Chinese Prom Attire Stirs Cultural Appropriation Debate." *Washington Post*, May 1, 2018. https://www.washingtonpost.com/news/morning-mix/wp/2018/05/01/its-just-a-dress-teens-chinese-prom-attire-stirs-cultural-appropriation-debate/?utm_term=.4e28e2196814/.

Scott, James C. 1987. *Weapons of the Weak: Everyday Forms of Peasant Resistance*. New Haven, CT: Yale University Press.

Scott, James C. 1998. *Seeing Like a State: How Certain Schemes to Improve the Human Condition Have Failed*. New Haven, CT: Yale University Press.

Scott, James C. 2012. *Two Cheers for Anarchism: Six Easy Pieces on Autonomy, Dignity, and Meaningful Work and Play*. Princeton, NJ: Princeton University Press.

Seely, Taylor, and Sean Rossman. 2018. "Mom of Utah Teen Who Wore Controversial Chinese Dress Explains Prom Photos." *USA Today*, May 2, 2018. https://www.usatoday.com/story/news/nation-now/2018/05/02/mom-girl-controversial-chinese-dress-cheongsam-prom-photos/572827002/.

Seljamaa, Elo-Hanna, and Pihla Maria Siim. 2016. "Where Silence Takes Us, If We Listen to It." *Ethnologia Europaea* 46 (2): 5–13. https://doi.org/10.16995/ee.1184.

Shuman, Amy. 1993. "Dismantling Local Culture." *Western Folklore* 52 (2–4): 345–64. https://doi.org/10.2307/1500094.

Shuman, Amy. 2005. *Other People's Stories: Entitlement Claims and the Critique of Empathy*. Urbana: University of Illinois Press.

Shuman, Amy, and Galit Hasan-Rokem. 2012. "The Poetics of Folklore." In *A Companion to Folklore*, edited by Regina F. Bendix and Galit Hasan-Rokem, 55–74. Malden, MA: Blackwell.

SIEF (Société Internationale d'Ethnologie et de Folklore). 2014. "What Is European Ethnology?" https://www.siefhome.org/videos/euro_ethno.shtml.

SIEF (Société Internationale d'Ethnologie et de Folklore). 2017. "What Do Ethnologists Do?" https://vimeo.com/237142052.

SIEF (Société Internationale d'Ethnologie et de Folklore). 2022. "Ethnological Sensations" [digital project]. Amsterdam: Société Internationale d'Ethnologie et de Folklore. https://www.siefhome.org/videos/ethno_sensations.

Silverstein, Michael. 1979. "Language Structure and Linguistic Ideology." In *The Elements: A Parasession on Linguistic Units and Levels,* edited by Paul R. Cline, William F. Hanks, and Carol L. Hofbauer, 193–247. Chicago: Chicago Linguistic Society.

Silverstein, Michael. 1981. "The Limits of Awareness." *Sociolinguistic Working Paper,* 84. https://eric.ed.gov/?id=ED250941.

Simpson, George Eaton. 1968. "Assimilation." In *International Encyclopedia of the Social Sciences,* edited by David I. Sills, vol. 1, 438–43. New York: Macmillan and the Free Press.

Skrydstrup, Martin. 2012. "Cultural Property." In *A Companion to Folklore,* edited by Regina F. Bendix and Galit Hasan-Rokem, 520–36. Malden, MA: Blackwell.

Spicer, Edward H. 1962. *Cycles of Conquest: The Impact of Spain, Mexico, and the United States on the Indians of the Southwest, 1533–1960.* Tucson: University of Arizona Press.

Spicer, Edward H. 1968. "Acculturation." In *International Encyclopedia of the Social Sciences,* edited by David I. Sills, vol. 1, 21–27. New York: Macmillan and the Free Press.

Stavrianakis, Anthony, and Gaymon Bennett. 2012. "On Concept Work." *Somatosphere,* September 25, 2012. http://somatosphere.net/2012/09/on-concept-work.html.

Stein, Gil, ed. 2005. *Archaeology of Colonial Encounters: Comparative Perspectives.* Santa Fe, NM: School of American Research Press.

Steward, Julian H. 1932. "A Uintah Ute Bear Dance, March, 1931." *American Anthropologist,* n.s., 34 (2): 263–73. http://www.jstor.org/stable/661655.

Steward, Julian H. 1955. *Theory of Culture Change: The Methodology of Multilinear Evolution.* Urbana: University of Illinois Press.

Stewart, Susan. 1991. "Notes on Distressed Genres." *Journal of American Folklore* 104 (411): 5–31. https://doi.org/10.2307/541131.

Stocking, George W. 1965. "On the Limits of 'Presentism' and 'Historicism' in the Historiography of the Behavioral Sciences." *Journal of the History of the Behavioral Sciences* 1 (3): 211–18. https://doi.org/10.1002/1520-6696(196507)1:3<211::AID-JHBS2300010302>3.0.CO;2-W.

Stocking, George W., ed. 1998. *Volksgeist as Method and Ethic: Essays on Boasian Ethnography and the German Anthropological Tradition.* Madison: University of Wisconsin Press.

Stocking, George W. 2010. *Glimpses into My Own Black Box: An Exercise in Self-Deconstruction.* Madison: University of Wisconsin Press. https://muse.jhu.edu /pub/19/monograph/book/1198.

Stoler, Ann, and Alex Golub. 2014. "Doing Concept Work: An Interview with Ann Stoler about the Institute for Critical Social Inquiry." *Savage Minds,* December 19, 2014. https://savageminds.org/2014/12/19/doing-concept -work-an-interview-with-ann-stoler-about-the-institute-for-critical-social -inquiry/.

Strauss, Sarah. 2002. "The Master's Narrative: Swami Sivananda and the Transnational Production of Yoga." *Journal of Folklore Research* 39 (2–3): 217–41. http:// www.jstor.org/stable/3814692.

Strong, Duncan. 1936. "Review of *The Pawnee Ghost Dance Handgame,* by Alexander Lesser." *American Anthropologist,* n.s., 38 (1): 112–13. http://www.jstor.org /stable/662540.

Sturm, Circe. 2011. *Becoming Indian: The Struggle over Cherokee Identity in the Twenty-First Century.* Santa Fe, NM: School of Advanced Research Press.

Sturtevant, William C. 1953. "Chakaika and the 'Spanish Indians': Documentary Sources Compared with Seminole Tradition." *Tequesta* 13:35–73. https://dpanther.fiu.edu/dpanther/items/itemdetail?bibid=FI18050900& vid=00013.

Sugden, John. 1999. *Tecumseh: A Life.* New York: Henry Holt.

Swan, Daniel C., and Michael Paul Jordan. 2015. "Contingent Collaborations: Patterns of Reciprocity in Museum-Community Partnerships." *Journal of Folklore Research* 52 (1): 39–84. https://doi.org/10.2979/jfolkrese.52.1.39.

Swanton, John R. 1907. "A Concordance of American Myths." *Journal of American Folklore* 20 (78): 220–22. https://doi.org/10.2307/534410.

Swanton, John R. 1910. "Some Practical Aspects of the Study of Myths." *Journal of American Folklore* 23 (87): 1–7. https://doi.org/10.2307/534319.

Swanton, John R. 1915. "Dr. Swanton's Reply." *American Anthropologist,* n.s., 17 (3): 600. http://www.jstor.org/stable/660517.

Swanton, John R. 1928. "Social Organization and Social Usages of the Indians of the Creek Confederacy." In *Forty-Second Annual Report of the Bureau of American Ethnology,* 23–472. Washington, DC: Government Printing Office. http://www .archive.org/details/annualreportofbu42smithso.

Swedberg, Richard. 2017. "How to Use Max Weber's Ideal Type in Sociological Analysis." *Journal of Classical Sociology* 18 (3): 181–96. https://doi .org/10.1177/1468795X17743643.

Synge, John Millington. 1992. *The Aran Islands.* New York: Penguin.

Tangherlini, Timothy. 1990. "'It Happened Not Too Far From Here . . .': A Survey of Legend Theory and Characterization." *Western Folklore* 49 (4): 371–90. https:// doi.org/10.2307/1499751.

Tauschek, Markus. 2011. "Reflections on the Metacultural Nature of Intangible Cultural Heritage." *Journal of Ethnology and Folkloristics* 5 (2): 49–64. https://ojs.utlib.ee/index.php/JEF/article/view/22593.

Tauschek, Markus. 2013. *Kulturerbe: Eine Einführung.* Berlin: Reimer.

Taylor, Colin F. 1988. "The Indian Hobbyist Movement in Europe." In *Handbook of North American Indians: History of Indian White Relations*, edited by Wilcomb E. Washburn, vol. 4, 562–69. Washington, DC: Smithsonian Institution.

Teske, Raymond H. C., Jr., and Bardin H. Nelson. 1974. "Acculturation and Assimilation: A Clarification." *American Ethnologist* 1 (2): 351–67. http://www.jstor.org/stable/643554.

Thompson, E. P. 1967. "Time, Work-Discipline, and Industrial Capitalism." *Past and Present* 38:56–97. https://www.jstor.org/stable/649749.

Thompson, Stith. 1929. *Tales of the North American Indians.* Bloomington: Indiana University Press.

Thompson, Stith. 1946. *The Folktale.* New York: Holt, Rinehart and Winston. http://hdl.handle.net/2027/inu.30000006134963.

Thompson, Stith. 1955–58. *Motif-Index of Folk-Literature: A Classification of Narrative Elements in Folktales, Ballads, Myths, Fables, Mediaeval Romances, Exempla, Fabliaux, Jest-Books and Local Legends.* Rev. and enlarged ed. Bloomington: Indiana University Press.

Thompson, Stith. 1961. *The Types of the Folktale: A Classification and Bibliography.* Helsinki: Academia Scientarum Fennica.

Thompson, Stith. 1965. "The Star Husband Tale." In *The Study of Folklore*, edited by Alan Dundes, 414–74. Englewood Cliffs, NJ: Prentice Hall.

Thompson, Stith. 1966. *Motif-Index of Folk Literature.* 6 vols. Bloomington: Indiana University Press.

Thoms, William J. 1996. "'Folk-Lore,' from 'The Athenæum,' August 22, 1846." *Journal of Folklore Research* 33 (3): 187–89. http://www.jstor.org/stable/3814673.

Thurston, Timothy. 2020. "Cultural Carriers and the Scientific Metaphors of Tradition in China." In *Centers/Peripheries: Connecting beyond the Binaries* [Conference Program for the 132nd Annual Meeting of the American Folklore Society]. Bloomington, IN: American Folklore Society.

Tolstoy, Leo. 1993. *How Much Land Does a Man Need? and Other Stories.* Translated by Ronald Wilks. New York: Penguin.

Tooker, Elisabeth. 1978. "Wyandot." In *Handbook of North Americas.* Vol. 15, *Northeast*, edited by Bruce Trigger, 398–406. Washington, DC: Smithsonian Institution.

Tooker, Elisabeth. (1964) 1991. *An Ethnography of the Huron Indians, 1615–1649.* Syracuse, NY: Syracuse University Press.

Townsend, Camilla, and Nicky Kay Michael. 2023. *On the Turtle's Back: Stories the Lenape Told Their Grandchildren*. New Brunswick, NJ: Rutgers University Press. https://doi.org/10.36019/9781978819184.

Trigger, Bruce. 1987. *Children of Aataentsic: A History of the Huron People to 1660*. Montreal: McGill-Queen's University Press.

Trowbridge, C. C. 1939. *Shawnese Traditions: C. C. Trowbridge's Account*. Occasional Contributions from the Museum of Anthropology of the University of Michigan 9, edited by Vernon Kinietz and Erminie W. Voegelin. Ann Arbor: University of Michigan Press.

Trower, Valerie Wilson. 2010. "Cheongsam: Chinese One-Piece Dress." In *Berg Encyclopedia of World Dress and Fashion: East Asia*, edited by John E. Vollmer, 142–46. Oxford: Berg. http://dx.doi.org/10.2752/BEWDF/EDch6023.

Tsing, Anna. 2000. "The Global Situation." *Cultural Anthropology* 15 (3): 327–60. http://www.jstor.org/stable/656606.

Tsing, Anna Lowenhaupt, Andrew S. Mathews, and Nils Bubandt. 2019. "Patchy Anthropocene: Landscape Structure, Multispecies History, and the Retooling of Anthropology: An Introduction to Supplement 20." *Current Anthropology* 60 (S20): S186–97. https://doi.org/10.1086/703391.

Tsosie, Rebecca A. 2002. "Reclaiming Native Stories: An Essay on Cultural Appropriation and Cultural Rights." *Arizona State Law Journal* 34:299–358. https://ssrn.com/abstract=1401522.

Tuck, Eve, and K. Wayne Yang. 2012. "Decolonization Is Not a Metaphor." *Decolonization: Indigeneity, Education and Society* 1 (1): 1–40. https://jps.library.utoronto.ca/index.php/des/article/view/18630.

Turgeon, Laurier, and Madeleine Pastinelli. 2002. "'Eat the World': Postcolonial Encounters in Quebec City's Ethnic Restaurants." *Journal of American Folklore* 115 (456): 247–68. http://www.jstor.org/stable/4129222.

UNESCO. 2018. "Fujian Tulou." https://whc.unesco.org/en/list/1113.

University Graduate School, Indiana University. 2004. University Graduate School Bulletin, 2004–2005. https://bulletins.iu.edu/iub/grad/2004-2005/grad045.pdf.

Urban, Greg. 2001. *Metaculture: How Culture Moves through the World*. Minneapolis: University of Minnesota Press.

Urban, Greg, Ernest Baskin, and Kyung-Nan Ko. 2007. "'No Carry-Over Parts': Corporations and the Metaculture of Newness." *Suomen Antropologi: Journal of the Finnish Anthropological Society* 32 (1): 5–19.

Urban, Greg, and Jason Baird Jackson. 2004. "Mythology and Folklore." In *Handbook of North American Indians*. Vol. 14, *Southeast*, edited by Raymond D. Fogelson, 707–19. Washington, DC: Smithsonian Institution.

Uther, Hans-Jörg. 2004. *The Types of International Folktales: A Classification and Bibliography, Based on the System of Antii Aarne and Stith Thompson*. Part 1, *Ani-*

mal Tales, Tales of Magic, Religious Tales, and Realistic Tales, with an Introduction. FF Communications 284. Helsinki: Suomalainen Tiedeakatemia.

Valentine, Lisa Philips, and Regna Darnell, eds. 1999. *Theorizing the Americanist Tradition.* Toronto: University of Toronto Press.

Valk, Ülo. 2021. "What Are Belief Narratives? An Introduction." *Narrative Culture* 8 (2): 175–86. https://doi.org/10.13110/narrcult.8.2.0175.

Valk, Ülo, and Marion Bowman, eds. 2022. *Vernacular Knowledge: Contesting Authority, Expressing Beliefs.* Bristol, CT: Equinox.

Virgil. 1995. *The Aeneid.* Translated by Charles J. Billson. New York: Dover.

von Sydow, Carl Wilhelm. 1948. *Selected Papers on Folklore.* Copenhagen: Rosenkilde and Bagger.

von Sydow, Carl Wilhelm. 1999. "Geography and Folk-Tale Oicotypes." In *International Folkloristics: Classic Contributions by the Founders of Folklore,* edited by Alan Dundes, 137–51. Lanham, MD: Rowman & Littlefield.

Wagner, Günter. 1931. *Yuchi Tales.* Publications of the American Ethnological Society 13. New York: G. E. Stechert.

Wallace, Anthony F. C. (1949) 1990. *King of the Delawares: Teedyuscung, 1700–1763.* Syracuse, NY: Syracuse University Press.

Wallace, Anthony F. C. 2003. *Revitalizations and Mazeways: Essays on Culture Change.* Edited by Robert S. Grumet. Lincoln: University of Nebraska Press.

Wallerstein, Immanuel. 1991. *Unthinking Social Science: The Limits of Nineteenth-Century Paradigms.* Cambridge, MA: Polity.

Wallerstein, Immanuel. 1996. "Open the Social Sciences." *Items* 50 (1): 1–7. https://items.ssrc.org/from-our-archives/open-the-social-sciences/.

Wallerstein, Immanuel. 2000. *The Essential Wallerstein.* New York: New Press.

Wallerstein, Immanuel. 2003. "Anthropology, Sociology, and Other Dubious Disciplines." *Current Anthropology* 44 (4): 453–65. https://doi.org/10.1086/375868.

Wallerstein, Immanuel. 2004. *World-Systems Analysis: An Introduction.* Durham, NC: Duke University Press.

Wallerstein, Immanuel. (1974) 2011a. *The Modern World-System I: Capitalist Agriculture and the Origins of the European World-Economy in the Sixteenth Century.* Berkeley: University of California Press. https://muse.jhu.edu/book/25877.

Wallerstein, Immanuel. (1980) 2011b. *The Modern World-System II: Mercantilism and the Consolidation of the European World-Economy, 1600–1750.* Berkeley: University of California Press. http://muse.jhu.edu/book/26070.

Wallerstein, Immanuel. (1989) 2011c. *The Modern World-System III: The Second Era of Great Expansion of the Capitalist World-Economy, 1730s–1840s.* Berkeley: University of California Press. http://muse.jhu.edu/book/26024.

Wallerstein, Immanuel. 2011d. *The Modern World-System IV: Centrist Liberalism Triumphant, 1789–1914*. Berkeley: University of California Press. http://muse .jhu.edu/book/25952.

Wallerstein, Immanuel. 2021. *The Global Left: Yesterday, Today, Tomorrow*. New York: Routledge.

Wallerstein, Immanuel, Calestous Juma, Evelyn Fox Keller, Jürgen Kocka, Dominique Lecourt, V. Y. Mudimbe, Kinhide Mushakoji, Ilya Prigogine, Peter J. Taylor, and Michel-Ralph Troullot. 1996. *Open the Social Sciences: Report of the Gulbenkian Commission on the Restructuring of the Social Sciences*. Stanford, CA: Stanford University Press.

Waselkov, Gregory A., with Jason Baird Jackson. 2004. "Exchange and Interaction since 1500." In *Handbook of North American Indians*. Vol. 14, *Southeast*, edited by Raymond D. Fogelson, 686–96. Washington, DC: Smithsonian Institution Press.

Weber, Max. 1949. *The Methodology of the Social Sciences*. Edited and translated by Edward Shils and Henry A. Finch. Glencoe, IL: Free Press.

Weber, Max. 1958. *The Protestant Ethic and the Spirit of Capitalism*. Translated by Talcott Parsons. New York: Charles Scribner's Sons.

Williams, Michael Ann. 2017. "After the Revolution: Folklore, History, and the Future of Our Discipline." *Journal of American Folklore* 130 (516): 129–41. https:// doi.org/10.5406/jamerfolk.130.516.0129.

Williams, Raymond. 1976. *Keywords: A Vocabulary of Culture and Society*. London: Croom Helm.

Willoughby, W. C. 1905. "Notes on the Totemism of the Becwana." *Journal of the Anthropological Institute* 35 (July–December): 295–314. https://doi .org/10.2307/2843071.

Wilson-Okamura, David Scott. 2003. "Virgilian Models of Colonization in Shakespeare's Tempest." *ELH* 70 (3): 709–37. http://www.jstor.org/stable/30029896.

Wimmer, Andreas, and Nina Glick Schiller. 2003. "Methodological Nationalism, the Social Sciences, and the Study of Migration: An Essay in Historical Epistemology." *International Migration Review* 37 (3): 576–610. https://www.jstor .org/stable/30037750.

Wissler, Clark. 1920. "Opportunities for Coördination in Anthropological and Psychological Research." *American Anthropologist*, n.s., 22 (1): 1–12. http://www .jstor.org/stable/660100.

Wood, W. Warner. 2008. *Made in Mexico: Zapotec Weavers and the Global Ethnic Art Market*. Bloomington: Indiana University Press.

Woodman, J. J. 1924. *Indian Legends, Being a Choice Collection of the Best Legends, Stories, and Traditions as Told by the Warrior and the Squaw to the Papoose and Showing How the Young Indian of the Olden Time Was Education, to Which Is*

Added Some Personal Narratives of Indian Captivity as Related by the Unfortunate Survivors. Boston: Stratford.

World Intellectual Property Organization. 2011. "Protecting India's Traditional Knowledge." *WIPO Magazine*, June 2011. http://www.wipo.int/wipo_magazine /en/2011/03/article_0002.html.

Worth, John E. 2012. "Enigmatic Origins: On the Yuchi of the Contact Era." In *Yuchi Indian Histories before the Removal Era*, edited by Jackson Jason Baird, 33–42. Lincoln: University of Nebraska Press. https://doi.org/10.2307/j.ctt1d9nqx5.8.

Wycoco, Remedios S. 1951. "The Types of North-American Indian Tales." PhD diss., Indiana University.

Yang, Jeff. 2018. "The Shocking Viral Reaction to a Prom Dress." *CNN*, May 2, 2018. https://www.cnn.com/2018/05/02/opinions/the-shocking-viral-reaction-to-a -prom-dress-yang/index.html.

Yasunobu, Ikeda. 2015. "Apple—Watch Sport." Flickr. https://www.flickr.com /photos/clockmaker-jp/17111109088.

Yeginsu, Ceylan. 2018. "Swedish Meatballs Are Turkish? 'My Whole Life Has Been a Lie.'" *New York Times*, May 2, 2018. https://www.nytimes.com/2018/05/02/world /europe/swedish-meatballs-turkey.html.

Zeitlyn, David. 2022. *An Anthropological Toolkit: Sixty Useful Concepts*. New York: Berghahn.

Zezima, Katie. 2014. "The Most Interesting Governor's Daughter in the Country." *Washington Post*, May 4, 2024. https://www.washingtonpost.com/news/the -fix/wp/2014/05/04/meet-christina-fallin-not-what-the-public-would-expect -of-a-politicians-daughter/?utm_term=.8798d4d10555.

Zhang Juwen. 2015. "Introduction: New Perspectives on the Studies of Asian American Folklores." *Journal of American Folklore* 128 (510): 373–94. https:// doi.org/10.5406/jamerfolk.128.510.0373.

Zhang Lijun. 2018. "Presentation, Representation, and Museumification in Heritage Tourism: The Case of Hongkeng Hakka Earth Building Folk Cultural Village." *Museum Anthropology Review* 12 (1): 5–13. https://doi.org/10.14434/mar .v12i1.20731.

Zhang Lijun. 2024. *Living in Heritage: Tulou as Vernacular Architecture, Global Asset, and Tourist Destination in Contemporary China*. Bloomington: Indiana University Press.

Zhang Lijun, Jason Baird Jackson, C. Kurt Dewhurst, and Jon Kay. 2022. "Basketry among Two Peoples of Northern Guangxi, China." *Asian Ethnology* 81 (1–2): 239–72.

Zhang Ruinan. 2018. "Qipao-Wearing Teenager Wins Support on Weibo." *China Daily*, May 4, 2018. http://usa.chinadaily.com.cn/a/201805/04/WS5aeba 209a3105cdcf651be24.html.

Ziff, Bruce, and Pratima V. Rao. 1997. "Introduction to Cultural Appropriation: A Framework for Analysis." In *Borrowed Power: Essays on Cultural Appropriation*, edited by Bruce Ziff and Pratima V. Rao, 1–27. New Brunswick, NJ: Rutgers University Press.

Zlatunich, Nichole. 2009. "Prom Dreams and Prom Reality: Girls Negotiating 'Perfection' at the High School Prom." *Sociological Inquiry* 79 (3): 351–75. https://doi.org/10.1111/j.1475-682X.2009.00294.x.

INDEX

Jason Baird Jackson is Ruth N. Halls Professor of Folklore and Anthropology at Indiana University Bloomington. He is author of *Yuchi Ceremonial Life: Performance, Meaning and Tradition in a Contemporary American Indian Community* and *Yuchi Folklore: Cultural Expression in a Southeastern Native American Community* and editor of *Material Vernaculars: Objects, Images, and Their Social Worlds.* A former museum curator and director, he has curated more than twenty exhibitions and remains active in museum anthropology and museum-based folklore studies.

For Indiana University Press

Sabrina Black, Editorial Assistant

Lesley Bolton, Project Manager/Editor

Gary Dunham, Acquisitions Editor and Director

Anna Garnai, Production Coordinator

Samantha Heffner, Marketing and Publicity Manager

Katie Huggins, Production Manager

Dan Pyle, Online Publishing Manager

Pamela Rude, Senior Artist and Book Designer

www.ingramcontent.com/pod-product-compliance
Lightning Source LLC
Chambersburg PA
CBHW031131270326
41929CB00011B/1584